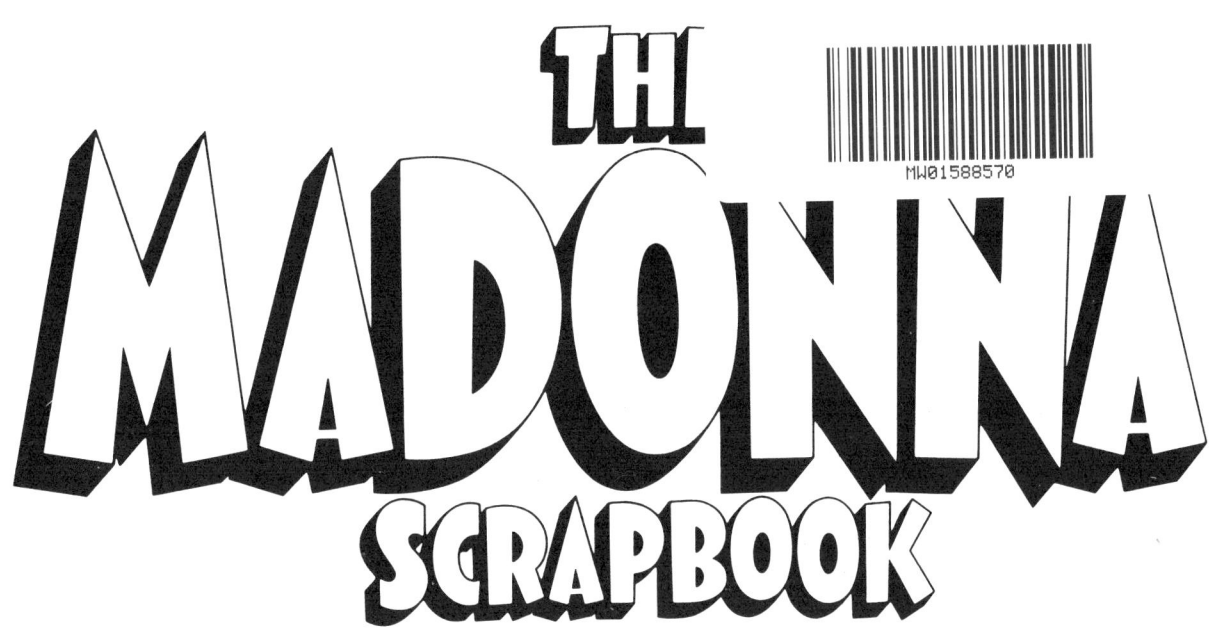

THE MADONNA SCRAPBOOK

LEE RANDALL

A CITADEL PRESS BOOK
PUBLISHED BY CAROL PUBLISHING GROUP

Copyright © 1992 by Lee Randall

A Citadel Press Book
Published by Carol Publishing Group
Citadel Press is a registered trademark of
Carol Communications, Inc.

Editorial Offices   Sales & Distribution Offices
600 Madison Avenue   120 Enterprise Avenue
New York, NY 10022   Secaucus, NJ 07094

In Canada: Canadian Manda Group
P.O. Box 920, Station U
Toronto, Ontario M8Z 5P9

All rights reserved. No part of this book
may be reproduced in any form, except by
a newspaper or magazine reviewer who
wishes to quote brief passages in connection
with a review.

Queries regarding rights and permissions
should be addressed to: Carol Publishing Group,
600 Madison Avenue, New York, NY 10022

Manufactured in the United States of America
10 9 8 7 6 5 4 3 2 1

Carol Publishing Group books are available at special discounts
for bulk purchases, for sales promotions, fund raising, or
educational purposes. Special editions can also be created to
specifications. For details contact: Special Sales Department,
Carol Publishing Group, 120 Enterprise Ave., Secaucus, NJ 07094

Randall, Lee.
 The Madonna scrapbook / by Lee Randall.
  p.   cm.
 " A Citadel Press book."
 ISBN 0-8065-1297-0
 1. Madonna, 1959-   . 2. Rock musicians—United States—
Biography.   I. Title.
ML420.M1387R36 1992
 782.42166'092—dc20
  [B]   92-14251
                                                     CIP
                                                     MN

Dedicated with love to the memory of Lia Ilgen, 1962-1989

ACKNOWLEDGMENTS:

Special thanks to Peter A. Davis, who whispered my name in the right ear. Thanks also to the following people, whose generosity and thoughtfulness helped make this book possible: Lynne Arany, Marie Bozzelli, Steve Brower, Norris Burroughs, Cheryl Clifford, Mary Flanagan, Monica Hardiman, Jan Hooks, Lynne Layton, Julia McFarlane, Alana Marinoucci, Anette Ohnikian at Conde Nast, David and Janille Randall, Sarah Tate Richmond, Bill Ryan (you outdid yourself!), Wiff Stenger, everyone at Weight Watchers Magazine (especially Mary Novitsky and Susan Rees), and Josleen Wilson, who has been a continual source of strength and inspiration throughout our friendship.

Introduction

The woman whom Madonna most reminds me of—and is infrequently compared with—is Mae West.

Forget the blond denominator. Forget, too, that West's ample bosom inspired the RAF to name life jackets for her ("because they bulge in all the right places") or that Madonna's oft-photographed breasts have been dubbed a national treasure.

Consider it. Mae West was a saucy, pushy, wickedly funny lady who "climbed the ladder of success wrong by wrong." She was gutsy and independent and fought tooth and nail to control her artistic destiny. When Hollywood patriarchs said, "Don't worry your pretty little head," West spat in their eyes and turned up as a major player in the male-dominated worlds of stage, film, and radio. West ignored convention and fought censorship—her overtly homosexual play was banned and *Sex* landed her in jail.

Then, too, Madonna and Mae are both Leos. Both come on strong; they're sexual predators, walking advertisements for hot-blooded female libido. They're both revered by gay men and feared by straight men, who are easily unnerved by salacious double-entendres, bawdy puns, and sassy physicality. Women long to be as up-front as these gals, and as much in control.

If Madonna's longevity equals Mae's—and it shows all the symptoms of robustness—we've only witnessed the first third of her career. There are always critics who insist Madonna has never had an original impulse but reworks hoary old themes and images. She's not drawing from a well, but a thimble, they say, and it's bound to go dry. I think Madonna has tapped right into the water table—she'll never run out of sap. Mae understood. She said, "It's not what you do, it's how you do it."

In less than a decade, Madonna has become a hypercelebrity. Why, in 1990 she bested Elizabeth Taylor, appearing on more magazine covers than any other celebrity. She's a potent symbol of the power of self-determination. And if she weren't so thoroughly Catholic, I'd get away with calling her the personification of America's Protestant work ethic—she is!

Madonna's an American hero straight out of Horatio Alger—a child touched by tragedy and hardship who, by dint of hard work and lucky breaks, zooms from the streets to a penthouse view. She's the picture in the dictionary alongside the word *success*.

What other living performer inspires such wildly disparate contemplation? They chronicle Madonna's most insignificant acts in the *National Enquirer*, *People*, and *Us*, and study the meaning of it all in journals like the *National Catholic Reporter*, the *New Republic*, the *Journal of Communication*, and *Forbes*. Madonna is scrutinized by students of popular culture—right now academic dissertations dissecting her are being scribbled at universities the world over.

There may be better-loved celebrities. But Madonna's in our face. She forces us to form opinions, even where we're happier ignoring the issues. As she sees it, "Somehow I feel that, as much as people complain and moan and groan and criticize me, they're affected by me. I've touched a nerve in them somehow."

What Madonna's career owes to Mae's precedent should be strikingly apparent in the words and images that follow. Be prepared to discover Madonna lives up to the standard set by another great iconoclast, Louise Brooks, who once told a lover, "If I ever bore you, it will be with a knife."

Lee Randall
Hoboken, 1991

CONTENTS

One:	**Young Adventurer**	8
Two:	**Adrift in New York**	16
Three:	**Bound to Rise**	28
Four:	**Struggling Upward**	42
Five:	**Facing the World**	60
Six:	**Try and Trust**	68
Seven:	**Strong and Steady**	82
Eight:	**Sink or Swim**	96
Nine:	**Shifting for Herself**	108
Ten:	**Luck and Pluck**	120
Eleven:	**The World Before Her**	130
Twelve:	**Do and Dare**	148
Thirteen:	**Making Her Way**	168

PHOTO: VINNIE ZUFFANTE / STAR FILE PHOTO

ONE: YOUNG ADVENTURER

"When I see my girlfriends with their mothers even now, I can't imagine—it's unfathomable what that sort of nurturing would have done for me."—Madonna

"When I was really little, my favorite thing to do—I suppose because I was sexually aroused—was to sit on the toilet backward. . . . somehow that would relieve me. . . . I also liked the idea of standing above the toilet and peeing."
—Madonna

When Madonna visited her mother's grave after twenty-one years, being Madonna, she brought a camera crew to record the spectacle. A ground mike picked up her whisper-soft musings: "You're nothing but dust now. . . . When I die, they'll bury me here." Madonna traced an imaginary channel alongside her mother. Cradling her head in both hands like a child napping, Madonna stretched out, and her cropped blond hair spilled across the marker that eerily bears her own name. For Madonna Ciccone, born in 1933, life ended abruptly in 1963. For her daughter, born in 1958, the future seems limitless.

Despite Madonna's protests to the contrary, the sequence is contrived. Yet it's the most emotionally affecting moment in her 1991 film documentary *Truth or Dare*. If this is manipulation, it's masterfully done. And it reiterates Madonna's theme that everything she's become, everything she's driven to achieve, is rooted in her mother's early death.

Madonna Louise Veronica Ciccone is a second-generation American. Her paternal grandparents emigrated from Pacentro, Italy, and settled in Pittsburgh. Her grandfather worked in the steel factories. Her father, Silvio (known as Tony), was the youngest of Gaetano and Michelina Ciccone's six sons and the only one to attend college. Intensely religious and deeply ambitious, Tony left Pennsylvania for Detroit and a job with Chrysler as an optics and defense engineer.

On the distaff side, Madonna's Fortin ancestors were French Canadian. Madonna senior grew up in Bay City, Michigan, where her daughter was eventually born August 16, 1958. Madonna and Tony met through her brother, an air force buddy of Tony's. Family legend claims they fell in love at first sight.

After a white wedding, Tony took a job with General Dynamics and moved his bride to the Detroit suburb of Pontiac. The family stayed there until he relocated to Rochester, Michigan, when Madonna was ten. Babies arrived in a steady stream, generally at the same time of the year: Anthony, Martin, Madonna, Paula, Christopher, and Melanie. Six kids, just like the sprawling family of Silvio's Pittsburgh boyhood.

Most of Madonna's early memories are bittersweet, tinged with loss and frustration. Her upbringing was bound by ironclad rules governing every aspect of behavior, enforcing a strict double standard dividing boys from girls, and girls into virgins or whores.

Certainly there were wild times, exuberant games with friends and family. "I think my parents pissed a lot of people off because they had so many kids and they never screamed at us," said Madonna. "My older brothers were very rambunctious and they would start fires in the basement or throw rocks at windows, and my mother and father would never yell at them. They would . . . put their arms around us and talk to us quietly."

Despite evidence to the contrary, Madonna claims the Ciccones lived in an integrated blue-collar neighborhood and that many of her childhood friends were black. She has said, "I was jealous of my girlfriends because they could have braids in their hair that stuck up everywhere. So I'd go through this ordeal of putting wire in *my* hair and braiding it so that I could make my hair stick up." Madonna told Arsenio Hall that throughout her childhood she longed to be black because her friends' parents seemed more easygoing and lenient.

Extremely *un*lenient Tony insisted his children attend church before school every day. They weren't allowed to watch television more than once a week and had a roster of daily chores. To his credit, Tony was no hypocrite. "My father was very strong. I don't agree with some of his values, but he did have integrity, and if he told us not to do something, he didn't do it either."

Talking to Carrie Fisher in 1991, Madonna revealed a history of alcoholism in her dad's family and deduced that some of his behavior fit the pattern of adult children of alcoholics. (Neither of her parents drank, but several of her siblings have been in and out of rehab.) A quiet man who kept his emotions largely hidden, Tony made an enormous impression on his eldest daughter. "He didn't give me advice, he just gave orders. . . . 'Do this or else.'" One of his "pearls of wisdom" was: "If it feels good, you are doing something wrong. If you are suffering, you are doing something right."

Tony "believed that making love to someone is a very sacred thing and it shouldn't happen until after you you are married. He stuck by those beliefs. . . . My parents were virgins when they got married. My mother was very religious, too." Tony thought the world would be a better place if more people chose virginity.

> *"Madonna is my real name. It means virgin, mother, mother of earth, someone who is very pure and innocent, but someone who's very strong." —Madonna*

It's unusual for an Italian daughter to be named for her mother, doubly so given their rare moniker. "My mother is the only other person I have ever heard of named Madonna. When I got involved in music, everybody thought I took it as a stage name. So I let them think that. . . . It's pretty glamorous." From the start, Madonna perceived her name as both blessing and challenge. "I thought, 'I belong in some special world. Madonna is a strange name.' I felt like there was a reason . . . like I had to live up to my name."

Madonna cherishes memories of her mother. Already a restless sleeper by age four, she'd steal into her parents' room and crawl into bed with them—over her dad's objections. "I think I must have done this a lot because they sat up in bed and said, 'Oh, no, not again,' and I said, 'Can I get in bed between you?' I always went to sleep right away when I slept with them. I felt really lonely and forlorn, even though my brothers and sisters were in my room with me. I wanted to sleep with my parents."

Madonna vividly recalls her mother's year-long illness. "She was a very forgiving, angelic person. My mother was sick for a long time so she was very weak, but she'd go on and do the things she had to, keeping her fear inside. She never complained."

Mrs. Ciccone was a radiation technologist, which makes Madonna wonder if she developed breast cancer because she wasn't protected on the job. Doctors initially misdiagnosed the disease, and by the time they reached a verdict of cancer, no amount of medicine or prayer could save the young woman.

The Ciccones' fight to normalize family life confused young Madonna. She didn't know better than to climb on her mother, beseeching her to play:

We picked on her all the time because we just didn't understand. But I don't think she ever allowed herself to wallow in the situation. [Once] I got really angry . . . and I remember pounding her back and saying, 'Why are you doing this?' Then I realized she was crying. I remember feeling stronger than she was. . . . I stopped tormenting her after that. That was the turning point when I knew. I think that made me grow up fast.

As the eldest girl, Madonna was especially close to her mom:

My mother dying was the single greatest event in my life and changed forever how I am. That's when the die was cast. I know if I'd had a mother, I would be very different. Mothers teach you manners and gentleness and a certain kind of patience. When my mother died, all of sudden I was going to become the best student, get the best grades. I was going to become the most famous person in the world, everybody was going to love me.

Within her family Madonna felt ostracized—"I thought I was a dog from hell." Her nickname was The Mouth—and it was frequently scrubbed with soap or taped shut. "I was considered the sissy of the family because I relied on feminine wiles to get my way. . . . My older brothers would hang me on the clothesline by my underpants. . . . Or they'd pin me down on the ground and spit in my mouth." She competed with her sisters so fiercely that they became adversaries rather than allies.

All the kids vied nonstop for their father's attention. Since he often worked two jobs, success called for drastic measures. Madonna's infamous exploits included jumping on tables for impromptu tap dances and sticking her hand in the stove's gas flame. "I realized I would only be noticed and heard if I made the biggest noise." The more Madonna misbehaved, the more she saw of her dad, though he was often grounding her at the time.

A series of housekeepers tried taming the Ciccones over the next three years, but Madonna was primarily influenced by her father and brothers. As a result, she wasn't dainty or genteel. "I did what [boys] did. I said what I wanted. I burped when I had to burp. When I liked a boy on the playground, I chased him. There was no one over me saying, 'Now, girls don't do that.'"

Unless you count the nuns who taught at her parochial school. Nuns fascinated Madonna. Their devout lifestyle and stylized black habits appealed to her dreamy side. "I saw nuns as superstars. Nuns were these superhuman, beautiful, fantastic people. I thought they were really elegant. They wore these long gowns, they seemed to glide on the floor, everyone said they were married to Jesus."

Madonna clung to a fairly dramatic view of religion: "When I was growing up, I was religious in a passionate, adolescent way. Jesus Christ was like a movie star, my favorite idol of all."

Nuns informed Madonna that a Good Catholic Girl didn't chase boys. Or hang upside down on monkey bars to expose her colorful undies. Or remove the top half of her school uniform on the playground. Or hike her skirt up over the desk during lessons.

Madonna claimed if she weren't a performer, she would have become a nun. "The reason I'm not a nun is because you can't take your own name. How could I change my name? I have the most holy name a woman can have. But if I *had* to change my name, I'd use my confirmation name, Veronica. I chose her because she wiped the face of Jesus, which I thought was really dramatic." Later, Madonna said she abandoned the notion of taking vows on discovering nuns were celibate.

Though she went wild, Madonna also stepped into the role of miniature wife and mother. "For three years before my father remarried, I clung to him. It was like: 'Okay, now you're mine, and you're not going anywhere.' Like all young girls I was in love with my father and I didn't want to lose him. I lost my mother, but then I was the mother; my father was mine."

She became positively phobic about leaving the house and loathed any separation from Tony—she even slept in his bed most nights. She was convinced a devil inhabiting their basement would grab her ankles when she climbed the open-tread stairs.

The kids always reckoned Tony would marry one of their housekeepers and put their money on a brunette Natalie Wood (and Madonna senior) look-alike. Instead, he fell in love with another housekeeper, a blonde named Joan. After their marriage the family swelled to eight with the arrival of Jennifer and Mario.

Madonna wasn't off the hook. "I felt like I didn't really have a childhood. I was forced to grow up fast. . . . I had a lot of adult responsibilities. I feel like all my adolescence was spent taking care of babies. I saw myself as the quintessential Cinderella. You know, I have this stepmother and I have all this work and I never go out and I don't have pretty dresses." Putting it bluntly, Madonna said she felt like the "unhired help."

Tony's marriage struck her as a second loss. First her mother was taken away, then her father. Madonna resolved to toughen up. She thought, "Okay, I don't need anybody. No one's going to break my heart again. I can stand on my own and be my own person and not belong to anyone." The bounce from "number one female" to daughter stirred up tremendous resentment, which Madonna took out on her rival. "I didn't resent having to raise my brothers and sisters as much as I resented the fact that I didn't have my mother. And that my ideal of my family was interrupted."

Madonna especially despised Tony's request that they call Joan Mom or Mother. "I remember it being really hard for me to get the word *mother* out of my mouth. It was really painful." With the acute clarity of hindsight, Madonna admits her stepmother was very young and utterly overwhelmed by the pressures of raising six rowdy kids plus two new babies. Joan was strict, but it was how she coped.

At age ten Madonna grew breasts ("The other girls in my class hated me"), got her period, and became more rebellious than ever, especially where she perceived injustice—which meant rebelling against her religious upbringing. Puberty intensified her interest in the opposite sex. "I was always very precocious as a child, extremely flirtatious. I was one of those little girls who crawled on everybody's lap. I flirted with everyone—my uncles, my grandfather, my father, everybody. I was aware of my female charm.

"Ours was a strict, old-fashioned family. When I was tiny, my grandmother used to beg me not to go with men, to love Jesus and be a good girl. I grew up with two images of a woman: the virgin and the whore. It was a little scary." Madonna understood that these images could be manipulated to her advantage: "I just knew that being a girl and being charming in a feminine way could get me a lot of things, and I milked it for everything I could."

The boys despised her shameless vamping, so it's ironic how desperately she ached for the prerogatives of masculinity. "I was insanely jealous of my older brothers. They didn't have curfews, they could pee standing up, they could take their shirts off in summer. . . . They had so much more freedom and I would just mope about that. . . . I wished I was a boy."

Silvio's adherence to Catholic doctrine and his delineation of correct female behavior thoroughly frustrated Madonna. "I was really annoyed that I couldn't wear pants to school or church. I kept saying, 'But why can't I love God the same way if I have pants on?' And [he] would always have these stock responses like, 'Because I said so.' . . . I'd be confused about who I was worshiping, God or my father?" Why can't I contact God directly? she wondered.

Like many lapsed Catholics Madonna often dwells on negatives, but sees a positive side. "Catholicism gives you an inner strength, whether you end up believing it later or not." She credits her indoctrination for a measure of her current success: "I don't know if this was more my father or Catholicism, but I was also raised to believe that idle time wasn't good. You always had to be doing something productive. . . . You always had to be challenging your mind or body, and that definitely shaped my adult life. . . . My father's strictness taught me discipline."

Challenge could replace Louise as Madonna's middle name. In 1969, for instance, she entered the school talent show. Madonna conceived, directed, produced, and costumed the act herself, borrowing heavily from TV's "Laugh-In." She leapt onstage in a bikini 'ala Goldie Hawn, her exposed skin covered by weird designs drawn in glowing green paint. As she undulated beneath a black light, The Who's "Baba O'Reilly" blared. Tony was mortified and read her the riot act back at home.

Madonna's peers didn't understand her any better. At dances boys never approached, so she'd boogie alone and cause such a fuss people cleared the floor to gape. She was an honor student who talked like a guttersnipe and won an undeserved reputation for promiscuity.

"When you're that aggressive in junior high, the boys get the wrong impression. They mistake your forwardness for sexual promiscuity. Then, when they don't get what they think they are going to get, they turn on you."

Madonna never discussed sex with Tony, so it fell to her stepmother to describe the birds and bees when Madonna began menstruating. "I was horrified. . . . I was washing dishes. Every time she said the word *penis* I'd turn the water on really hard so it would drown out what she said. I thought what she was telling me was horrifying."

Joan's brief explanation of sex ("just that a man has a penis and a woman has a vagina") was tailored to reinforce that much-prized value—virginity. She forbade tampons before marriage, claiming they were tantamount to intercourse. Madonna turned to her older friend Moira for guidance, but something about the lesson went awry. The first time Madonna tried a tampon, "I put it in sideways and was walking around paralyzed one day."

In *Truth or Dare*, Madonna insisted Moira finger-fucked her as a kid and Moira pleaded total amnesia. By her admission, Madonna and her school chums experimented sexually at slumber parties, venting their natural curiosity. Like plenty of girls they played naughty Barbie and Ken games. In fifth grade Madonna stole her first kiss from a boy she fancied named Tom Marshowitz, cornering him in back of the school.

As a young teen Madonna guarded her virginity by wearing a dark blue turtleneck bodysuit to mixed-sex parties. Though she made out with boys, her virtue lay safely hidden behind layers of protective cloth. At fourteen Madonna went all the way in the backseat with her longtime steady, Russell Long. Succumbing in a car was a tad clichéd. Doing so in a Cadillac was pure Material Girl.

Madonna test-drove identities. She tried the Brownies but binged on cookies and got in trouble. Briefly a cheerleader, she forgot to leave her brain in the locker room and soon tired of their bubblehead mentality. Even as a rebel she ran aground. Twice she snuck off to rock concerts—Elton John and David Bowie—and twice she got snagged and grounded. Madonna was also a Michael Jackson wannabe: "I thought, 'I can do everything he can do, only I'm a girl.'"

She adored old movies. "I loved Carole Lombard and Judy Holliday and Marilyn Monroe. They were all incredibly funny and they were silly and sweet. I saw myself in them, my funniness and my need to boss people around and at the same time be taken care of. My knowingness and my innocence."

Forbidden to watch much television at home, Madonna snuck off to friends' houses to bone up on cultural developments and succumbed to girlhood crushes on the era's heartthrobs—David Cassidy, Bobby Sherman, the Monkees. Living in the Motor City, she was a natural devotee of the Motown sound. She adored "innocent child voices like Diana Ross. . . . I practically swooned when I heard Frankie Lymon's records."

Madonna also gushed over Nancy Sinatra's hit, "These Boots Are Made for Walking." It made her feel "like I was going to get out there and take a bite out of the big forest." A voice in her head whispered "that the world was mine, that it was a stomping ground for me, full of opportunities. I always had the attitude that I was going to go out into the world and do all the things I wanted to do."

In junior high Madonna appeared in a classmate's Super 8 film. Her now-famous navel made its screen debut when the young auteur filmed an egg frying on her stomach. She acted in school plays throughout high school, often in starring roles.

Another of Madonna's enthusiasms was tortured poetry by authors like Anne Sexton, Sylvia Plath, and "any really depressed women." She worshiped Anne Sexton. "My sister and I used to read all her poems when we were in high school because she looked like our mother. She talks about death a lot and breast cancer and mothers, all these death images that we were obsessed with."

The more she looked around, the less Madonna knew what she wanted. "You want to identify with somebody as you're growing away from being a child. . . . In my school there were the hippies. . . . I didn't identify with them because I thought they were extremely lazy. . . . I was a cheerleader for a little while, but I couldn't agree with [their] sensibilities." Her sense of self lacked focus.

She spent the summer between eighth and ninth grade working up a new fashion statement. She and a girlfriend bought bullet bras and stuffed them to bursting, then crammed themselves into tight sweaters. "We wore tons of lipstick and really badly applied makeup and huge beauty marks and did our hair up like Tammy Wynette." Dressing up made Madonna feel mature and sophisticated, but her stepmother said she looked like a floozy.

When Madonna was in tenth grade at Rochester Adams High, she befriended a girl whose smart, offbeat looks intrigued her. The girl was a ballet dancer and took Madonna along to class. There she met Christopher Flynn, a forty-something, gay, Catholic dancer who ran his own ballet school. Madonna admits, "I latched onto him like a leech and took everything I could from him."

Flynn and dancing changed everything. "Before I started feeling devoted to dancing, I didn't really like myself very much. I didn't think I was beautiful or talented. I spent a lot of time loathing myself and not feeling like I fit in and hating the authority of my parents. When I started having a dream, and working toward that goal, having a sense of discipline, I started to really like myself for the first time. Then that just carried over into everything."

Madonna told the *Advocate*, a popular gay monthly magazine:

After my father, the most powerful, important relationship in my life was with Flynn. I didn't understand the concept of gay at that time. All I knew was that [he] was different from anybody else. He was so alive. He made you proud of yourself, just the way he came up to me and put my face in his hand and said, 'You are beautiful.' No one had woken up that part of me yet. I was too busy being repressed by my Catholic father.

Flynn became her mentor, surrogate father, imaginary lover, and chief inspiration. "He made me push myself. He was constantly putting all that stuff about New York in my ear." Flynn took Madonna to gay nightclubs, where she immediately felt at home. What a contrast to Adams High! These men were "more free about themselves than all the blockhead football players I met in high school." Even so, Madonna still wished she were a boy—"just so *somebody* would ask me out on a date!"

Now, Madonna's perspective altered radically:

> Until that point I kept seeing myself through macho heterosexual eyes. Because I was a really aggressive woman, guys thought of me as a really strange girl. I frightened them . . . I felt inadequate around them, and I felt not beautiful, and I felt like I could never fit in with prom queens and cheerleaders and the perfect girls. . . . When Christopher introduced me to this life, I suddenly thought, "That's not the only way that I have to be."

Her fashion statement this time was the European hippie look, complete with short, spiked brown hair, pierced ears, unshaven armpits and legs, ripped-up clothes, and a diet of nuts and berries. Even Flynn said, "She was kind of far-out. . . . We would go to gay bars and she and I would go out and dance our asses off. People would clear away and let her go."

After graduating with honors in 1976, Madonna attended the University of Michigan at Ann Arbor on a dance scholarship. Her rebelliousness undaunted, she'd belch during barre exercises, scratch herself, and generally act out. Another time, itchy and overheated, she whined that she would rather come to class in just a bra. As she explained it, "I was a real ham [and] did everything I could to get attention and be the opposite of everyone else."

While in Ann Arbor, Madonna met Steve Bray, a musician moonlighting as a waiter at the popular Blue Frogge disco. "It was the first time in my life I asked a guy to buy me a drink. He was all soulful and funky looking. You couldn't help but notice." Madonna trailed Steve to gigs when he played drums for an R&B combo, but still imagined her future lay in dance. Though she had briefly studied piano as a kid, Madonna couldn't (and doesn't) read or write music.

Goaded by Flynn, Madonna fixated on New York—and no hometown sweetie could keep her down on the farm. It was the first of many times she'd sacrifice a relationship to her career. "I think that I probably did make [Steve] feel kind of bad, but I was really insensitive in those days . . . totally self-absorbed."

Steve had an inkling that Madonna wasn't easily contained. "She stood out," he recalled. "Her energy was really apparent." Whatever heartache their breakup engendered, the friendship between these two cronies has weathered the storms and flourishes to this day.

Madonna mustered enough cash for one-way airfare and set off to spend the summer in Manhattan. It was her first plane trip.

TWO: ADRIFT IN NEW YORK

"I prayed for seventeen years to get out of the Midwest, and I don't want to go back."—Madonna

"I'm tough, ambitious, and I know exactly what I want."—Madonna

Madonna's arrival in New York had all the earmarks of a low-budget teen-runaway-meets-a-bad-end flick. But a lucky star shielded her from harm. Madonna landed at La Guardia Airport in the summer of 1977, wearing her winter coat and lugging a suitcase full of dancing gear. As the oft-repeated story goes, she had either $35 or $37 in her pocket, jumped into a cab, and commanded the driver to deposit her in "the center of everything." He left her in Times Square.

She wandered toward Lexington Avenue and a hopping summer street fair. A curious man tagged after her, watching Madonna explore Forty-second Street. He inquired about the heavy coat. She blithely explained about arriving from out of town without friends, money, or a hotel reservation. He offered her a place to stay. Madonna accepted. She camped at his apartment rent-free for two weeks and he even fed her breakfast. "He didn't try to rape me or anything. He showed me where everything was. It was perfect."

She won a tryout for a study scholarship with Alvin Ailey's distinctly unprestigious third company but found her classmates maddening. "I thought I was in a production of *Fame*. Everyone was Hispanic or black, and *everyone* wanted to be a star." Madonna defected to study under Pearl Lang, a Martha Graham disciple. (Lang was married to Joseph Wiseman, the actor who played Dr. No in the eponymous James Bond film.) Madonna studied with Lang for a few months, then left in a flurry of ill will, though their artistic differences have never been detailed.

Some of her critics bitch that Madonna never paid her dues. Their accusations largely ignore these early New York days when Madonna lived hand-to-mouth, improvising out of her suitcase, sleeping in a series of dodgy digs in unsavory neighborhoods. She lived alongside transients and junkies in smelly rooming houses, ate sparingly (frequently composing her vegetarian meals from garbage cans), and wore clothes she found or inherited from acquaintances.

She wasn't too proud to ask for handouts. "I'd let some poor sucker take me out to dinner and then I'd go, 'Can I borrow a hundred dollars?' I was always borrowing." In that respect, she was a lot like Truman Capote's Holly Golightly, a comparison not lost on Madonna. "The character I identified with most was Holly, because when I first came to New York, I was lonely, lived by myself, was going to parties and not fitting in."

Though Madonna went home for a few months, she returned to Manhattan quickly despite Tony's strenuous objections. "For five years after I left home I barely spoke to him," she said. The breach widened when he visited the Big Apple and Madonna's tenement home. "The first apartment I ever had all by myself was on Fourth Street and Avenue B, and it was my pride and joy because it was the worst possible neighborhood I could ever live in." Dad's horror was as good as cement. Madonna wouldn't budge.

Madonna kept it together with a succession of minimum-wage jobs until she heard she could make from $10 to $35 an hour posing nude for art classes.

I modeled for a lot of art schools . . . and the nude is essential . . . for a person in beginning study; they have to draw the anatomy of the human body. . . . So, when I did this, a lot of people wanted me to start modeling privately for them. . . . I could hang out a lot more and work a lot less. I got to know these people in a friendly kind of way. They became like surrogate mothers and fathers for me. . . . Then, they'd say they knew a great photographer and he's doing an exhibit on nudes and he'd like to do some pictures . . . and for the photography sessions I'd be paid a lot more than drawing. I consider the nude a work of art. I don't see pornography in Michelangelo, and I likened what I was doing to that.

Czechoslovakian émigré Martin Schreiber is one of the photographers she posed for. His Madonna nudes were published in *Playboy* and collected in two of his books. They met on February 12, 1979, when she showed up to model for a course he taught at Parsons, called Photographing the Nude. "She was a determined young woman," he said. "She was strong emotionally and she had ambition. I felt that nothing or anyone was going to stand in her way." Madonna's unadorned beauty and popcorn-induced slenderness made a welcome change from the mostly "lumpy" models who paraded through Schreiber's studio. "I think she's quite beautiful now, but she had a different kind of beauty then."

Lee Friedlander also photographed Madonna in the late seventies and called her a good model, very streetwise and self-confident. Today Friedlander's highly praised work hangs in the Museum of Modern Art; he's received a Medal of Paris and three Guggenheims.

Though the press tried—still tries—to incite scandal, there's nothing prurient about the photographs. Schreiber remarked, "[They] have nothing to do with sex or exploitation. . . . Nudes have been in art for centuries. We are fascinated by the human form, by our bodies, and that fascination won't stop."

> *"Fear was my catalyst. It was the desire to get through all those things—I kept saying, Okay, this is hard, this is scary, but I'm going to make it—that kept me going."—Madonna*

Rather more exploitative was the no-budget movie *A Certain Sacrifice*, which filmed sporadically between 1979 and 1981. *Rolling Stone* called it "Madonna's dirty laundry," and she confirmed her unhappiness with it by suing unsuccessfully to block a video release. *Sacrifice* is a wretched, amateurish product that even die-hard fans do best viewing with a finger on the fast-forward button. The production values on this sixty minute, Super-8 film are abysmal. It's out of focus, choppily edited, and the sound veers between inaudible dialogue drowned in crackling static to heavy-handed music that tries to induce spine-tingling chills and simply delivers an earache.

It got mixed reviews. The *New York Post* said,

Who's that girl? An unknown and uncredited Madonna models fashions for the *Village Voice* in the early 1980s.

From the personal collection of Curtis Zales

The 10 Best Buys in Vintage Clothing

Old Clothes You Can Wear as Real Clothes

By Amanda Mayer Stinchecum

Photographs by Fred Seidman

How about a genuine Adrian jacket? The couture details are so exquisite, who cares if the original skirt is gone? Mismatched suits are in. Bought at Harriet Love, 412 West Broadway; worn by rock performer Madonna.

A lot of people know that shopping for antique (dare we call them used?) clothes workmanship is even more startling. Pay particular attention to wear and general condition; if a piece of clothing is

Harriet of Harriet Love, 412 West Broadway, suggests accessories as a go

"Madonna is hot as a pistol, she's sexy as hell." The *Philadelphia Daily News* joked, "This is not *Bambi*." The *Film and Video Independent* called it "a bizarre story of urban terror and ritual barbarism." *Spin* called it "a melodrama of surprising intensity and value."

A Certain Sacrifice, billed as "a new musical," was the brainchild of Stephen Jon Lewicki. Madonna stars as free-living Bruga, who leads a band of sex slaves devoted to her pleasure. She falls in love with Dasheel, a suburban refugee-cum-philosopher. Dasheel meets an obnoxious lout named Raymond Hall, who inexplicably connives to ruin him.

First, Hall gets Dasheel booted from his apartment. Later, he follows the lovers to their favorite diner, trails Bruga to the toilet, rapes her, and flees. Bruga collects her sex slaves in a stretch limo and kidnaps Raymond. In the ensuing musical number (sans Bruga) Dasheel sacrifices Raymond at a satanic Black Mass.

Later, when they're making love, Dasheel smears Bruga with a cup of Raymond's blood (it looks like a Slurpee) while she writhes ecstatically beneath him. The film ends happily, with a shot of the lovers frolicking like innocents.

A Certain Sacrifice raised eyebrows on its release because Madonna appears topless during an "orgy" scene. When Bruga tells her sex slaves the party's over, they retaliate by strutting their stuff to remind her what she's forsaking. The orgy features a little frontal nudity, but there's nothing suggestive here. The sex slaves prance in a circle. Bruga slithers. There are shots of hands rubbing thighs. An average episode of *Knots Landing* is more salacious.

It's worth noting that one of Bruga's acolytes is played by Angie Smits, who together with Madonna and the Gilroy brothers would form the band called The Breakfast Club.

According to Lewicki, "I started off with the idea of a human sacrifice and worked my way back to Madonna!" He thought she'd be perfect as a dominatrix. "She was exactly what I was looking for—this kind of nasty, sexually charged, at the same time vulnerable female." The film took three years to cobble together because Lewicki kept running out of funds. Though Madonna lost enthusiasm for the movie, she, too, was chronically short of cash. Lewicki's offers of money up front persistently lured her back.

Watching *A Certain Sacrifice*, fans can see classic Madonnaisms were already fully formed. Here's the little-girl gaze, the fingernail biting, the hand in her mouth—a roster of feminine ploys perfected as Daddy's Girl. They turn up in the "Lucky Star" video and much of Madonna's early work.

Madonna's rise as a musician in the early 1980s is usually characterized as a steady climb over the bodies of her ex-lovers. None of the men themselves level the charge—they're remarkably loyal. Even Steve Bray, who has reason to be angry, stands up for Madonna, saying, "Exploited? . . . That's resentment of someone who's got the drive. It seems like you're leaving people behind or you're stepping on them, and the fact is that you're moving and they're not. She doesn't try to be that polite. She doesn't care if she ruffles someone's feathers."

Apparently Dan Gilroy doesn't feel used either. "I think a lot of people feel exploited by Madonna, but

The exploitation film Madonna tried—and failed—to suppress when she hit it big.
Memorabilia courtesy the Bill Ryan Archives.
Photo by David Palmore.

then again everyone's got so many expectations about a relationship with her. She's very intense immediately with somebody, very friendly."

By the early eighties Madonna knew the shortest distance between obscurity and fame wasn't dancing, but music. Every child of the sixties knew how quickly a hit song and catchy look transformed shop assistants and art school students into superstars. If Norris Burroughs (see box page 172) nudged Madonna toward singing, Dan Gilroy pushed her over the edge.

Rumor has it Madonna's first words to Gilroy were, "Aren't you going to kiss me?" One version of this meeting has Gilroy underwhelmed, while another says he kissed her and swooned. They met at Norris Burroughs's Rites of Spring party in May of 1980 and began dating immediately. Madonna and Gilroy got along terrifically well, but once again career came first. When two French producers promised, "We'll make you a star," and offered a free trip to Paris, Madonna packed her bags.

If you missed them, Patrick Hernandez's fifteen minutes of fame were spent singing "Born to Be Alive" on the disco circuit. The hit was produced by Jean Claude Pellerin and Jean Van Lieu, who itched to transform another unknown into a sensation. While auditioning back up dancers and singers for Hernandez's act, the Jeans found Madonna and decided to make her their next protégée. "I was in seventh heaven. I kept thinking, 'I can't believe it. Somebody *noticed* me,'" she said. The Svengalis whisked her to a flashy Paris apartment and paid all her living expenses.

Madonna wanted for nothing. Jean and Jean sprang for the best of everything and paraded her around town as a newfound Piaf they'd rescued from the gutter. They wrote her a dance tune and tried to refashion Madonna in their image of a disco diva. They erred by leaving Madonna with time on her hands—time to feel manipulated and misused, time to feel lonely, time to resent the fact that they had other projects on the boil, time to get up to mischief.

She revenged herself by raising hell. "I felt like the poor little rich girl. Once again I was forced into the role of enfant terrible. All I wanted to do was make trouble, because they stuck me in an environment that didn't allow me to be free."

Madonna took her clothing allowance and spent it on black leather. She put safety pins in her ears. She dated scores of boys, favoring exotic punks on motor scooters. She spent every evening in Parisian nightclubs and skipped daytime business meetings. Fast living caught up with her—she got pneumonia.

Six months later, no amount of francs or threats could entice Madonna to linger. Fed up, depressed, and diseased, she flew back to New York and Dan Gilroy, who was still burning a torch. Throughout her Parisian stay Gilroy had sent a steady stream of endearing, romantic letters. "His letters were so funny. He'd paint a picture of an American flag and write over it, like it was from the president, 'We miss you. You must return to America.' He really made me feel good."

Madonna moved in with her close friend Martin

> *"I certainly wasn't born with a perfect body. I'm five feet four inches and I feel like a shrimp—I probably look taller 'cause I've got such a big mouth."—Madonna*

Burgoyne, an illustrator who did some of her early twelve-inch record jackets. They rented adjoining apartments on the Lower East Side. Madonna jumped ship after her place was robbed by some teenagers and moved to Thirteenth Street. Burgoyne followed when *his* place was vandalized by the same mob two days later.

Going to Paris convinced Madonna to channel her energy into music, and, well, *Gilroy was a musician*. . . . Dan shared an abandoned synagogue in Corona, Queens, with his brother Ed. The space doubled as living quarters and rehearsal hall, littered with instruments, amplifiers, and band paraphernalia. Dan taught her to play drums, and she'd practice for five or more hours at a time while he went to work. Since she was spending the lion's share of her time with them, Madonna convinced the brothers to let her live at the synagogue.

Life was sweet. Madonna wrote songs, got a musical education, and hustled her contacts. "It was one of the happiest times of my life," she said. "I really felt loved. Sometimes I'd write sad songs and [Dan] would sit there and cry." According to Gilroy, Madonna started each day with a quick cup of coffee, then staged telephone blitzkriegs, blistering the wires with calls to anyone and everyone who could jump-start her career.

Along with Ed Gilroy and Angie Smits, Madonna and Dan were The Breakfast Club. Madonna drove the band crazy—she wanted to rehearse nonstop. She also wanted to soak up all she could about the recording industry. "I just took over in the sense that I said, 'What do you know? Teach it to me.' I took advantage of the situation. I wanted to know everything they knew because I knew I could make it work to my benefit."

Typically, Madonna dreamed big. "I started thinking record deals, making records and doing shows and stuff like that. And . . . most of the people you have to deal with are men, and I think I was just naturally more charming to these horny old businessmen than Dan and Ed Gilroy."

The Breakfast Club, with Madonna on drums, played all over the Lower East Side earning minimum wages that were split four ways. Those band members who had jobs hung on to them. Money was precious. Sometimes they'd scramble around hunting for loose change behind seat cushions and in corners before going out to haggle for food with local vendors.

But backing the group on drums didn't feed Madonna's massive need for attention. She pestered them to let her sing and to play her compositions. Meanwhile she drew close to Angie Smits, whose sartorial influence rubbed off. Gilroy recalled, "Angie dressed really sexy with see-through clothes and she moved sensuously on-stage. Madonna began to do these things, too. She was dark haired then, but she saw Angie's long blond hair got the attention. . . . Maybe that contributed to her finally going blond."

By all accounts Madonna's affair with Gilroy went kaput after a year, torn apart by her ambition and his conflicting loyalties. Should he side with his brother and their original vision of the band, or fall in with his determined lover's radically different goals? Madonna said, "I knew Dan and Ed were afraid that I was going to steal all the attention, so I thought . . . 'I'm going to have to leave and front my own band.'" It was a sad breakup. In 1982, Madonna moved back into Manhattan to go solo.

Madonna's style had evolved along with her

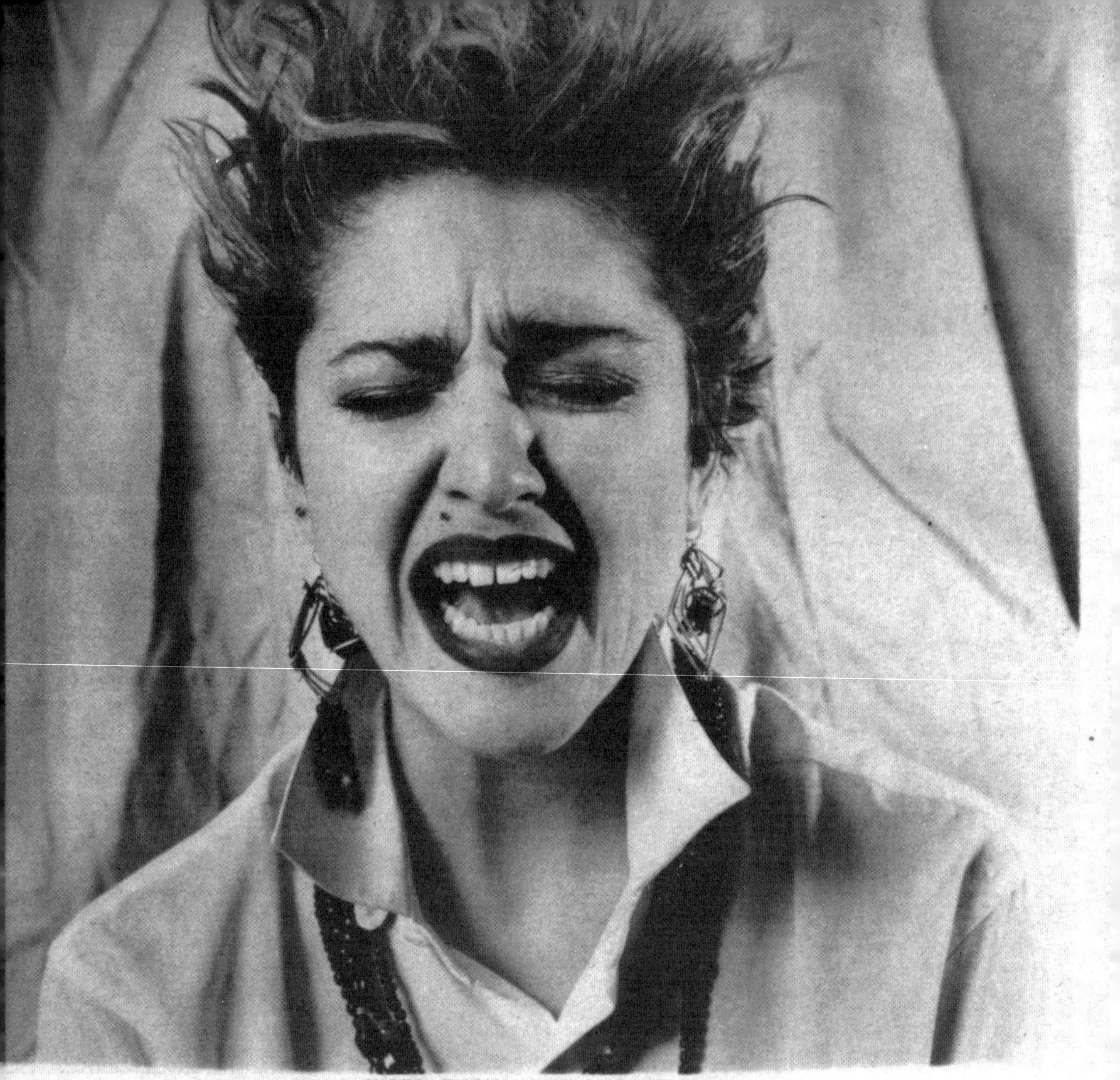

MADONNA PHOTOGRAPHED BY LAURA LEVINE.
CAMERA—NIKON

arted making records using records. ho w... it?

of, say, FRANK SINATRA JR. performing his latest recording. The Scopotone did

and over and over. They repeat them more than the top 10 on tightly formatted AM dio. MTV must have their reasons for remarkably restrictive policy and they bably quite similar to the rationale

rock and roll club has been heavily wired for TV. I really can't see going to a night club to watch television, but I have watched just because it's there. There's not much to watch. Most tapes are hi tech

Why's she screaming? A rave mention in Andy Warhol's *Interview* is every New Yorker's dream come true.

From the personal collection of Curtis Zales

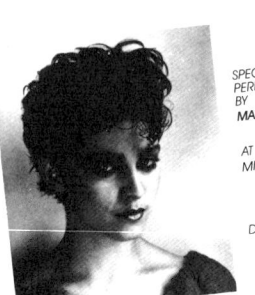

SPECIAL PERFORMANCE BY MADONNA

AT MIDNIGHT

DJ: ADRIAN

HEINRICH SCHILLING INVITES YOU TO
AN EVENING OF BOTANICAL ENCHANTMENT

DESIGN AND DECORATION CONCEIVED BY DANIEL HENDLIN • EARTHLY DELIGHTS, SOHO WITH ASSISTANCE FROM FRANK O'DONNEL

PLANTS • BRIAN SLOAN • METRO PLANTS, FT. LEE, N.J.

$12 ADMISSION WITH INVITATION

UNDERGROUND 860 BROADWAY (17 ST.) 254-4005
THURS. NOV. 19, 1981 11 PM A NIGHT TO REMEMBER

Madonna's earliest performances were in downtown clubs like the Underground.

music, and both were drawn from her encounters with club kids, graffiti artists, and their ilk. "It always comes from the street—people who aren't in show biz at all. Latin and black kids from the Lower East Side and the Bronx. I like clothes you can move about in—I don't like it when someone looks as if they're glued into their outfit."

She may have been experimenting with peroxide about now. Early photographs show a scraggly head of hair that's partly matted, partly spiked, a bit braided, even shaved. Madonna's still more brunette than not, but blond's building.

Madonna moved a lot and often stayed near the Music Building opposite Madison Square Garden, which was really a series of rehearsal spaces. She'd play all day, wait until the last band left, then settle down for a fitful night's sleep amid amplifiers, mixing boards, and electrical cords.

I lived a lot in the garment district where no one was allowed to live. It was for offices and factory warehouses and stuff, and there was no hot water. There wasn't even a fucking shower. Finally I had to leave because there was no heat. It was winter and I was sleeping on the floor surrounded by space heaters, and I woke up engulfed in flames.

A heater set fire to the rug and Madonna unthinkingly threw water on it—disaster with an electrical fire. Leaping flames caught her nightgown so she ditched it, threw on some clothes, and bolted. "All my important things, like tapes and instruments, were already over at the Music Building, three blocks away—and I went over and started sleeping there."

It was tough keeping a band together, but her good luck held when Steve Bray decided to move to New York to play drums professionally. He agreed to team up with his old girlfriend, who admitted, "He was a lifesaver. I wasn't a good enough musician to be screaming at the band about how badly they were playing."

The hard-rocking group went through many incarnations and names, like Modern Dance, the Millionaires, and Emmy. From the start she wanted to call the band Madonna, but the others resisted—far too egotistical, they said.

As Bray remembers, there was plenty of resentment toward Madonna, most of it coming from her peers. She made no secret of her belief that the other musicians she heard rehearsing were lazy and destined for obscurity. Her popularity quotient was low, her friends few.

Still in thrall to Chrissie Hynde and Debbie Harry, Madonna sang a blend of hard rock threaded with New Wave, but she was moving toward the infectious dance music blaring from ghetto blasters. She and Bray produced an early demo of "Burning Up" that caught the attention of Camille Barbone. Barbone and partner Adam Alter were launching Gotham Management, and Madonna was an early client. They put Madonna on salary and helped her get an apartment on the Upper West Side.

Camille Barbone claimed she and Madonna were as close as sisters. Maybe she didn't know about Madonna's problem with her blood relations! Camille was

> "When a girl leaves home at eighteen, she does one of two things. Either she falls into saving hands and becomes better, or she rapidly assumes the cosmopolitan standard of virtue and becomes worse."
>
> —Theodore Dreiser, Sister Carrie

both awestruck and amazed at how needy Madonna, at the height of her waif period, could be. By Camille's reckoning, she got behind the singer 200 percent—emotionally, professionally, and financially—only to be dumped unceremoniously when Madonna found something better.

Madonna wanted to play funk and Camille wanted rock and roll. "Although I'd agreed to do rock and roll, my heart was no longer in it. Soul was my main influence and I wanted my sound to be the kind of music I'd always liked. . . . I wanted it to be direct. . . . I loved to dance and all I wanted to do was make a record that I would want to dance to, and people would want to listen to on the radio."

Camille wanted absolute artistic authority. Madonna despised taking orders. The singer and Gotham parted angrily. "I lost everything. My demo tape was the property of Gotham Management. I was living back on the street and sleeping in studios, and I'd have to walk around in the same clothes for weeks."

By day, Madonna and Bray wrote songs, recording them when they could sneak into studios. By night they toured the clubs. The trendiest spots in the early eighties were the Roxy, Studio 54, and Danceteria. Each club was "hot" on a different night, so you planned your itinerary around the scene. Danceteria, a multi-level club on West Twenty-first Street, attracted a hip, white, Saturday-night crowd presided over by deejay Mark Kamins. He had a collection of dancing "groupies" who monopolized the dance floor. One of them was Madonna Ciccone.

THREE: BOUND TO RISE

"I think most people who arrive are takers. They take at the beginning of their lives, then if they have good character, they realize that they've been pigs and they try to pay back some of it."
—Katharine Hepburn, New York Times, August 1991

"I'm just a Midwestern girl in a bustier."—Madonna

Breaking off with Gotham Management was like picking a "Do Not Pass Go" card in the game of career Monopoly. Madonna dusted off and started over. "I knew record companies wouldn't listen to my demo, so I started taking it round the clubs and giving it to deejays." She had an ally in Danceteria deejay Mark Kamins, also a part-time beau. "Madonna was special," he remembered. "She had her own style and a tremendous desire to perform for people. When she started tearing up the dance floor, there'd be twenty people getting up and dancing with her. She was innocent, ambitious, broke, and confused. She was living a hard life."

Madonna played Kamins the four-track demo of "Everybody" she and Steve Bray produced. Kamins liked it and tried it out on his Danceteria crowd, who responded enthusiastically. So Kamins financed a remix, then shopped the tape among his industry contacts. Michael Rosenblatt of Sire spotted Madonna's star quality and brought her to the attention of Seymour Stein.

Sire Records, a division of Warner Inc. run by industry lifer Seymour Stein, had a reputation by the late seventies as the home of hip New Wave acts like The Pretenders, The Talking Heads, Depeche Mode, The Smiths, and The Ramones.

Stein's energy more than matches Madonna's. His knowledge of music—every artist, every hit, every lyric, every label—rivals the encyclopedia. In 1986, Madonna said, "He's more interested in the music than whether he's going to get platinum records out of it. Every time he signs someone he's taking a chance. And there aren't many people in the entertainment industry who do that anymore."

Stein was in Lenox Hill Hospital undergoing treatment for endocarditis when he heard the demo. He was impressed enough to invite Madonna to the hospital for a meeting. "I had this idea that I was going to meet some really sort of cold person in a suit and tie. And here Seymour was wearing boxer shorts and goofing around in his hospital room. He had a big ghetto blaster . . . [and] played my songs right while I was there in front of me, raving, 'It's great, it's great.' . . . I thought the guy was nuts. But he liked my music, so I won't complain."

Like others before and since, Stein was mesmerized by Madonna's presence—even more so than her music—so he offered $5,000 for three twelve-inch singles. She went into the studio over Easter and emerged with a finalized version of "Everybody," which Kamins showcased at Danceteria.

This was really a second audition with Sire so they'd put their money behind an album and some videos, so Madonna hired backup dancers, one of whom was buddy Martin Burgoyne. She poured on the moxie, dancing with abandon. Her act was a sizzling success.

Sire sent her around to play at clubs, but now instead of singing live she'd lip-sync. Many fans were amazed to find out Madonna was a white woman; her voice and material sounded black. "My first two hits were hits only on black stations, and it wasn't until 'Borderline,' which was my third release, and that's also the first video I had on MTV, that they crossed over to the white pop stations. People didn't know what I looked like before, and I was only played on black stations, but I still considered that I was very successful."

Throughout the early eighties, Madonna relied heavily on the kindness of friends, many of whom were downtown artists who went on to become name brands. According to Andy Warhol's diary, Madonna had a brief fling with Jean-Michel Basquiat before either of them hit the big time. A few years later Jean-Michel kicked himself because Madonna "got so big and he'd lost her."

Though newly solvent, Madonna didn't run wild. "The first expensive thing I bought was a Roland synthesizer. The next big money I got was publishing money for writing songs. . . . The first extravagant thing I bought that I felt guilty about was a color TV. I never had a TV before in the seven years I lived in New York. When I grew up, I didn't even have a color TV."

She followed "Everybody" with a twelve-inch version of "Burning Up," and a video, directed by Steve Baron, whose credits include Michael Jackson's "Billie Jean," "Cuts Like a Knife" for Bryan Adams, and Joe Jackson's "Stepping Out." It featured Kenny Compton, her boyfriend of two-something years, as a demonic driver aiming his car at Madonna. Instead of running away she gyrated in the road, yanking at her bodice and singing her song of incendiary love. Proving that life imitates art, Compton dumped Madonna just after the shoot.

But Madonna's lucky star kept beaming. She made friends with John "Jellybean" Benitez, the ineffably cool deejay from a club called The Funhouse. They circled each other warily, neither overwhelmed with the other's sex appeal, and approached romance in baby steps. "She didn't bowl me over at first," explained Jellybean. "We were attracted to each other, but we were just playing with each other." Because both worked long, unusual hours, they courted over the telephone.

"Burning Up" and "Physical Attraction" were club hits and successful on the dance charts. Sire wanted an album fast, so in 1983 *Madonna* was conceived—though not without labor pains. Mark Kamins and Steve Bray each swore *he*'d been promised the producer's job by his good friend and former lover, Madonna. Both were stunned when she announced Reggie Lucas would produce.

Madonna said, "I was really scared. I thought I had been given a golden egg. In my mind I thought, 'Okay, Mark can produce the album and Steve can play the instruments. It was really awful, but I just didn't trust him enough." Steve broke with Madonna. He told her she had no morals and stormed off. Ironically, he wound up playing with Dan Gilroy's Breakfast Club and cut an

Dancing at the Third Annual APLA benefit for AIDS.

Photo courtesy of Ron Galella

At this marathon the dance cards are filled by the charitable pledges.

Photo courtesy of Ron Galella

album with that group.

Even with Bray out of the running, Madonna didn't think Mark could handle an entire album. Kamins was hurt, but that anger was ameliorated by writing royalties for "Physical Attraction" and "Borderline," and producer's credit on "Everybody." "Sure I was hurt," he said. "At the time I felt stepped on. But I don't think there's a mean bone in her body. Maybe a knuckle, but not a mean bone."

Madonna never apologizes for her ambition. "It comes down to doing what you have to do for your career. I think most people who are attracted to me understand that, and . . . take that under consideration. You'd think that if you went out with someone in the music business they'd be more understanding, but people are the same wherever you go. Everybody wants to be paid more attention to."

She insists all her former boyfriends still love her and would eagerly take her back. "I wish I were a million different people so I could stay with each boyfriend while moving on to another one. I learn more, want more, and suddenly—that person isn't enough." Some people smirkingly suggest Madonna hasn't enough cells in her body to divide among former lovers. Rumors of her promiscuity may be exaggerated. Still, Andy Warhol once gossiped to his diary: "Keith Haring said that when Madonna was staying [with him], sleeping on his couch, the stories he could write about the people she had sex with."

Reggie Lucas was known for working with songbirds Roberta Flack and Stephanie Mills. Lucas envisioned Madonna as more of a pop artist than a disco singer and pushed her to achieve a mainstream sound. The impressive roster of songs on *Madonna* are "Lucky Star," "Borderline," "Burning Up," "I Know It," "Holiday," "Think of Me," "Physical Attraction," and "Everybody." Of the eight tunes, five were penned by Madonna, including the hit "Lucky Star." She dedicated the album to her dad.

Madonna's lyrics were supersimple and relied heavily on repetition. Her readiness to employ puns to convey double entendres is glaringly obvious, and most of the songs stick to rock's standard theme, romance. Knowing what we do about her childhood, it's interesting how often she's heard whining that the object of her affection (or lust) isn't paying enough attention to her.

Madonna made a quick trip to London promoting "Everybody." For her Camden Palace debut she wore a white T-shirt, red tartan shorts, a sweater vest, four or five belts, and her trademark rag ribbons wrapped around blond-streaked short hair. While not the opulently decorated look that sparked a legion of wannabes, she'd clearly stepped in that direction. This was a far cry from the style of her rarely seen live-performance video for "Everybody," shot in New York's Paradise Garage.

Madonna and her dancers are dressed like urban guerrillas. Her streaky hair is bound in rags and she's decked out in baggy multipocket khaki pants, a midriff-skimming brown T-shirt, and a big fisherman's vest with still more pockets. The dark, moody video moves slowly compared with the energetic minifilms fans are now accustomed to. The lethargy's heightened by an endless singsong refrain: "Everybody, come on dance and sing. Dance and sing, get up and do your thing."

One of Madonna's most exuberant hits almost

didn't make it onto the album. "Holiday," penned by Curtis Hudson and Lisa Stevens (of Pure Energy) and mixed by Jellybean, had been rejected by several great singers, including Mary Wilson and Phyllis Hyman. A last-minute crisis resurrected the song when Madonna's rendition of "Ain't No Big Deal" was cut from her album. Frenzied, she turned to Jellybean.

"Madonna called up and said she was short a song," he remembered. Benitez played the "Holiday" demo, and she decided to go with it. It took him "a week of twenty-four-hour days" to get the cut ready. "Holiday" made an impact in the clubs, so it aced out "Lucky Star" to become the first album single. "Ain't No Big Deal" eventually surfaced on the compilation *Revenge of the Killer B's, Volume 2.*

Madonna moved slowly at first, but Madonna didn't lose faith. "I know this record is good, and one of these days Warner Bros. and the rest of them are going to figure it out." She loved the album's energy level—"My dream was to make a record that I would want to dance to myself"—but wasn't satisfied she'd found her artistic groove. "I didn't realize how crucial it was for me to break out of the disco mold before I'd nearly finished the album. I wish I could have gotten a little more variety in there." It was curtains for Reggie Lucas.

Meanwhile the romance-cum-working relationship with Jellybean thrived. It stayed solid as long as their careers moved at the same pace. "My career has exploded within the industry and hers has exploded on a consumer basis," said Benitez early in 1985. "We're both very career oriented, very goal oriented." Madonna took Jellybean to her home that Thanksgiving—a dating first. They had to sleep separately, however, since Tony's strict rules about sexual conduct apply until you die. Madonna said she and Jellybean didn't sneak around after dark because her dad's room was in the middle!

In August 1983, the lovers moved into a SoHo loft. Madonna described it as "two thousand square feet, with wooden floors and windows on every wall. We had a bed, a table overlooking the street, and lots of mirrors for my choreography."

By the following April she was in the studio with Nile Rodgers polishing off *Like a Virgin*. Reggie Lucas joked, "It's funny about that thing with Kamins. The same thing that happened to him pretty much happened to me on her second record, when they hired Nile Rodgers." Rodgers was the hot producer famous for bringing a funky beat to David Bowie's mega-successful album *Let's Dance*.

Madonna enjoyed collaborating with Rodgers because he was open. He didn't hide information or ignore her input. "It wasn't until my first album was three-quarters of the way done that I realized, 'Hey! I know a lot more about this than I'm allowing myself to speak out about.' So I started going backward and stripping the songs down and making them more sparse.... When we got to the second album, I had a lot more confidence in myself."

That confidence made Rodgers's job harder. He found her a challenge to work with. "She didn't stumble across her success. She knows what she's doing. She's more temperamental than anyone I've ever worked with.... Some people do it and it's a drag because they don't have the talent to back it up, but when Madonna does it, it's because something's really bothering her.... Madonna assuredly isn't one to mince words."

Exiting the Michael Jackson concert with John "Jellybean" Benitez.
Photo courtesy of Ron Galella.

Benitez might have told him *that*. He's said, "Madonna makes all her own decisions. No one tells her what to do. She has other people carry out different things for her that might be awkward for her as an artist to do, but Madonna basically is Madonna. She knows what she wants and she goes after it."

One of the things Madonna wanted was Michael Jackson's manager. "Jackson transcended almost every level and appealed to everyone, and he had conquered the world. I thought, 'I want his manager.'" She flew to Los Angeles and convinced Freddy DeMann to come see her perform at Studio 54. It was a nerve-racking night. She knew he disliked Prince's overt sexuality and worried that her provocative act might sour the deal. Would he approve? He did and announced: "Madonna will be a female Michael Jackson." It wouldn't be the first or last time Madonna followed in Jackson's footsteps.

In 1991, DeMann said, "I remember when she first walked into my office. . . . She came in and I was absolutely smitten by her. She had three problems that day, three pressing problems, and I said, 'I'll make three calls and take care of your problems.' And I did it. The next day she called with five problems. The next day she had eight. The next day ten. . . . Madonna has that ability to grab you by the lapels and soon all you can think about is her." He stopped working for Jocko and started working for Madonna.

Instead of releasing the newly completed *Like a Virgin*, Sire pulled more singles off *Madonna*, including remixed dance versions of its most popular tunes. By Jellybean's calculations, they sat on *Virgin* for at least eighteen months. Sire was lucratively rewarded when "Holiday" became an unexpected Christmas hit and leapt into the top twenty. Once the album took off, *Madonna* went platinum and stayed high on the charts more than forty weeks. The Blonde One was understandably thrilled. "It had been hard making it as a woman . . . so when it finally happened, I thought to myself, 'You deserve it.'"

Madonna continued playing nightclubs. That May she performed at Paradise Garage at a party honoring her buddy Keith Haring. As publicist Liz Rosenberg said, "You could almost feel like you were a star when you were singing to tracks for five thousand screaming maniacs at the Paradise Garage." It worked for Madonna—at first. "To me that was the world. That's what I loved, nightclubs and discotheques. And then when the mass audience started catching on to who I was, it was like, 'Oh, I guess that *wasn't* the whole world.'"

All along Madonna kept one eye open for acting opportunities. She didn't get the Lori Singer role in *Footloose*, but won a bit part in *Vision Quest*. Directed by Harold Becker, *Vision Quest* stars Matthew Modine as a high school wrestler who starves himself into a lower weight class for the privilege of wrestling an archrival. It's a classic coming-of-age saga, complete with a manly rite of passage and sexual initiation.

Madonna essentially plays herself performing "Crazy for You" and "Gambler" in the nightclub where boys meets girl. Don't blink if you're hoping to catch her.

> *"I'm considering doing a song with Billy Idol, if you can believe it. Maybe a soul cover. That would be good, because we're both white and plastic and blonde." —Madonna*

In 1984 New York's arbiter of who's hot and who's not put Madonna front and center!

From the personal collection of Curtis Zales

Madonna's appearance is brief and inconsequential. At least she's in good musical company; the sound track features plenty of hot rock and roll, including Journey performing the lead cut. Her ballad "Crazy for You" recurs as the movie's "love theme" and plays in the background during a classic love montage—five minutes of swanning about holding hands in scenic locales before their inevitable lesson in comparative anatomy.

The Madonna of *Vision Quest* is fully evolved—long blond hair with serious dark roots, plenty of jewelry, and a multilayered costume that manages to leave her best parts bare.

Some biographies say the film's producer, Jon Peters, introduced Madonna to Barbra Streisand, but in September of 1991 Streisand told *Vanity Fair* they met through her lifelong friend Cis Corman, now the president of Streisand's production company, Barwood Films. In the early 1980s she was a casting director.

To illustrate her point about different types of stardom, Streisand brought up that introduction:

> There's a very interesting need for "stars" and "divas." Madonna is very good at that. She "plays" the part . . . [Cis] calls me up . . . and says, "I found this girl and she reminds me of you." . . . This was before she had had a hit record or anything. We took her out for a Chinese meal, and the funniest thing is she *orders a whole fish!* When I go out with people, I don't order lobster or steak. I mean, that takes chutzpah to order a whole fish. I was knocked out by her chutzpah. . . . This girl is out there.

Madonna found Streisand "enthusiastic and encouraging."

Though it was still early in the game, Madonna already displayed the instinctive cunning that makes her a topflight businesswoman. On November 7, she attended *Greener Pastures* at the Brooklyn Academy of Music with dates Keith Haring and Andy Warhol. Later, Warhol asked Madonna if she was interested in making a movie. "She was smart," he reported. "She said that she wanted more specifics, that she just didn't want to talk and have her ideas taken. She's very sharp."

What gave her first album its longevity? First, Madonna had crossover appeal. She was played on both pop stations and "urban contemporary" stations—i.e., stations catering to blacks. But more than anyone, Madonna owes her success to MTV. The first album sold over 6 million copies because Madonna's strong visual presence put her over to fans. She wouldn't even tour for another year.

Madonna never underestimated the power of television—it brought her to the masses. "If I didn't have a video, I don't think all the kids in the Midwest would know about me," she said. "It takes the place of touring. Everybody sees them everywhere. That really has a lot to do with the success of my album." And they partially satisfied her urge to act: "I always wanted to be a movie star and I've studied acting, which is a natural progression for anyone who's been onstage a lot. And videos, if they're good, are a short form of cinema."

"Borderline" (1984) was her first MTV video, the one that officially made her a star. "Borderline" tells the story of a pretty, streetwise girl discovered by a fashion photographer. The video splices images of Madonna hanging with the homeboys and girls, versus Madonna glammed up for the camera in the photographer's studio. She comes close to losing her boyfriend and gaining the photographer, but returns to the pool hall and vamps her beau all over again.

Another early video, "Lucky Star," was a veritable Sears catalogue of the future fashion craze. Studious wannabes could pick out the netting, fingerless gloves, crucifixes, rubber bracelets, and low-heeled boots that would become their uniform for the next few years. Best of all, everything was sold at the mall—and nothing about Madonna was irreversible, like a tattoo. You could don it or ditch it at will.

I like to look the way Ronnie Spector sounds: sexy, hungry, totally trashy. I admire her tonal quality. I don't have a deep, throaty voice or a womanish voice when I sing. I think my voice sounds innocent and sexual at the same time. That's what I try to tell people, anyway; but they always misconstrue what I mean when I say "sexual innocence." They look at me and go, "Innocent, huh?" They think I'm trash.

Madonna mania took off at the tail end of 1984 with the release of *Like a Virgin* and the video. Her rise perfectly mimicked Michael Jackson's solo career. He released *Thriller* in 1982 but didn't sell a trillion copies until millions of TV viewers caught the Motown special in May of 1983. Jackson's innovative dancing stole the show. Suddenly Jackson was *it*.

Now the girl who'd been a Jackson wannabe discovered that, like her idol, she was simply a few steps ahead of herself. And like Jackson, she zoomed into the collective consciousness because of a televised image.

The "Virgin" video was shot on location in Venice during the summer of 1984. It introduced fans to Madonna's now-infamous wedding dress—with its Boy Toy belt, yards of crucifix ornamentation, and miles of sheer gauze. The dress spoke more of Frederick's of Hollywood than *Brides* magazine, and Madonna's sultry, forthright stare was like a closed caption for the hearing impaired. She milked it, too, writhing like a sex-starved cobra across the polished floor of a Venetian palazzo and in the prow of a gondola.

"We felt that Venice symbolized so many things, like virginity. And I'm Madonna, and I'm Italian," she explained. The video was directed by Mary Lambert, who did "Glamorous Life" for Sheila E. Like "Borderline," "Virgin" relied on alternating images of Madonna the bride and Madonna the dancing gondolier. This penchant for opposites remains a constant theme throughout Madonna's video career.

During the video she's trailed by a lion. Perhaps it was chosen to symbolize the savage nature of passion. Perhaps it was Madonna's way of paying tribute to the mascot of Venice and its patron, St. Mark. Whatever the reason for its inclusion, he positively terrified her.

"The lion didn't do anything he was supposed to do, and I ended up leaning against this pillar with his head in my crotch. . . . I thought he was going to take a bite out of me, so I lifted the veil I was wearing and had a stare-down with the lion, and he opened his mouth and let out this huge roar. I got so frightened my heart fell in my shoe."

On September 14, 1984, even before the record's release, Madonna performed "Virgin" on the MTV music awards. Her live television debut started a debate that won't die. She appeared atop a giant wedding cake, rigged out in full Boy Toy regalia. After kicking off her high heels, she descended the cake writhing, squirming, and singing. Earthbound and shod, Madonna brought the performance to a climax by humping her veil and rolling around on the floorboards. One cameraman aimed his lens between her loins to offer America a prolonged look at Madonna's underwear.

When Madonna finished, hostess Bette Midler wisecracked, "Now that the burning question of Madonna's virginity has been answered, we are free to go on to even more *gaping* questions."

Critics tore apart Madonna's "sledgehammer sensuality." Mary Lambert defended the imagery: "I don't see any way to be subtle with a song like that. Madonna's not subtle. She's singing about sex." Madonna, on the other hand, insisted she *wasn't*.

Anyone who's truly listened to the lyrics of "Like a Virgin" knows how consistently they're misinterpreted. "I was surprised how people reacted to the song because I was singing about how something made me feel a certain way—brand-new and fresh—and everyone else interpreted it as, 'I don't want to be a virgin anymore.' That's not what I sang at all."

Sometimes it's not what you sing, it's the way you sing it.

Madonna was an official superstar. In November of 1984 while filming *Desperately Seeking Susan*, she appeared on the cover of *Rolling Stone* for the first time. That December, when filming completed, she checked into the tony Rancho La Puerta spa near Tijuana to relax and work out. Around now, according to Benitez, "she became obsessed with keeping her body in shape." Her dedication was apparent to everyone working on the film. They'd often shoot into the wee hours, but Madonna always began her new day with a four-thirty A.M. workout prior to the six-o'clock call. As Susan, she munched junk food on camera, but spit it out when Seidelman yelled, "Cut." Tastebuds aside, Madonna and Susan had much in common.

Madonna and Rosanna Arquette hotly denied rumors that they were at each other's throats filming *Desperately Seeking Susan*.
Memorabilia courtesy the Bill Ryan Archives.
Photo by David Palmore.

FOUR: **STRUGGLING UPWARD**

"I always had a great interest in films, and the thought that I could only make records for the rest of my life filled me with horror. Judy Garland did it . . . and if actress Sissy Spacek can be a country singer, then why can't I be an actress?"—Madonna

"There are two things that have no limit. Femininity and the means of taking advantage of it."—Jeanne Moreau in La Femme Nikita

Desperately Seeking Susan was directed by Susan Seidelman, whose *Smithereens* won accolades at Cannes in 1982. *Susan* was made for just $5 million and tells the story of a bored New Jersey housewife, Roberta Glass (Rosanna Arquette), who reads personal ads hoping to capture the excitement missing from suburban life. She's obsessed by the romance between the elusive Susan and the adoring Jim.

Susan's lifestyle is a far cry from Roberta's. Within the film's first few minutes Susan slips away from an Atlantic City tryst (after stealing the earrings, money, and silverware), parades through New York in abbreviated, see-through clothes, bathes in a sink at the Port Authority, and, in the words of writer Stephanie Brush, "gives us an encyclopedic display of antisocial behavior."

Consumed with curiosity about a series of mysterious ads, Roberta travels into Manhattan to catch a glimpse of the lovers. She trails Susan on a shopping spree and buys a trendy jacket Susan has traded for boots. When Roberta's conked on the head and wakes up with amnesia, she believes she is Susan. By now Susan's life is in danger. The earrings she stole were already hot, her weekend lover is dead, and a team of gangsters won't hesitate to snuff her to get the antiques.

Roberta/Susan is sheltered by Jim's friend Des (Aidan Quinn), an earnest projectionist who lives in a Chinatown loft. Madonna/Susan teams up with Roberta's hot-tub-selling husband to find Roberta.

Susan showcased plenty of hot talent, including Aidan Quinn, Laurie Metcalf, Mark Blum, Richard Hell, John Turturro, Annie Golden, John Lurie, and Ann Magnuson. It was designed as Arquette's star vehicle, but filling Susan's role proved difficult, and the woman who won the part walked off with the film. Seidelman auditioned over two hundred actresses before hearing that Madonna was interested. The singer was invited to test for the role.

According to Midge Sanford, one of the producers, "Madonna had this presence you couldn't get rid of. We kept going back to her screen test." Seidelman called Madonna "nervous and vulnerable and not at all arrogant—sweet, but intelligent and verbal, with a sense of humor. . . . She has the kind of face you want to look at blown up fifty times. . . . I didn't choose her because she was a rock star, I'm interested in interesting people."

Madonna liked the screenplay. It reminded her of the screwball comedies she adored. "I just love those films where the woman gets away with murder, but her weapon is laughter. And you end up falling in love with her." She envisioned herself reinventing the stylish roles popularized by Carole Lombard and Claudette Colbert in the thirties.

Madonna's celebrity quotient was rising fast, but stardom didn't inoculate against stage fright. "I had a few scenes where I was really shittin' bricks. A few times I was so nervous I opened my mouth and nothing came out."

The mood on the set was tense. Buzz in Hollywood and on the street called this "the Madonna movie." Gossipmongers played up sparks that supposedly flew between Madonna and Arquette while they loudly claimed to be boon companions. Nevertheless, some of Arquette's dissatisfaction made it to print: "I told them that if *Susan* was going to be a two-hour rock video, I didn't want to be part of it. A disco-dance movie wasn't what I signed on to do." In reality, the biggest conflicts flared between Seidelman and actors Arquette, Quinn, and Metcalf. It's said that Seidelman lacked the knack of stroking her talent.

When it came time to promote the film in spring of 1985, Rosanna told *Rolling Stone*, "We were really tight. . . . Madonna taught me a good lesson, because she just laughs off bad press. They think they're hurting her, and she just laughs." Arquette did admit she was "freaked out" that Orion pictures was promoting *Susan* as Madonna's film, but concluded, "I think her performance is really good. All I'm saying is, 'Let her be an actress.'"

Madonna was prepared to do just that, so she worked extremely hard at *not* being a rock star. "It was hard to get [them] to take me seriously. . . . I think they were shocked when I showed up every morning like clockwork." As she always did in new surroundings, Madonna took advantage of people's expertise and set herself the task of learning all she could about movie-making.

If Madonna had qualms about acting, she had no such doubts about her look. Santo Loquasto was costume and production designer for *Desperately Seeking Susan*. In 1977, he won a Tony Award for *The Cherry Orchard*, and he was nominated for an Oscar for Woody Allen's *Zelig*. His experience and impressive credentials didn't daunt Madonna for a minute. Loquasto wanted to give Susan a "West Side" look—antique fifties dresses and such. Madonna objected.

They battled it out and reached a compromise that fairly reeked of Madonna's downtown aesthetic. From dancer's leggings and midriff-baring lace tees, to boxers worn with garters and clanking jewelry, Susan's look screams Madonna. In one scene she sports a bright orange cutoff sweatshirt with the initials MC on the front and #6 on the back. Someone's idea of a joke? Madonna also did her own hair and makeup for the film.

Photographer Herb Ritts first met the singer when he shot the movie poster. He remembered, "She marched in with this little cigar box full of jewels and trinkets that she wanted to wear. She knew exactly how she wanted to look. I liked that."

The movie got more Madonna and less Arquette with the inclusion of her song "Into the Groove." As she explained it:

We needed a song that had a really good dance beat . . . and I brought in this tape we had been working on . . . I had no intention of using it in the movie. So I brought it in and we played it, and we had to do take after take and pretty soon everyone was starting to like the song. . . As the film got nearer to the end and they were doing the final cuts, Susan called me up and said, "We were trying to find another song for that scene and we just think yours really works.

Madonna agreed, figuring the song didn't interfere with her characterization. She was smart enough to recognize it undermined her goals. "I have a big audience of kids for my music, and you know how they use sound tracks to push movies. . . it's really a drag, because I'm trying to establish myself as an actress, not as a singer making movies."

Though *Desperately Seeking Susan* opened in just 269 theaters, it grossed $20 million over the first three days thanks to a predominantly teenage audience. The film appealed to Madonna wannabes as well as older women enchanted by the fantasy element of the plot and the love story between Arquette and Quinn.

Susan received a lot of press because its producer, director, writer, and top stars were women. Plus, it was an independent film that earned money. Quirky and silly, the film reflected Seidelman's affection for New York: "I'm infatuated with New York. It's not the buildings. It's the people you see walking the streets."

Bad blood between Madonna and Rosanna? Rosanna Arquette was a guest at Madonna's 1985 wedding. And in 1991, she told *Details* that she'd never yet used a body double, but if approached to do any more nude scenes, "I'll ask Madonna to be my legs." Arquette shrewdly perceived the great paradox of Madonna's personality: "Madonna goes right for it and she gets what she wants. I admire that a lot. But I think behind all that is a little tiny girl inside."

In January, "Like a Virgin" went to number one on the U.S. singles chart. On January 28, 1985, Madonna and Jellybean Benitez attended the American Music Awards at the Shrine Auditorium in Los Angeles. Her hair was long and mostly blond. She wore a *bustier* with suspenders, lots of rosaries, black fingerless gloves, and bracelets. Madonna collected an award for the *Like a Virgin* album, released in late 1984. It entered the charts at number seventy but flew to number one with the arrival of the new year.

Like a Virgin opened with "Material Girl" and featured the songs—about half of them cowritten by Madonna and Bray—"Angel," "Like a Virgin," "Over and Over," "Love Don't Live Here Anymore," "Dress You Up," "Shoo-Bee-Doo," "Pretender," and "Stay." Madonna's liner notes thank lawyer Paul Schindler, publicist Liz Rosenberg, and such friends as Steve Bray, Maripol, and Martin Burgoyne. Extraspecial thanks go to: "My family for nurturing my strange behavior. Freddy DeMann for knowing what to do with it. Jellybean. Goo Goo Ga Ga." She dedicated the album to the virgins of the world.

For all the goo-gooing, Madonna's affair with Jellybean was through. Madonna found the romance very tiring—indeed everything about stardom was tiring, and she had nothing left to give. Benitez, like her other exes, insisted he wasn't used. A loyal friend, he called

Madonna "a diamond in the rough" and added, "I know a lot of her ex-boyfriends and I don't think she used them or me. She took advantage of opportunities given her. Other people do the same thing."

With the collapse of this relationship Madonna announced she would probably never marry. "I can't conceive of living happily ever after with one person. I change so much and so my needs change also." Well, change she did in just a few months' time.

As her career exploded, public debate over Madonna's image and her place in rock's pantheon escalated. To this day, America can't get over Madonna's look and occasionally startling behavior. She points out that there's nothing new under the sun. The guys plowed this ground eons ago. "I get bad press for being overtly sexual. When someone like Prince, Elvis, or Mick Jagger does the same thing, they are being 'honest, sexual human beings.' But when I do it, it's, 'Oh, please, Madonna, you're setting the women's movement back a million years.'" Critic Dave Marsh agreed: "She presents herself as very tough and sluttish, which people seem able to accept very easily from Mick Jagger, but not from her."

Nineteen eighty-four was dubbed "a year of triumph for rock's new women." Every magazine ran stories on the new female singers and compared Madonna to Cyndi Lauper—always unfavorably. Those who saw Madonna's rise as a steady climb over the prone bodies of lovers dubbed her "McDonna—over 1 million served." Everyone agreed her image overwhelmed the music and said maybe that wasn't such a bad thing, given her abilities.

Comparing Madonna to Lauper has, to borrow a criticism leveled at Madonna's work, a central dumbness. In a field crowded with male talent, no one suggests choosing between, say, George Michael and Michael Jackson. There's no rule that the world contain only *one* heavy metal band at any given time. Or one rapper.

Perhaps the onslaught of female talent panicked America's arbiters of taste? At least critics who despised Madonna's voice ("like Minnie Mouse on helium") attacked on the basis of talent and artistry, not gender. One critic who caught the irony behind Madonna's act wrote: "Madonna suggested that dance music could be sung with the quietly humorous implacability of one of her unacknowledged influences, Leslie Gore."

Cyndi Lauper complained, "I hate when they pit woman artist against woman artist" and defended her supposed rival: "How can you criticize a woman for having a sexuality when men for years and years have been singing about nothing else? Madonna's just doing her thing. My thing happens to be different. Women have a sexuality that shouldn't be suppressed."

Nonetheless, critics persistently set Lauper and Madonna at opposite ends of the spectrum marked Politically Correct. Lauper, they decided, raised valid questions about female sexuality, while Madonna, to quote Ken Tucker, "not only didn't reject the woman-as-sex-object stereotype, she took it to new heights." Detractors vilified her as a "prefeminist anachronism whose come-hither posturing both exploited and trivialized her sexuality." *Vanity Fair*'s James Wolcott noted, "Madonna has been vilified in the rock press as if she were an invitation to a gang bang."

Robert Pattison, in *The Triumph of Vulgarity*,

Desperately seeking detente?

Photo courtesy of Ron Galella

Hugging the award for her Number One album, *Like a Virgin*.

What *me* insecure? Madonna's got a firm grip on bear and beau.

Portrait of a winner.

points to the long historical tradition of artists who used their sexual adventures as an extension of their art. He offered Oscar Wilde, Rimbaud, Verlaine, and Shelley as examples. And, he said, "a cunning rock star nourishes the fantasy that he's sexually omnivorous." Students of popular culture along with rock writers point out that nearly all music videos promote carnal desirability as the be-all and end-all in life.

E. Ann Kaplan, contemplating Madonna's style in her book *Rocking Around the Clock*, described it as "a cross between a bordello queen and a bag lady. . . . [She] combines unabashed seductiveness with a gutsy kind of independence. She is neither particularly male nor female identified and seems mainly to be out for herself." Kaplan saw Madonna as the rare woman who boldly demanded men's desire while simultaneously refusing to lose herself in any man's identity. Wolcott concurred: "Virginity is mine to claim, is Madonna's message. I'm pure as long as I belong to myself."

Camille Paglia, the author of *Sexual Personae*, a self-confessed Madonna fanatic and herself no stranger to controversy, called the early look "a brazen, insolent, in-your-face street style. . . . From the start there was a flamboyant and parodistic element to her sexuality, a hard glamour she had learnt from Hollywood cinema and its devotees, gay men and drag queens."

Madonna spoke out: "For so long people have been telling girls there are certain ways they mustn't look if they want to get ahead in life, and there I was dressing in a forbidden way and obviously in charge of my life and career. I was saying I can look sexy if I choose to and still be smart." Tony, are you listening?

How did she explain the wedding dress, Catholic iconography, and Boy Toy belt buckle? Characteristically, she replied honestly and humorously. Sometimes too humorously. Madonna didn't do herself any favors by joking that she regarded losing her virginity "as a career move," or declaring her overwhelming ambition was "to rule the world." On other issues she gave her comments more weight:

With the crucifixes I was exercising the extremes that my upbringing dwelt on. Puttingthem on the wall and throwing darts at them. . . . Crucifixes are sexy because there's a naked man on them. When I was a little girl, we had crucifixes all over the house, as a reminder that Jesus Christ died on the cross for us. . . . I liked the way they looked and what they symbolized, even before they were fashionable. . . .

I have always carried around a few rosaries with me. . . . One day I decided to wear it as a necklace. I thought, 'This is kind of offbeat and interesting.' I mean, everything I do is sort of tongue in cheek. . . . It isn't a sacrilegious thing for me. . . . When I went to Catholic schools, I thought the huge crucifixes nuns wore around their necks were really beautiful. . . .

I used to love hanging out with graffiti artists. . . . Everybody had a tag name they would write on the wall. . . . The thing was to see how much you could 'throw up' your name everywhere. One day I just thought of BOY TOY . . . everybody thought it was funny.

> "I'm considering doing a song with Billy Idol, if you can believe it. Maybe a soul cover. That would be good, because we're both white and plastic and blond."—Madonna

I've been called a tramp, a harlot, a slut, and the kind of girl that always ends up in the backseat of a car. If people can't get past that superficial level of what I'm about, fine.

Madonna's fans were far too busy snapping up seventy-five thousand copies of her record each day to ponder *why* they loved her. They just did. But she had a theory: "What kids see in me is another rebel kid who says what she wants and does what she wants and has a joy in life. The girls that dressed like me all got the joke—it was the parents who didn't."

Because she had struggled for identity, Madonna empathized with her fans. "Young people seem to be obsessed with not liking themselves," she commented. Her message was love yourself the way you are and keep a positive outlook on life. "What they see more than anything is that I was a little girl from Michigan and I had a dream and I worked really hard and my dream came true. I believed in myself and . . . children really need to have those kind of people to look up to."

In February 1985, *Vision Quest* hit movie theaters. This didn't affect Madonna one bit. That same month she made her "Material Girl" video and met Sean Penn. *These* two events indelibly altered her life.

"Material Girl," written by Peter Brown and Robert Rans, was a goofy little tune that perfectly epitomized the eighties rich-is-better mind-set. Madonna delivered the song with a real camp sensibility, accentuating the limitations of a flawed voice that Michael Musto called "paper thin, slightly nasal, but somehow sexy." Stephanie Brush got the joke. She wrote, "Madonna designed herself to be a parody of a sex object, and the song 'Material Girl' has got to be the longest-running musical put-on since Randy Newman's 'Short People.'"

For the video, directed by Mary Lambert, Madonna chose to delve into the Monroe archives again by recreating the "Diamonds Are a Girl's Best Friend" sequence from *Gentlemen Prefer Blondes*. It was a bold stroke, parodying a parody, but Madonna's never lacked confidence.

Decked out in a nearly identical hot-pink gown, surrounded by male dancers, Madonna reenacted Marilyn's number with a few new twists. First, and most important, she altered the story. *Gentlemen Prefer Blondes* was the saga of blond bombshell Lorelei Lee's pursuit—and capture—of an extremely rich beau. In the framing story of the video, Madonna played a much-sought-after actress (the "nice girl") who's bored with expensive tributes and ultimately falls for an average Joe. In the musical portion, Madonna played an acquisitive ("bad") songstress and vamp.

The audience, however, knows this paramour, played by Keith Carradine, is really a rich, powerful movie director. And because Madonna's so obviously in control, we know she knows. But defending herself against the "Material Girl" tag when it followed her off the screen, Madonna persistently reminded interviewers that the poor man won her in the end.

With "Material Girl," Madonna played to both men *and* women. John Fiske, author of *Reading the Popular* wrote, "Madonna invites women to find pleasure in her toying with chorus boys just as much as she invited men to find pleasure in her sexual body." At one point, Madonna knocks down a dancer and walks over his

Beulah, peel me a grape . . .
Photo courtesy of Ron Galella

Partying at the Palladium in New York.
Photo courtesy of Ron Galella

prostrate figure, the very picture of triumph. The lady's in control, and she can't be bought or bribed. Appeal to her vanity but don't insult her intelligence—if she wants you, she'll let you know.

"Material Girl" was our first peek at how adeptly Madonna could borrow images—from television, films and videos, art, magazines, etc.—and give them her own spin. This magpie sensibility proved to be a hallmark of her career. "I'm a sponge," she said. "I soaked up everything in my life and this is how it manifested itself." The *Village Voice* noted, "By becoming a pastiche object and poking fun at that object without degrading it, Madonna reveals that the honor behind her celluloid heroes, as well as herself, is brains."

When Madonna needed a stylist for the video, someone suggested Marlene Stewart, an L.A.-based costume designer. Their meeting launched a collaborative friendship. Stewart was already designing sexy black lace dresses so the two shared a wavelength. Marlene Stewart would design twelve costumes for the Who's That Girl? tour, create Madonna's wedding dress, and provide some clothes for "Blond Ambition." Interestingly, Stewart didn't always design the costumes from scratch but she never bought retail. "Even though Madonna starts fashion trends, I prefer to dig around thrift shops, rental shops, or make something for her, rather than buy something that's in the stores. As a designer, I prefer to have her wear something that's unique."

Madonna and Sean Penn are both fire signs. Their birthdays are one day apart, hers on August 16, his the 17th. Their tempestuous three-and-a-half-year marriage, as full of passion as one would expect from two Leos, was very much in keeping with the stormy unions endured by Madonna's cherished heroines. Frida Kahlo, Tamara de Lempicka, and Georgia O'Keeffe, three artists whose lives preoccupy Madonna, were all strong women married to equally strong men. Each fought for her artistic identity in the midst of marital tempests. Like her heroines, Madonna was about to face trial by fire.

Before meeting Madonna, Penn was engaged first to Pam Springsteen (Bruce's sister), then to actress Elizabeth McGovern. His reputation in Hollywood was one of dynamite talent locked inside a powder-keg personality. Madonna knew of his escapades, but admired him nonetheless. At one point she declared, "Sean, to me, is the perfect American male. I'm inspired and shocked by him at the same time." She predicted he'd die young.

> *"She only pretends to be a gold digger. Remember, I have seen the other side of Madonna."*—Christopher Flynn

Sean managed to get onto the set of the "Material Girl" video and snag a few minutes of Madonna's time. She told *Cosmopolitan:* "The director was a friend of Sean's and she knew that he sort of had a crush on me. . . . So I looked down and noticed this guy in a leather jacket and sunglasses kind of standing in the corner, looking at me. And I realized it was Sean Penn, and I immediately had this fantasy that we were going to meet and fall in love and get married."

Madonna had been standing at the head of a long flight of stairs, waiting for the electricians to set up their lights. Drawing upon the drama such a staircase affords, she swept past Penn with feigned nonchalance. "I just said, 'Hi.' And he kept hanging around. Hours had gone by, and it had gotten dark, and I saw him poke his head around the corner again, and I was like, 'Oh, *you're* still here?' So I went outside to talk to him." They tossed questions back and forth—the more outrageous the better. As Sean left, Madonna presented him with a single rose.

After their meeting, Sean's story goes, he and a friend were flipping through a book when it spontaneously opened to the quote: "She had the innocence of a child and the wit of a man." Sean and the buddy exchanged significant looks. "Go get her," the friend counseled. Sean pursued.

On their first date he took her to a party at Warren Beatty's house. "I remember meeting a lot of movie stars that night," she said. "Mickey Rourke, all these people. It was an auspicious evening. I met my friends Sandra Bernhard and Warren Beatty on the same evening. Sean was introducing me to all his friends." Sensible of her Marilyn fixation, Sean drove Madonna to Westwood to see Marilyn's crypt. They marveled at Joe DiMaggio's floral tribute, that symbol of love everlasting.

Just as their romance was getting off the ground, Sean left for Tennessee to film *At Close Range* with Christopher Walken. Meanwhile Madonna's career went stratospheric. Throughout winter and spring she dominated the *Billboard* charts and her videos were played in such heavy rotation that punsters dubbed MTV Madonnavision.

In March 1985, *Desperately Seeking Susan* came out. Reviewers kicked up a big fuss over Madonna's performance. *New York* magazine's David Denby (in a rare moment of amity toward her) pronounced Madonna "the most interesting thing in the movie." He added, "Madonna looks confident enough to crunch boulders.... A coarse erotic object, Madonna is a caricature of the movie femmes fatales of the past. But she wants to play that role so badly—she's so demanding of your adoration—that you would have to be a perfect bear to resist."

Films in Review said, "Madonna gives the role a certain sleazy authority." The *Village Voice* proclaimed, "Madonna has enormous authority. With her meaty little body, flared nostrils, and lewdly puckered lips, she's imperiously trampy—just walking down the street she seems X-rated." Andy Warhol admired Madonna's performance because it was so lifelike: "Madonna doesn't have much to do. She doesn't talk in the first part. But later on she does some good things, she sleeps in the bathtub and dresses up and shoplifts."

Judith Crist said, "Madonna seems to be dripping self-confident savvy from every pore and glitter spot." *Variety* pointed out that "thinking women" were resisting the film because of Madonna's involvement, but urged feminists to set aside these prejudices. "Madonna not only turns in a rounded, interesting performance, but the whole picture reflects the fact that none of the producers, director, or writer is named Joe or Sam."

Many reviewers decided Madonna barely had to act to portray Susan. Most proclaimed that a movie star was born. Hollywood came a courting. With the eyes of the nation upon her, it was the perfect moment to tour.

Except for the club kids and the MTV awards audience, no one had seen Madonna perform live. It's a testament to her popularity and the power of television that her albums went triple platinum without concert backup. By the middle of 1985, Madonna had sold 16 million singles. She raked up seven top-twenty singles in seventeen months in the States, and eight top-ten singles in Britain.

Freddy DeMann shrewdly decided to book Madonna into smaller concert halls rather than stadiums so that she could make contact with the fans. When tickets for her three June dates at Radio City Music Hall went on sale, fans bought 17,622 seats in thirty-four minutes. The previous world record for speed was held jointly by Elvis Costello and Phil Collins, whose fans took a comparatively leisurely fifty-five minutes to buy every seat in the house.

Madonna was slated to visit twenty-seven cities over seventeen weeks, and the concerts were accompanied by a merchandising blitz that would have made R. H. Macy proud. Concession stands hawked Madonna jewelry, T-shirts, posters, and more. In stores throughout the nation her Wazoo clothing line made a hit with thousands of wannabes desperately in need of lacy leggings, fingerless gloves, cropped shirts, and extroverted underwear.

The Beastie Boys opened with a thirty-minute set, but most wannabes missed it. They gathered in the ladies' room to rat their hair and adjust every lacy layer, leaving their moms back at the seats. Madonna came onstage in a madcap Technicolor jacket, purple lace leggings, turquoise knit skirt rolled down to expose the tops of her hose, a purple bra barely covered by a sheer lace tee, pounds of bracelets, two-inch false eyelashes, a floppy hair bow, and several ropes of religious jewelry. On her feet were low-heeled, ankle-high boots. To the adult eye she looked more cartoon than coo-ca-choo.

Later she donned black bicycle shorts, a fringed skirt and gloves, sleeveless vest, cropped top, and sunglasses, which conveyed a slightly raunchier message.

The first date was in Seattle on April 9, before three thousand wildly excited adolescents. Michael Goldberg, reviewing the concert for *Rolling Stone*, described her as a pinup girl come to life. Madonna plowed through thirteen of her hits in a klunky, on-the-job-training manner, proving that "she's not some perfect, unattainable sexual icon; she's a real person, like her fans." Goldberg estimated nearly 80 percent of the girls in the audience had dressed like the star. By the time Madonna hit San Francisco, twenty-dollar T-shirts were selling one a minute, and a concessioner claimed her stuff sold more than The Stones, Springsteen, or Duran Duran.

The show relied heavily on sexual innuendo. Madonna carried a boom box onstage and announced, "Every lady has a box. My box is special. Because it makes music. But it has to be turned on." For her encore of "Virgin" and "Material Girl" Madonna donned the controversial wedding dress and crawled between her guitarist's legs. Then she asked the crowd, "Will you marry me?" Naturally they shouted, "Yes!" At the end of "Material Girl," loaded down by tributes of cash, jewels, and fake fur, Madonna asked the crowd, "Do you think I'm a material girl? Well, I'm not. Take it, it's been nothing but trouble. I don't need money. It's the root of all evil. I need love!"

The Detroit show, released as a video, showed Madonna in a nostalgic mood, obviously overwhelmed by emotion. She said, "There's no place like home. . . . I was never elected the high school queen or anything, but I sure feel like one now." The show ended when her father's voice boomed, "Madonna, come down off that stage this instant."

"Daddy, is that you?"

"Come down this instant."

"But Daddy, I'm having a good time."

"You heard what I said."

At one Michigan concert, Tony himself dragged Madonna offstage.

After every show Madonna called Sean in Tennessee for a thirty-minute long-distance chat.

Critics spilled a lot of ink on the wannabe phenomenon. Many wondered how Madonna—boldly strutting the gifts of puberty—attracted such a young crowd of girls. Rock writer Richard Jackson marveled, "Her success is based on some of the oldest sexual ploys in the business, but her fans are mostly girls!" Another rock critic Georgia Christgau speculated that Madonna's earthy honesty defused the sexual threat. Dave Marsh wrote, "Madonna, almost alone among all the current women rockers, seems to be having a good time without forcing the issue."

Madonna herself said, "If you can't make jokes about yourself, then you're not going to be happy. You'll be the saddest person that ever lived. In my concerts there are so many moments when I just stand there and laugh at myself."

The fans, polled for magazine stories, called Madonna a "free spirit" who did whatever she pleased sartorially and got away with it. One teen said of her adaptation of Madonna's look, "You catch more men's eyes this way." Another said, "Madonna's living out our fantasies. She's able to do something our parents would never let us get away with. That whole slut image, it's usually just the guys who get to do that." Madonna told wannabes they didn't need men to enjoy their bodies—and the message made an impact.

Naturally detractors continued to fume that Madonna used her body to gain riches and fame. So what, she countered. "As long as I am riding high on the charts, I don't care if they call me a tart or a slut. I am proud of my trashy image."

Then she utterly confounded them with this brain teaser: "I know the aspect of my personality, being the vixen, the heartbreaker, and the incredibly provocative girl is a very marketable image. But it's not insincere. You just can't take it seriously."

Washington Post columnist Richard Harrington was one of the first to write a prescient, intelligent defense of Madonna in May 1985. He reasoned that her music wasn't important or meaningful, but had the virtue of accessibility. He defended her: "With Madonna, what you see is what you get, and if you miss the point of her, you're missing the obvious. Her fashions and performance may be libidinous, but they're not demeaning. . . . [She's] in total control and that makes a lot of people—men in particular—uncomfortable." She is not a bimbo, he said. "Bimbos suggest that their purpose is to fulfill men's fantasies; Madonna suggests her purpose is to fulfill her own. . . . She smolders so openly that anyone getting burned never learned the adage about hot stoves, but she hardly seems ruthless."

In May, *Rolling Stone* ran a swimsuit spread featuring Madonna posing like Marilyn Monroe—just

Performing sure wears a girl out . . .
Photo courtesy of Ron Galella

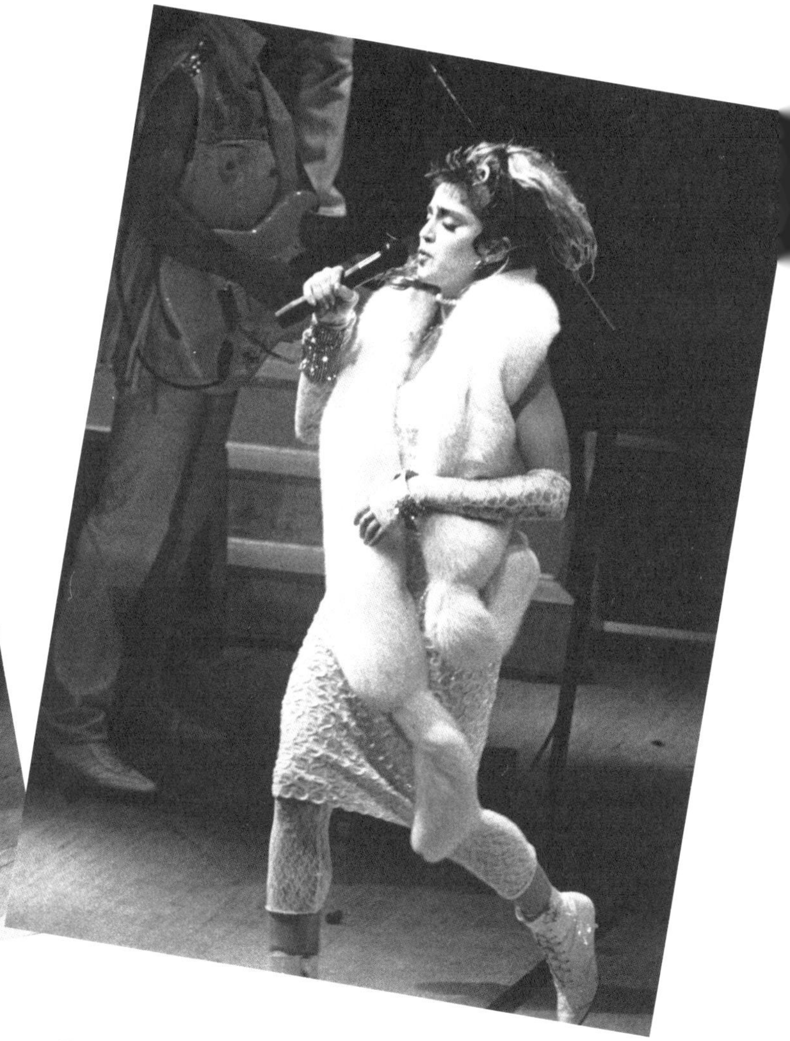

Collecting a tantalizing tribute.
Photos courtesy of Ron Galella

Photo courtesy of Ron Galella

"Hello, New York!" Madison Square Garden, January 11, 1985.

Memorabilia courtesy the Bill Ryan Archives.

Strutting her stuff on the Like a Virgin tour.

another notch on the peroxide bottle for Madonna, who was busily appropriating Monroe's images for herself.

Midway through 1985 a group of Washington wives headed by Tipper Gore founded the Parents Music Resource Center (PMRC). They advocated a rating system similar to the movies, with parental warning stickers on albums dealing with sex, satanism, and other "adult" topics. Madonna was singled out as one of the performers who created pornography. The PMRC filmed a commercial depicting a little girl playing with a doll, singing the words, "Like a Virgin." A stern voice-over warned parents about the evils inherent in this pop tune.

Discussing censorship in 1985, Madonna said: "Most of the lyrics in my songs have double entendres or lots of different meanings, so if you're thinking in a purely sexual way—I'm not using any offensive words or profanity at all. I'm not naming anything." Nor was she describing sexual acts the way, for instance, Prince had in "Head." "Prurience is in the eye of the beholder," she insisted.

The tour reached New York in June. Macy's department store celebrated with a Madonna look-alike contest on the sixth and convinced her pal Andy Warhol to be a judge. He reported that only about one hundred girls showed up so the event took less than forty minutes. He gave higher marks to that night's performance:

> The show was so great. Just so simple and sexy and Madonna is so pretty. Now she's thinner and just so great. And afterwards we went downstairs where there was a private party. . . .They were teasing her about her false eyelashes, saying they were bigger than Louise Nevelson's. And everyone was so thrilled, the waiters were on the floor. She was drawing cocks on Futura's pants.

After her New York shows Madonna zipped downtown to Steve Rubell's glitzy new Palladium nightclub. On June 11, after her third performance, Rubell and partner Ian Schrager threw a party in her honor. They bathed Madonna in rose petals dropped from the ceiling, swathed the rooms in white cloth, and dressed their waitresses in wedding gowns.

Flush with success, Madonna bid $1.8 million for an apartment at the prestigious San Remo on Central Park West. The co-op board, fearing the addition of a notorious celebrity to their ranks, turned her down.

Suddenly *Playboy* and *Penthouse* announced they'd unearthed shocking nude photographs of the Material Girl. "Since my tour I haven't had a moment's peace from the press," she whined. When reporters realized she was dating Sean Penn, their scrutiny intensified.

Madonna missed her freedom. She went from an exuberant, outgoing woman with a lilt in her step to someone scurrying along with her head down, avoiding people's glances, avoiding photographers. To protect herself, Madonna hired a bodyguard and started flying first class.

"The thing that annoys me more than anything about paparazzi is that they feel that they have put you where you are." They loved to hide and pop out unexpectedly, as if the element of shock contributed somehow to the beauty of the finished product. "It's like a teeny heart attack every time it happens. Every time I go running. . . I'm gliding along listening to music and all of a sudden they jump [out]. They're always scaring me, so I have to deal with that constant fear. I feel like they just might as well have taken a gun out and shot me."

By mid-1985 Madonna was certifiably rich and famous—fast discovering fame's downside.

Photo courtesy of Ron Galella

FIVE: FACING THE WORLD

"I feel like he is my brother or something. In fact when I squint my eyes, he almost looks like my father when he was young."—Madonna

"When I married Madonna, I certainly didn't expect the kind of ruckus that occurred in the media."—Sean Penn

During the summer of 1985, Warner rereleased the *Madonna* album and the upbeat tune "Holiday" went top twenty again on both sides of the Atlantic. On July 8, *Time* magazine announced the engagement of Madonna Louise Ciccone, twenty-six, the "belly-button-baring rock phenomenon," to Sean Penn, twenty-four. Just two days later *Playboy* and *Penthouse* hit the stands. On the thirteenth Madonna performed at Live Aid in Philadelphia before ninety thousand concertgoers and billions worldwide. On July 15, *Time* announced Sean Penn had been arrested on two counts of assault and battery after allegedly attacking an English photographer and reporter stalking the lovers in Nashville. Penn was released on $1,000 bond and threatened with a $1 million civil suit by the two journalists.

In the midst of it, Madonna and Sean planned their wedding.

Live Aid was two simultaneous concerts, one in Philadelphia, the other at London's Wembley stadium, consisting of over seventeen hours of broadcast time. The rockfest continued Bob Geldorf's effort to raise money for Ethiopia, which began in 1984 with Band Aid's recording of "Do They Know It's Christmas," which raised nearly $13 million. American singers chimed in as U.S.A. for Africa and produced "We Are the World" the following January.

Live Aid was beamed to 140 countries via satellite and accumulated $85 million in pledges. Prior to the concert date promoters had accumulated about $7 million in ticket and merchandise sales, plus another $7 million for broadcast rights.

Bette Midler got off another zinger at Madonna's expense, introducing her as "a woman who pulled herself up by her bra straps and has been known to let them down occasionally." Looking puffy and startlingly overdressed for a hot July day, a redheaded Madonna barreled onstage in Philadelphia and bulldozed through her set, shaking a red tambourine and her booty with wild abandon. She belted out "Holiday," "Into the Groove," and "Love Makes the World Go Round."

> I remember the sun burning in my face, which was a strange experience because I'm used to performing at night and I was really hot and . . . people were screaming, 'Take it off, take it off!' And I said, 'I ain't taking *shit* off! I don't want you to hold it against me in five years.' Before I went on, I really thought, 'I can't do this.'. . . I was so

unsure. . . . There were those *Playboy* pictures and I'd just gotten engaged to Sean and I really wasn't sure of myself. So I decided to be a warrior and it worked, and that was the first time that I really understood my power.

This visible strength and courage won Madonna many new fans, and their dollars kept record sales strong throughout the summer. Another bonus from Live Aid was an introduction to her idol Chrissie Hynde. They met backstage and hit it off immediately. They had things in common. Both are vegetarians, both record for Sire, both are strong, outspoken women.

About those nudes. As *Time* wrote, "Discovering that Madonna had posed nude early in her career is a bit like learning that the blond pop siren streaks her hair." Given her overheated image, what's most surprising is how tame those photographs—relics of her art school modeling sessions—turned out to be.

To hear Bob Guccione tell it, "*Playboy*'s photographs were coarse, uncomplimentary, and rather like scraping the bottom of the barrel." Guccione claimed he had first dibs when compiling his feature, though other sources say he tried to buy the *Playboy* photos for $100,000. Guccione also offered Madonna a cool million to pose for a new, exclusive layout. When she refused, they sent advance copies of the magazine to Sean Penn, though their reasoning is unclear. He'd undoubtedly seen Madonna nude by this juncture.

The magazines and photographers reaped big profits. *Playboy* printed 5.9 million copies—350,000 above normal, while *Penthouse* shipped 5.2 million issues instead of their usual 4.9. Schreiber and Friedlander, whose work appeared in *Playboy*, won't say what price they got (in the $100,000 range), but they only paid Madonna $25 for the entire lot. It was a testament to Madonna's success—and fans' curiosity—that both magazines became collector's items.

Though she bluffed her way through it, the scandal devastated Madonna. Luckily Sean was on hand to reassure her that everything blows over in time. In retrospect, she's quite philosophical: "I felt really out of control. I feel silly that I ever got so upset. . . . You think it's the end of the world, and then one day it's not. . . . I would have preferred that those photos weren't printed, because obviously the way they were promoted wasn't very flattering to me, but when people actually saw them, they thought, 'What's the big deal here?'"

Again in 1987 and as recently as September 1991, *Penthouse* published additional Madonna nudes. By now, however, the novelty has worn off since Madonna's given us many nude and seminude views of her well-toned physique, posing `a la Marilyn or as her rambunctious self for such renowned lensmen as Herb Ritts and Steven Meisel.

Sean never proposed, exactly. To hear Madonna explain it, "Sean asked me to marry him, but he didn't say it out loud. I read his mind. So I read his mind back to him."

The couple were staying at a Tennessee inn during the shooting of *At Close Range*. One Sunday morning Madonna began the day in her usual rowdy fashion by jumping up and down on the bed. "All of a sudden he got this look in his eye and I felt like I just knew what he was thinking. I said, 'Whatever you're

"I ain't taking *shit* off!"
Photo courtesy of Ron Galella

The Woman Warrior conquers Live Aid.
Photo courtesy of Ron Galella

Publisher Bob Guccione sent Madonna's then-fiance Sean Penn copies of these nudes when she refused a cool million to pose again.
Memorabilia courtesy the Bill Ryan Archives.
Photo by David Palmore.

thinking, I'll say yes to.' That was his chance. So he popped it." Madonna, a woman of her word, said yes. That settled, they trundled off to 7-Eleven for a sack of celebratory jawbreakers.

What attracted Madonna to Sean? Was it physical? Madonna always told interviewers her favorite physical type was the Latin variety with dark skin and full lips. Far from a portrait of blond, squinty-eyed, mini-lipped Penn. Given her history, many theorists cut to the chase, openly wondering how Penn could advance Madonna's career.

Susan Seidelman felt the attraction was good old-fashioned love: "She could have had anyone she wanted. If it was just for the sake of getting married, she could have married someone richer, better looking, and more politically connected than Sean. I don't think she needed Sean in an opportunistic way. Movie people were already beating down her door."

Martin Burgoyne explained: "The other relationships weren't right because they weren't fifty-fifty. This one is. Neither one of them is in control; she can learn from him and he can learn from her."

Madonna told Carrie Fisher: "It was really a romantic thing. We were madly in love with each other, and we decided quite soon after we started seeing each other that we were going to get married." Like many another lover, Penn got a tattoo—albeit a discreet one—to honor his lady. It's a daisy (his nickname for Madonna), located on his toe.

Surely Madonna wasn't marrying for security—she was worth millions, though she downplayed that aspect of her life. "What interests me is what happens in my confrontations with people every day and in my performances. . . . Not figures on a piece of paper or how much money I have in the bank. . . . I always said I wanted to be famous, I never said I wanted to be rich."

Yet Penn undeniably offered quick access to the Hollywood "A" list and a certain legitimacy. Sean is the son of director Leo Penn and former actress Eileen Ryan. He started acting as a teen and within a few years was hailed as a new Brando with unlimited potential. Penn lived in Malibu and hung out with a cool Hollywood crowd, a mixture of Brat Packers and older performers with deep Hollywood roots. Through Penn, Madonna met such people as *At Close Range* director James Foley (who eventually directed her "Live to Tell" video and *Who's That Girl?*), Warren Beatty, Diane Keaton, and many others.

> *"I'd rather walk through fire than walk away from one."—Madonna*

Certainly Sean was someone to *talk* to. For all his hotheaded outbursts, Penn is an intelligent, if tortured, young man who writes poetry in his spare time.

The hot-pink invitations read:

Please Come to Sean and Madonna's
Birthday Party on the Sixteenth of August
Nineteen Eight-Five
The Celebration Will Commence at Six o'clock P.M.
Please Be Prompt or You Will Miss Their
    Wedding Ceremony
The Need for Privacy and a Desire to Keep You Hanging Prevents the Los Angeles Location From Being Announced
Until One Day Prior*
R.S.V.P. by August 3 to:
    Clyde Is Hungry Productions
    6521 Leland Way, Hollywood, CA 90028
    (213) 460-6208
    *Please include a phone number where you can be reached

Before the wedding they had his and her

Never before published photos of Madonna's first performance ever in 1980, New York City!

From the personal collection of Curtis Zales

From the personal collection of Curtis Zales

Bussed by a wellwisher after her first club date.

From the personal collection of Curtis Zales

Back then, Madonna was unfussy and unmadeup—a far cry from Blond Ambition.

Looking for more than disco, Madonna plays the legendary Max's Kansas City, home-away-from-home for the Warhol crowd.

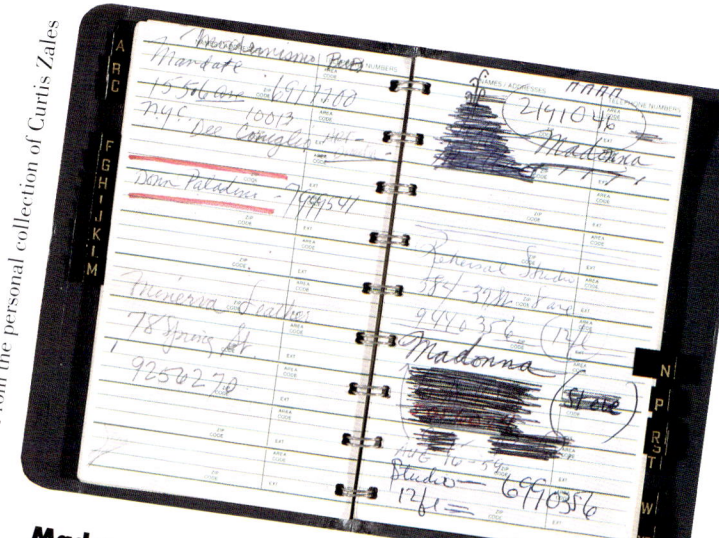

From the personal collection of Curtis Zales

Madonna's phone numbers way back when!

the Madonna story 4
LUCKY STAR

Madonna has never been a girl to hang about waiting for things to happen. If she wants something she gets on and does it. And she's not one to let relationships get in the way.

In the wake of her early recording career lay old boyfriend Dan Gilroy and his band The Breakfast Club; another longtime friend, drummer Steve Bray; and producer and lover Mark Kamins.

All had helped her. But as her situation changed she let them go.

It was a pattern of play that would continue. Madonna may have had a recording contract, plus a 'name' producer in Reggie Lucas, and her first single ready to go. But when her career demanded it she wouldn't hesitate to make the necessary changes again...

HISTORY IN THE WAITING

With her singing career now properly underway, Madonna continued performing – but not with a band. Instead she'd hop onstage at dance clubs and sing to backing tracks or lip-sync, spicing up her performance with the sort of lusty dancing that has now become her trademark.

It was at one of these shows that producer Reggie Lucas first saw her new act.

By Christopher Connelly

In 1984 New York's arbiter of who's hot and who's not put Madonna front and center!

From the personal collection of Curtis Zales

From the start, teenagers were Madonna staunchest fans.

From the personal collection of Curtis Zales

"In this early pairing with her frequent iconographer, Herb Ritts, Madonna "gets it white.""

Years before "Love Song," tabloids had a field day linking these God-obsessed rockers.

From the personal collection of Curtis Zales

Madonna went high profile to promote the release of *Shanghai Surprise*.

Moviegoers found this freebie at the box office in May of '91, part of the media blitzkrieg hyping *Truth or Dare*.

Her look is sleek but the mannerisms still speak of a lost little girl. . . .

From the personal collection of Curtis Zales

bachelor parties. Nile Rodgers's girlfriend, Nancy Huang, hosted Madonna's at her New York flat. The to-do was enlivened by the arrival of six men in drag. Several days later the celebration continued at the Tropicana, a female mud-wrestling club.

Sean's bash, August 14, convened in a party room at L.A.'s Roxy nightclub. Entertainment was courtesy of Kitten, a stripper with staggeringly zaftig dimensions of 42-24-36. Kitten reported: "[Sean's] very nice. He reminds me of a little boy, like he's eight years old and he's got so many cookies he doesn't know what to do with them." She brought the house down stripping to "Material Girl." An expert on such matters, Kitten judged the night tame by bachelor-party standards.

Sean and Madonna were married on her birthday at Kurt Unger's lavish Malibu home perched on a bluff overlooking the Pacific. They had the bluff blessed by a priest, but the two lapsed Catholics were married in a civil ceremony by Judge John Merrick.

Invited guests numbered around two hundred, but the uninvited caused more commotion. A phalanx of helicopters manned by tabloid photographers buzzed overhead throughout the ceremony, drowning out the couple's vows. Though guests passed through a security check and special guards scanned the property with infrared binoculars, none of their precautions were a match for the aerial onslaught of these determined journalists. As one guest said, "No one knew they were married until they kissed."

"It was almost too much," said Madonna. "I mean, I didn't think I was going to be getting married with thirteen helicopters flying over my head. It turned into a circus. In the end I was laughing. You couldn't have written it in a movie." Sean, rumor has it, took potshots at the helicopters with a pistol and scrawled an obscenity into the Malibu sand big enough for passengers in the choppers to read. He greeted guests with the wisecrack, "Welcome to the remake of *Apocalypse Now.*"

Madonna's dad gave her away, and sister Paula was maid of honor. Director James Foley, wearing lime green and sporting George Michael stubble, was best man. Sean wore a double-breasted, off-the-rack Gianni Versace suit.

Madonna was a vision in white—well, antique white, confected by Marlene Stewart. Madonna's hair was caught in a French twist, and she held her veil on with a black bowler hat. She wore a single long earring and an antique pearl bracelet. Perhaps the most eccentric element of her costume was the Miss America-type sash draped across her shoulders. It featured dried roses wrapped in silver and pink metallic tulle dripping with gold threads and pearls. According to Stewart, "We wanted a fifties feeling, something Grace Kelly might have worn." Stewart was especially proud of Madonna's shoes—Louis XIV pumps with pearls and little gold-plated roses encrusted with jewels.

The house and grounds were decorated in white, from tents and bunting covering Unger's tennis court to the tablecloths and table decorations. The centerpieces were gold-and-jewel-studded high-heeled shoes on embroidered cushions. A coincidence, or another message from the girl who thought she was Cinderella?

Spago catered the fiesta, delivering pounds of curried oysters, fancy pizzas, rack of lamb, lobster ravioli, swordfish, and baked potatoes bulging with sour cream and caviar. Cristal champagne flowed unstintingly. The five-tier hazelnut wedding cake was adorned with sugar flowers.

When it came time to cut the cake, Madonna turned to Cher and inquired, "You've done this before. Do you just cut one piece or do you have to slice up the whole thing?" The question baffled Cher, who said, "As if I'd know!" Madonna passed slabs of cake in her hands and smeared some on Sean, who retaliated by smearing it back.

Guests danced under a white tent to the sounds of the big band era. Madonna enlisted the help of archivist Michael Ochs, who helped pull together a selection of music that encompassed such talents as Bing Crosby, Ella Fitzgerald, Sarah Vaughn, and Cole Porter.

The guest list read like Robin Leach's black book. Jamie Foley brought Diane Keaton. Cher, resplendent in a violet wig, came with then-fiancé Josh Donen. Andy Warhol, Keith Haring, Martin Burgoyne, Steve Rubell, Rosanna Arquette, and Harry Dean Stanton came. So did David Letterman, Judd Nelson, Carrie Fisher, Emilio Estevez, and David Geffen. Not to mention Timothy Hutton, Tom Cruise, Martin Sheen, Crispin Glover, and Christopher Walken. Madonna's many siblings, parents, and grandmother were also on hand to watch her shout her wedding vows.

To celebrate their short four-day honeymoon, Sean and Madonna drove up the Pacific Coast Highway. They spent at least two nights at Carmel's Highlands Inn where they registered as M. Osch. Their room, 429, held a king-size bed, spa bath, fireplace, and balcony overlooking the ocean, at a cost of $225 nightly. For refreshment, the newlyweds ordered masses of smoked salmon, fresh berries, and champagne from room service.

When they returned to Hollywood, the Penns settled into a $3.5-million Malibu estate with a state-of-the-art security system, though Sean joked they'd be better off installing gun towers!

Though their wedding made headlines nationwide, Madonna was probably right when she commented, "No one wanted us to be together."

"Madonna will be out of the business in six months. Her image has completely overshadowed her music." So prophesied Paul Grein, a *Billboard* editor, in March of 1985. At the same time, manager Freddy DeMann correctly hailed Madonna as "the 'It' girl of the 1980s."

Now Madonna's star burned with such intensity that even she broke a sweat. *A Certain Sacrifice* director Steven Jon Lewicki speculated, "Madonna loves to have the camera pointed at her. She needs a lot of attention. . . . That's the deepest need that I think she has as a person. She's probably a very fulfilled person right now because she has the entire world looking at her."

In reality, the Penns were far less fulfilled than frustrated. Sean and Madonna lived under a microscope lens. Their daily routine was constantly interrupted by photographers, interviewers, and adoring fans.

In October, Sean faced a judge in Nashville to settle July's assault charges. He was fined a hundred dollars and received a ninety-day suspended sentence.

On November 14, Madonna went solo in New York and showed up at Yoko Ono's dinner party for Bob Dylan. Andy Warhol was there and told his diary, "Madonna arrived and . . . said she was so relieved her husband, Sean, wasn't with her so she could really have fun. And she felt uncomfortable without her shoes because she didn't have socks—she said she'd feel more comfortable with her top off than her shoes off." Another report said Madonna wandered into the kitchen where Dylan and David Bowie were deep in discussion. She fled to the living room and blurted, "Thank God there's somebody here to talk to—there are only old folks in the kitchen."

For a while, being in love with Sean centered Madonna and gave her strength. "I feel calmer now than I ever have before. What that means is that I can really concentrate on the important things. . . . Now that I'm in love, all the songs I write I feel like I do it all for him . . . I think, 'Would he like it?' . . . So love inspires me, and Sean inspires me."

Being Madonna, she proceeded to tell the interviewer that books, movies, butlers, janitors, and children inspired her, too!

As ever, Madonna was hard at work. The songs in question would become her 1986 album, *True Blue*, an album that would spark more controversies and unveil Madonna's most breathtaking look to date.

SIX: TRY AND TRUST

"Growing up I admired the kind of beautiful glamorous woman—from Brigitte Bardot to Grace Kelly—who doesn't seem to be around much anymore. I think it's time for that kind of glamour to come back."—Madonna

"There's nothing behind her other than instinct and impulsiveness. She's unlocked enormous pent-up yearnings for a glamorous image. She's hooked onto a moonbeam."—Director James Foley

The new year, 1986, started exotically in China where Madonna and Sean went to film their joint acting enterprise, *Shanghai Surprise*. Backed by George Harrison's Handmade films for $15.5 million, *Shanghai Surprise* was intended as a romantic adventure. They dreamed of recreating the magic of *The African Queen*. Ultimately the finished product (and ensuing media circus) smelled more like a Taylor/Burton fiasco than a cinema classic.

Madonna remembered arriving in Shanghai after a disorienting flight that lost them a day. "We were supposed to go to sleep, but we couldn't sleep, and we ended up just walking around in the streets on this steel-cold morning. It was still dark out, and the streets were filled with people doing t'ai chi."

Her blond hair—long and wavy like a proper movie star's—attracted tremendous attention, and Madonna was equally captivated by the Chinese. "They hang their wash out—put a stick out the window and put their clothes on the stick, and they're frozen in the air. When it gets light out, people are traveling around with buckets, a huge chunk of meat, and a head of cabbage, their food for the day."

Mutual fascination quickly soured. The Penns discovered Shanghai lacked the necessary atmosphere for a period film, so they had to relocate to Macao. *Shanghai Surprise* was based on a novel called *Faraday's Flowers* and cast Penn as a small-time crook adrift in the Orient. Madonna played prim Gloria Tatlock, a missionary who enlists his aid in locating a half-ton shipment of opium that's been missing more than a year.

What possessed Madonna to tackle the role of a missionary knowing the guffaws that it would invite? In 1987 she told *American Film:* "To the public, the roles they've seen me do in videos are me. To me, they're characters that part of me is in. After I did *Desperately Seeking Susan,* people went, 'Oh, she's really playing herself,' and I thought, 'That means I have to play an opposite character to convince everyone.' Which is a trap."

Sean and Madonna had approval on every aspect of the film. They chose director Jim Goddard based on a recommendation from Martin Sheen, but later complained that his television-only background left him woefully short of the expertise necessary to handle a feature film. "I thought it was a great script, and the idea of going to Shanghai was exciting, and the idea of working with my husband was exciting to me because he's a great actor. But sometimes everything goes wrong."

The production moved to Hong Kong, where they hoped to find more of the gritty, back-alley look of the late thirties. The bay city swarmed with journalists, many of them English, trailing the Penns day and night. Fans followed them too, shouting, "We want Madonna!"

To complicate matters, the locations they wanted were controlled by Chinese gangsters. Madonna recalled: We were at one location for eighteen hours and there was only one little road to it. They blocked it off. So, it's two o'clock in the morning, it's cold, we're tired, we have to get up the next morning at six, and we couldn't get out of there because this guy was parked, and he wanted fifty thousand dollars. That went on every day. And nobody would help us.

Everyone predicted working together would drive the couple to divorce court. "A lot of people were saying that's a sure way to end a relationship . . . and I had all these feelings of insecurity. But I've seen Sean work with other people, and—a lot of people have said it—he's a very giving actor. . . . Strangely enough, we never got along better." That's probably because they adopted such an "us against them" attitude toward everything and everyone involved in the film.

The Penns took turns "being strong" and buoyed one another's spirits throughout the tense shoot. There were other problems besides relentless reporters. Many of the cast and crew developed food poisoning, rats lurked beneath the trailers, and Madonna found her lightweight cotton wardrobe no match for freezing temperatures. Madonna tried to find strength in the biblical quote "This, too, shall pass." "I kept saying, 'I can't wait till I can look back on this, I can't wait.'"

In Macao, Sean and Madonna had a suite on the eighteenth floor of the Oriental Hotel. Though the entire floor had been combed for cameras, tape recorders, and reporters, they were stunned to encounter a journalist "in the door of our hotel room." He was Leonel Borralho, an employee of *Hong Kong Standard*. When Sean saw him there, camera poised, he went ballistic. "What are you doing here? Who let you in? Can't you see my wife is trembling?" Someone, perhaps Sean, twisted the camera strap around Borralho's neck, causing some damage. Borralho responded with a million-dollar lawsuit.

"Sean's whole image was sort of blown up into this impossible person out of control," said his exasperated wife. The film's publicist, Chris Nixon, suggested Sean and Madonna bite the bullet and pose for some photographs to appease the press. Infuriated, Penn had Nixon fired.

A reporter even popped up in the hotel sauna asking if Madonna was having a good time! "What? Being harassed? No. We didn't think we'd have any problems here," she replied. Thoroughly fed up, Madonna let loose with some unflattering comments about her fans, whom she imagined as "boring people leading boring lives. Then they read in the paper reports detailing the lives of celebrities—their every move. They admire them and end up fantasizing about them." George Harrison felt compelled to do some on-site-damage control so he flew to the Orient to chat with the Penns.

If Madonna and Sean expected a more civilized reception when they arrived in London in late February, they were delirious. At the *airport* a reporter bounced off Madonna's limo fender and wrote a story entitled

Leaving the Muse restaurant with Alek Keshisian.

Photo courtesy of Ron Galella

"Maimed by Madonna" that insinuated she'd ordered the driver to mow him down. Next, a set of Polaroids of the stars went missing and the newlyweds went on strike, refusing to report to the set until the matter was resolved.

By March 6, the situation was so stressful that George Harrison called a press conference for seventy-five reporters at London's private Kensington Roof Gardens club. An extremely subdued Madonna appeared, but no Sean. He was there in spirit, since nearly every question harped on his volatile nature. The reporters were so vicious that Harrison blew up, calling them a bunch of animals.

Madonna showed great loyalty to Harrison. "He's a great boss, very understanding and very sympathetic." Harrison clearly understood the pressure she was under and traded war stories of his Beatle days in an effort to get her to lighten up. When reporters asked if she'd like to apologize, Madonna replied, "I have nothing to apologize for." The phrase mockingly echoed all the next day on British radio.

When *Shanghai Surprise* was released, it redefined the term *bomb*. The nicest critics called it a silly piece of fluff. The *Cleveland Plain Dealer* called the movie "awesome in its awfulness, momentous in its ineptness, and shattering in its stupidity." Box office was terrible—after three weeks it had earned just over a million dollars. Audiences avoided it strenuously.

Unlike *Desperately Seeking Susan*, which garnered lukewarm overall notices but won Madonna good personal reviews, critics were distinctly unimpressed with this performance. A critic for the *Milwaukee Journal* said Madonna "acts and emotes with all the conviction of a guest in a sketch on a Bob Hope special." Penn's reviews were equally devastating. What really surprised critics was the utter absence of sexual chemistry between the two stars. If they couldn't *act* like lovers, what must their home life be like?

Madonna blamed others. "If it was *directed* poorly, you can't imagine how poorly it was *edited*. . . . The film was edited as an adventure movie and they left out all the stuff that was its saving grace. They cut all my major scenes down to nothing, which made me look like an airhead girl without any character."

A day after her return Madonna began recording her third album, *True Blue*. She was slated to film Blake Edwards's *Blind Date*, but the agreement went sour. "I was supposed to have approval of the leading man and the director, and they didn't tell me they'd already hired Bruce Willis." She never explained what, if any, objections she had to Willis. Probably Madonna was peeved that the studio undermined her control. Backing out of the project was one way of saying don't cross me.

For *True Blue*, Madonna collaborated closely with Steve Bray and Patrick Leonard, coproducing and writing nearly all the songs on the album, which Jon Pareles called "a checklist of music styles," including a retro sound, a Spanish tune, a ballad, and a dance tune. Sometimes Bray or Leonard played a tune that gave Madonna a certain feeling or inspiration. At other times she'd think up characters and a situation then write their song. Madonna boasts that she and Leonard have never spent more than three hours composing a tune.

True Blue, dedicated "to my husband, the coolest guy in the universe," includes "Where's the Party," "True Blue," "La Isla Bonita," "Jimmy Jimmy," "Love Makes the World Go Round," "Papa Don't Preach," "Open Your Heart," "White Heat," and "Live to Tell." The last song was prereleased as a single to coincide with the April opening of Penn's movie *At Close Range* and became an instant, if unpredicted, hit for Madonna, who wasn't generally considered a balladeer. To compose the haunting lyrics, Madonna "thought about the relationship with my parents and the lying that went on."

Madonna rode roughshod over every note on the new album. Her motto was: "Time is money and the money is mine." But her longtime collaborators remained hugely impressed by Madonna's instincts and talents. Pat Leonard said, "I found out after the first song or so that if you listen to what she says, it instantly becomes a 'Madonna' record—her instincts just turn it into that, no matter what producer she's working with." He feels Madonna's attention to her favorite parts—bells and the bass line—are what make a song hers.

Leonard took a lot of flack from peers who accused him of wasting his time working with a lightweight talent. "She's a nice person. She's smart. She's dedicated. She's fucking talented as hell. She's prolific. She's compassionate. She's not this person everybody thinks she is."

Two songs on the album pay homage to Madonna's favorite actors. "Jimmy Jimmy" is her tribute to James Dean: "I used to fantasize that we grew up in the same neighborhood and that he moved away and became a big star." "White Heat" is dedicated to James Cagney.

In April 1986 the citizens of China witnessed their first aerobics demonstration as fifty women in exercise tights and leotards paraded and puffed for ninety minutes in a Beijing square. The music? Madonna and Michael Jackson, naturally!

On April 12, Sean and Madonna were at Helena's with friends. David Wolinski, a musician/songwriter who's worked with Madonna, was also there with another party. On his way out he stopped to say hello. Penn erupted, throwing Wolinski to the floor with a cracking thunk. It took several people to keep Penn from smashing Wolinski's head in with a chair. The unprovoked incident terrified its many witnesses because Penn seemed truly homicidal, completely out of control. Madonna convinced Wolinski not to sue, but the L.A. city attorney's office prosecuted anyway. Sean paid a $1,700 fine and received a year's probation.

Sean's hair-trigger mood swings fueled the gossip mill, which churned out daily divorce rumors. "From the time we got married [the press] couldn't make up their mind: they wanted me to be pregnant, or they wanted us to get a divorce," Madonna said. "That put a lot of strain on our relationship, too, after a while. It's been a character-building experience, and a test of love to get through all of it."

At Close Range premiered on April 16 at Westwood's Bruin Theater. In *Rolling Stone*, Fred Schruers joked that it took "what looked like a phalanx of wrathful Hitler Youth seemingly jacked up on atropine and PCP" to keep the paparazzi and reporters at bay. The post screening party at Helena's was a star-studded affair attended by the likes of Don Johnson, Michelle Phillips, Harry Dean Stanton, and Charles Bukowski. Sean was on superlative behavior.

What *is* Sean's problem with fans and the press?

Sean feels celebrity is "totally ridiculous and defeats the whole purpose of acting." Madonna courted celebrity so her tolerance was higher:

> I've been dealing with the media since the very beginning of my career, and Sean never really had to. I wanted it, and I was sort of ready to deal with it, and he wasn't. That's all there is to it. I would rather see some harmony taking place than all the violence—and when I say violence, I don't mean necessarily hitting, but people screaming and tugging at you. I don't like any of that.

She pointed out that singers establish themselves on a much more intimate basis with fans than actors do. "When you're a singer, obviously it's you. That's what music is all about. . . . You're saying, 'This is me,' so people know you intimately. . . . When you are singing a song you are making yourself very vulnerable. It's almost like crying in front of people."

Called upon to defend Sean's explosive tendencies, Madonna said:

> He wants to protect me—he sees a lot of people being, in his eyes, disrespectful to me—or wanting to start rumors . . . to create an untrue image of me. As inefficient as his methods might be, he has a way of thinking, an integrity, and he sticks with what he believes in, no matter what. There's not many people who do that.

At some level Sean impressed his wife. "I liked his public demonstrations of protecting me. In retrospect I understand why he dealt with the press the way he did . . . but it's a losing battle. He'll defend you to the death—it's very irrational, but also noble." Most candid photos of the era feature the Penns tented by jackets, or walking with their hands up, eyes averted, as if to ward off the camera's lens.

True Blue instantly sold 2.5 million copies upon arrival in stores June 15. Reviews were mixed. The *Christian Science Monitor* said, "Deep inside the hype. . . . lies a rich understanding of what creates motion in both physical and imaginative terms," and called her musicianship "intelligent." *Rolling Stone* said *True Blue* was a reflection of and appeal to Madonna's blue-collar roots, "full of immigrant-stock hustle." They called the album sturdy and dependable without actually saying "good," concluding: "Like every other brainy move from this best of all possible pop Madonnas, it sounds as if it comes from the heart."

If people were lukewarm about her album, people went berserk over Madonna's sleek platinum-blond look, which borrowed heavily from Jean Seberg, an actress she'd long admired. Her very blond (good-bye roots) hair was cropped short. Gone, too, were the pounds of clanking jewelry that inspired a million wannabes. Madonna told the *New York Times*, "I got sick of wearing tons of jewelry—I wanted to clean myself off." The new image was "very innocent and feminine and unadorned. It makes me feel good."

The old look meant big business for Madonna's friend Maripol, whose New York shop, Maripolitan, on Bleeker Street was packed with teenyboppers. When Madonna stripped down, Maripol went bankrupt.

> *"Madonna is a lovable punk: cynical, street-smart, funky, sexy, fundamentally idealistic, indestructibly self-respecting."—David Sigerson in Rolling Stone*

Madonna's new look—still lingerie-heavy—didn't bother Frederick's of Hollywood. According to John Chapman, their general merchandising manager, *bustier* sales went up 40 percent when Madonna became a household name.

David Sigerson wrote in *Rolling Stone*, "Madonna has played America's public morals like a virtuoso, building from starlet to megaslut to bad girl with a heart of gold to New Honest Woman." In *Vanity Fair*, Michael Gross swooned, "All make-overs should be like this. The gooey girl has become a glamour queen.... Madonna is proclaiming herself the rightful inheritor to the long-vacant throne of blond ambition." He described Madonna in rapturous cadences, doting on her mole, her milky white skin "gleaming with all the limelight it has soaked up," her eyebrows, her svelte figure. The accompanying Herb Ritts photos are America's first hint of the intense love affair developing between Madonna and the camera.

> I wanted to change my clothes. You wait for things to cool off. You wait for your image not to be plastered up everywhere.... If you've got a product, you promote it.... If you spend a couple of years wearing layers ... you get the urge to take it all off and strip yourself down and cut your hair all off just for relief.

Perhaps only Madonna could finesse a move of convenience into a polished fashion statement.

One wonders if Sean had a hand in it. Madonna once said: "Sean was like my father in a way. He patrolled what I wore. He'd say, 'You're not wearing that dress. You can see everything in that.' But at least he was paying attention to me. At least he had the balls."

Madonna didn't exactly lack balls herself. Even as she recorded "Papa Don't Preach," she predicted the controversy it would ignite. Like her last-most-controversial song, "Material Girl," "Papa" wasn't written by Madonna, but by Brian Elliot. (Though the album sleeve credits her with "additional lyrics" we never learn what they are.)

The song is sung by a pregnant teenager trying to break the news to her dad, explaining that she's chosen to have the baby and marry its father. *Newsweek* correctly predicted that "Papa" would have mothers across America wringing their hands. Teens who were already pregnant found the song uplifting and supportive.

Alfred Moran, then executive director of Planned Parenthood, protested: "The message is that getting pregnant is cool and having a baby is the right thing and a good thing and don't listen to your parents, the school, anybody who tells you otherwise.... The reality is that what Madonna is suggesting is a path to permanent poverty." Moran argued that Madonna had more impact on teenagers than anyone since the Beatles and asked Warner Bros. to donate approximately 25 percent of the song's earnings to programs promoting responsible sexual behavior.

In a *Washington Post* editorial that September, Ellen Goodman called the song a commercial for teen pregnancy. "The happily-ever-after image has about as much to do with the reality of adolescent motherhood as Madonna's figure has to do with pregnancy." She feared the song and video overromanticized a serious issue and worried it would confuse girls in the midst of making their own choices.

For the first and only time in her career, pro-lifers backed Madonna.

Madonna maintained that the song simply described a young woman making a decision in life. "To me it's a celebration of life. It says, 'I love you, Father, and I love this man and this child that's growing inside me.' Of course, who knows how it will end? But at least it starts off positively."

The video sends violently mixed messages. In the verse portion, Danny Aiello plays Madonna's father, a single parent in a working class community on Staten Island. She's a real daddy's girl, caught between currying her father's favor and moving on to adult relationships. The story's resolved on a life-affirming—and family-affirming—note. Aiello doesn't denounce his daughter as many traditional Italian fathers would. He embraces her, offering love and support.

But disturbing this bittersweet imagery is the vision of Madonna, black clad in skin tight capri pants and a dangerously low-cut *bustier*, dancing against a black backdrop during the chorus, her red lips, white skin, and platinum hair the only spots of color. She spins and bounces. The sophisticated, sexual image is anything *but* troubled teenager. Mostly, it's suspenseful—her top is so small, her movements so frenzied, one can't help wondering when her breasts will cut loose.

Not surprisingly, academics have had a go at deconstructing this Madonna video. E. Ann Kaplan saw the twin images as another depiction of "good" versus "bad," blurring the demarkation between virgin and whore. The video's heroine, Kaplan concluded, "is *neither*, but rather a sexy young teenager, in love and pregnant, and refusing to conform to social codes." Kaplan makes an interesting point: "It is important that the reconciliation only happens because the *father* decides to relent, the heroine simply refusing to be what he demands; she insists on being herself."

An article in the *Journal of Communications* (Spring 1990) described a study on race and gender by Jane D. Brown and Laurie Schulze. They screened the video for a group of male and female, racially mixed students at three universities. Afterward they were asked a series of questions. Brown and Schulze discovered that "almost all the white females and nearly as many white males said that 'Papa' is about teen pregnancy, [but] a large proportion of the black students thought that the 'baby' of which Madonna sings is her boyfriend, not an unborn infant." Black viewers were more likely to see the video as a story about the relationship between father and daughter, with pregnancy as a secondary topic.

Publicist Liz Rosenberg said, "Madonna's singing a song, not taking a stand. Her philosophy is people can think what they want to think."

Madonna replenished the women-sex-power debate with her startling video for "Open Your Heart," directed by Jean-Baptiste Mondino, who later broke his one-video-per-performer rule to direct "Justify My Love."

"Open Your Heart" portrays Madonna as a peep-show dancer raunchily working over a bentwood chair in the tradition of Marlene Dietrich's Blue Angel. She's wearing a shiny black *bustier*, its projectile breasts tipped in gold sequins and tassel—more like arrowheads than objects of desire. At first, Madonna's hair is short, raven black. Slowly she arches her neck, running her hands up and up and up until she scrapes off the black wig, revealing her whitest hair ever.

While Madonna dances for her customers (who include a gay male couple and a woman in drag), a boy lingers outside the theater, transfixed by her image on a billboard poster but barred from entry because he's so young. At the video's end Madonna emerges dressed identically to the youngster in an androgynous gray suit, and the two dance off like twin souls.

By now it was de rigueur for everyone to have a go at Madonna's image-dense video. Camille Paglia wrote:

"Open Your Heart" . . . remains for me not only Madonna's greatest video, but one of the three or four best videos ever made. . . . [It] is a brilliantly mimed psychodrama of the interconnections between art and pornography, love and lust. . . . [She] has cured theills of feminism by reasserting woman's command of the sexual realm.

Musicologist Susan McClary noted:
The leering patrons are rendered pathetic and grotesque . . . the usual power relationship between the voyeuristic male gaze and object is destabilized. . . . The video is risky, because for all those who have reduced her to a "porn queen in heat," there she is: embodying that image to the max.

Shelagh Young, in an article called "Feminism and the Politics of Power," argued that Madonna teaches women their sexuality need not be passive:
When Madonna confidently returns the fetishist's gaze while wearing his favorite sexual accessories, she reveals herself to be in the possession of knowledge; she *knows* because she has looked and is now *looking back*. This parody of a classic pornographic peepshow reveals the sophistication of a new young female audience that knows the difference between feeling powerful and feeling powerless.

Madonna said:
I think for the most part men have always been the aggressors sexually. Through time immemorial they've always been in control. So sex is equated with power. It's scary for men that women would have that power, and I think it's scary for women to have that power—or to have that power and be sexy at the same time.

"Open Your Heart" pushed a lot of buttons. Was Madonna thumbing her nose at those who claimed she used her body as currency to buy acceptance, power, and love? Was the video pornography or a critique of pornography? Was the little boy her son? Underage lover? Brother? Fan? What about her *bustier*, which wasn't gentle or inviting? For some women, the sight of Madonna's lithe form, so different from the "Virgin" body, prompted a return to celery sticks and carrot shavings. There was something here to unsettle everyone!

On the home front, the couple now known as S&M busied themselves with projects ranging from buying a New York apartment near Central Park and rehearsing a play to fistfights and lawsuits.

Madonna's emotions were additionally strained by Martin Burgoyne's disclosure that he had AIDS. Now he began to decline. Madonna was one of several good friends, including Keith Haring, who pitched in to organize a benefit to help pay Martin's hospital bills.

By August the Penns were fine-tuning David Rabe's play *Goose and Tom-Tom*, which played for select audiences (but not the public) at the Mitzi Newhouse Theater in Lincoln Center for three nights at month's end. The press was banned, though reports filtered out that Madonna, as a gangster's moll, was terrific. Andy Warhol told his diary he'd been uninvited from the performance on August 28 because the owner of *Interview* was considered press. On August 30, he went anyway with one of Martin Burgoyne's tickets.

Warhol told the diary:

The best thing about the play was the costumes, which were done by Kevin Dornan. . . . Madonna changes outfits all the time, from one beautiful one to another one. . . . The play was like a Charles Ludlam, abstract. Madonna was good when she wasn't trying to be Judy Holliday or Marilyn. She chewed gum through the whole two hours and I did, too. She was blowing bubbles and everything.

Backstage, friends gathered in the star's dressing room, where they had fun devouring a huge chocolate bunny from Kron. Warhol, a notorious hypochondriac, was touched by Madonna's behavior: "Everybody was eating it, and Martin was, too. And it's so sad, he has sores all over his face, but it was kind of great to see Madonna eating the leg, too, and not caring that she might catch something. Martin would bite and then Madonna would bite."

After performances the Penns stopped at West Side eateries like Columbus Cafe or The Ginger Man, where the press invariably tracked them down. Sean typically cursed but let it go. Then on August 29, he erupted and swiped at some photographers with a shopping bag. When that didn't cow them, he lashed out, spitting and hitting.

The incident made the *New York Post:* "Bad Boy Sean Penn was at it again over the weekend—he got into a wild brawl with photographers." As they reported it, at least six photographers trailed the Penns from the restaurant to their sixty-fourth Street apartment, prompting Sean's angry reaction. He spat. A photographer spat back, and Sean swung the shopping bag into shutterbug Anthony Savignano's face. While Sean threatened Savignano with a slow, painful death, Madonna screamed, "Stop, Sean, stop!" Penn caught Savignano in a headlock. Someone grabbed Penn by the throat, but he managed to punch Vinnie Zuffante before the combatants were separated.

For the closing-night party at Sardi's, on August 30, the Penns relied on the muscle of a crew of beefy bodyguards. This couldn't have pleased Madonna, who cherished dreams of normalcy. She told an interviewer, "I don't go around in limousines, I don't have bodyguards. I like to be pretty low-key."

By mid-September, Madonna was back on the West Coast. She appeared at the Wiltern Theater at the Second Commitment to Life Gala for the L.A. AIDS Project. She introduced Joe Namath and joined the assembly gathered to honor Elizabeth Taylor's contributions to AIDS awareness. Sean wasn't there.

In October, Madonna saw the premiere of *The Mission*, starring Jeremy Irons and Robert De Niro at New York's Ziegfeld Theater. October 14 was "True Blue" Day on MTV. They sponsored a competition for the best

Ducking out of Sardi's after the party for *Goose* and *Tom-Tom*.

Photo courtesy of Ron Galella

Photo courtesy of Ron Galella

Seconds later, Sean started swinging.

viewer video of the song, with the winner collecting $30,000 and dinner with Madonna.

In *Reading the Popular* John Fiske noted that teenagers who dressed like Madonna "aligned themselves with a source of power." In his discussion of the winning viewer videos Fiske points out that "frequently the pleasures Madonna offered her fans were associated with moments of empowerment."

One viewer video shows students overpowering their tyrannical teacher, forcing him to admit Madonna is great. Another tracks the growth of two children, an American girl and a Russian boy. Pen pals as kids, they eventually become leaders of their respective countries. By declaring their love, they settle the cold war.

The third video begins with a classic train scene—the boy sets off on a journey. Instead of running home to weep, his girlfriend cheerfully bops off with a female friend to spend a fun afternoon trying on clothes. Every outfit conjures a new type of boy to the door, but they reject them all. When the boyfriend returns, the video culminates in a shot of the two girls and the boy walking off holding hands. As the camera pulls back it reveals the "rejected" boys hanging on to the second girl's arm in a long line.

Fiske said these videos and fans' comments demonstrate that controlling one's appearance transcends fashion to become a way to dictate social relations and social identity. "The sense of empowerment that Madonna offers is inextricably connected with the pleasure of exerting some control over the meanings of self."

As October ended, the *National Enquirer* ran a cover story announcing that one of Madonna's former roommates was dying of AIDS. They claimed Sean was terrified and furious with Madonna because she had been intimate with him. That roommate, of course, was Martin Burgoyne.

In November, Madonna began filming *Who's That Girl?* (originally called *Slammer*) in New York. She participated in a fashion show at Barney's, modeling a black leather minidress with fishnet stockings, topped by a Martin Burgoyne hand-painted jeans jacket. Iman also modeled, wearing a Keith Haring jacket. The evening benefited AIDS patients at St. Vincent's Hospital in Greenwich Village. By now Madonna's short bob had gone from white to yellow with definite roots, the look she'd maintain to play Nikki Finn.

At the end of November, Martin Burgoyne died at home. Throughout his illness Madonna remained a true and loyal friend, giving generously of her time, love, and money. He did not go gently. In 1991 she told Carrie Fisher: "It was the ugliest, most horrible thing I've ever seen. I was in the room with my best friend when he died. I was absolutely, positively horrified."

Unfortunately the movie faced setbacks, too. It was too cold to continue filming in New York, so production moved to Los Angeles, where set designers busied themselves changing street signs to make it double for Manhattan.

Madonna graced the December cover of *Life* resplendent in gold. Bruce Weber's photographs paid homage to Marilyn Monroe and offered readers a rare glimpse of the eight Ciccone kids united in a big bear hug. Though relations with her family were on an upswing, Madonna's marriage seemed iffy. The press delighted in calling Sean her "on-again, off-again" husband.

Probably only Sean and Madonna know exactly when their problems started, and what they really were. Not all the pressure came from within. "When you're always being watched, you almost want to kill each other," Madonna said.

Still, she found marriage quietly fulfilling: "I did the wash a lot. I liked folding Sean's underwear. I liked mating socks. I love taking the lint out of the lint screen." Because they kept two careers on the boil, Sean often joked that they *both* needed a wife. He got perverse pleasure from bringing friends through the house when Madonna was particularly grungy and in the midst of housework. Then he'd taunt, "Look at her! She's one of the richest women in America!"

Stepping out on behalf of AIDS victims.

Photo courtesy of Ron Galella

Iman sports Haring, Madonna a Burgoyne original.

Photos courtesy of Ron Galella

SEVEN: STRONG AND STEADY

"People who listen to Elvis Costello hate me."—Madonna

"She doesn't know 'wait.' She doesn't know 'later.' She knows 'now.'"—Harry Crews

Who's That Girl? (1987) was Madonna's "reward" for not getting to do *Blind Date*. Once again, the script for this exuberant, physical comedy reminded her of a glorious screwball comedy, notably *Bringing Up Baby*. She was thrilled to be working with the director she considered a friend and a true genius. James Foley, who directed two of her videos, was just as excited and predicted a big film career in Madonna's future. "The form is big enough, she was made for wide-screen Technicolor. And she is precociously talented."

The twin nature of her character, Nikki Finn, appealed to Madonna, who staked her entire career on dualism. "There was just something about [Nikki]—the contrasts in her nature, how she was tough on one side and vulnerable on the other—that I thought I could take and make my own," she said. "There's a little bit of you in every character that you do. I think I had something in common with Susan . . . and I think I have a lot in common with Nikki . . .but it's not me."

As the film opens, Nikki is getting out of jail. She's been there four years, framed for a murder rap. On the proviso that she head directly to Philadelphia and stay there, Nikki wins parole. But this is no angel. She keeps posters of Elvis and James Dean on her cell wall, smokes, sports a tattoo, and generally misbehaves. Nikki talks in a screechy little voice (Madonna's interpretation of Cyndi Lauper doing Betty Boop?) and walks with a mincing hobble, as if afraid of outdistancing that tiny voice.

Griffin Dunne plays Loudon Trott, a stuffy tax lawyer poised to enter high society by marrying the boss's daughter, Wendy Worthington. Worthington's so eager to get Nikki out of town that he sends Trott to personally escort her to the bus.

But Trott's also fetching a rare jungle cat for the firm's other senior partner, who runs a private zoo. The cat's ensconced in the backseat of a Rolls-Royce Loudon's been given to drive when he meets Nikki. Not surprisingly, she's unwilling to return to Philly straight away. Not, at least, until she finds the guy who set her up.

The remainder of the film is a preposterous (meant to be madcap) romp through high and low society, as the trio (man, woman, cat) flee the forces of good and evil. They're tailed by undercover cops and colorful criminals hell-bent on eliminating Nikki. The crowning absurdity is a sword fight that interrupts Loudon's wedding, leaving him free to marry Nikki and establish a Critter Crisis Center.

The movie was shot during late 1986 and part of January 1987. In contrast to *Shanghai Surprise*, Madonna was well liked by the crew and got on well with her fellow actors. Foley said, "Everyone on a crew observes the tone the star sets, and Madonna emanated such a sense of ease and dignity it filtered clear down to the caterer. She's curious as hell, too—about lights, scripts, people's names." In return for her attentiveness, the crew fawned over Madonna. "They'd run around getting her boxes to sit on, and when it got cold, they'd build her a little booth with a heater and she'd sit in there like a princess and love it. She's the greatest flirt of all time."

This time Madonna coped admirably with the cougar—really four cougars—which is surprising given her experience with the Venetian lion.

Costar Griffin Dunne was smitten with Madonna's performance in *Goose and Tom-Tom*, so he looked forward to acting with her. Dunne soon discovered they had very opposite styles. Instead of causing a rift, they used the friction to enhance their roles. "She likes her first take best," Dunne explained. "I think my best is around the fourth. . . . On the set she'd use this talent she has for grating on my character's nerves—talking nonstop between takes—and I'd look at her and I really *would* go: 'Who is this girl?'"

On January 26, Madonna made a surprise appearance at the American Music Awards at Los Angeles's Shrine Auditorium. She turned up alone, wearing a breathtaking sheath made of opalescent froth that hugged her body like glue, and picked up an award for Favorite Female Video Artist.

Rumors about marital rifts were as puffed up as Madonna's bank balance. If she spent a night away from home to be close to the film set, the next day's headlines announced her divorce. "From the time we got married, people wanted our marriage to fail. And that did put a lot of strain on our relationship. . . . A lot of the times, the press would make up the most awful things that we have never done, fights that we never had. Then sometimes we would have a fight and we'd read about it, and it would be almost spooky, like they'd predicted it or bugged our phones."

Probably the hardest part of any marriage is the daily stress of cohabitation, especially when the couple cherishes dissimilar notions about housekeeping. Madonna, a control and neatness freak, admitted she found some of Sean's habits exasperating. "He loved to ball up clothes. I'd say, 'You twisted a Versace suit into a ball and *I can't bear it!*' I would follow him and take his things and hang them up. He'd say, 'Leave me alone. I want to do it this way.' But I just couldn't stand it."

Madonna even overcame her aversion to dogs and bought Sean a puppy—half Akita, half wolf—that he named Hank. "I hated dogs. But I always have to confront things I hate," she said. The dog was from a litter that a hairdresser working on *Who's That Girl?* put up for adoption. Madonna saw puppy pix, heard Sean's wistful, "Oh, I wish we could get a dog," and her heart melted.

"I thought that would probably be a great thing to do, buy Sean a dog. . . . [I] brought it home and said, 'Come outside, there's somebody out here wants to meet you.' When he saw this dog, he looked like he was going to start crying. . . . It was like I'd just had a baby, and Sean saw it and just like died over it. He took it everywhere with him, he wanted to sleep with it."

Madonna wasn't over the moon about Hank. "They pee in the house, and they get dog hair on your clothes. It's like having a kid, only kids wear diapers, and later on in life they learn how to say decipherable words."

Filming *Who's That Girl?* on location in L.A.

Photo courtesy of Ron Galella

In character as Nikki Finn.

Photo courtesy of Ron Galella

With director Jamie Foley, her hubby's best man.

Photo courtesy of Ron Galella

Loudon scolds Nikki for yet another misdemeanor.

Photo courtesy of Ron Galella

That Nikki's tutu much!

Photo courtesy of Ron Galella

When the couple had to be apart, they ran up enormous phone bills and exchanged love letters. "To me our love feels like a huge hand that comes around my whole body," Madonna told a British deejay. "Sometimes it's all furry and warm, and sometimes it's all scratchy and it hurts."

Before year's end it would scrape like sandpaper. First, a photographer spotted Sean dining with a blonde. Penn went berserk and allegedly pointed a gun at the photographer, whose sensible fear of death kept him from recording the moment on film. Later, during the making of *Colors*, directed by his friend and hero Dennis Hopper, Sean wound up behind bars after he attacked a film extra who had the temerity to chance a candid photo. Coming hot on the heels of Penn's sentencing in the Wolinski brawl, this constituted a violation of parole. To make matters worse, Penn got pulled over on a DWI just weeks later. The long arm of the law was flexing its meaty biceps.

While Madonna was in Japan kicking off her Who's That Girl? tour in June, Sean received a sixty day jail term for parole violations. He managed to wangle a deal to serve the time in two thirty-day blocks in order to fly to Germany and do a film with his father. Sean also paid to serve his time at Bridgeport, California, in a far nicer prison than the Los Angeles County Jail. Unfortunately, during the in-between period when he should have been in Germany, Sean was spotted in New York dining and window-shopping with Madonna, in town for an AIDS benefit. The press and the California authorities were not amused.

Madonna's marketing savvy said "saturate," so she coordinated the movie, album, and Who's That Girl? tour to overlap. Though she'd sworn "never again" after the grueling "Virgin" tour, Madonna planned to play eighteen cities on three continents—performing for upwards of 2 million fans. It's possible she collected more than $500,000 a show.

"I told my manager the only way I would do the tour was if I could make it interesting for myself. Because that was the challenge; being able to make a show interesting in a stadium where it's impersonal. I wanted to make it really personal." Madonna promoted the tour with a flourish, debuting on "The Tonight Show," where she strenuously denied divorce rumors.

Indeed, Madonna seemed to rely on her husband as much as ever. "When I was putting my tour together, it was always in the back of my mind: 'I wonder what Sean will think of this?' He's extremely opinionated and has really high standards, and that sometimes pushed me into making decisions I wouldn't have otherwise made. . . . I really respect his opinion; he has great taste and is a very brilliant man.

"I was crazy about him from the beginning," gushed Madonna. "I think you learn to deal with insecurity and feeling threatened. I think the longer we're together, and the more we grow to love each other, the more stable we'll feel. . . . I can't say that nothing will ever go wrong, but I would hope that ultimately our love would be stronger than anything that happens on the outside."

To get into shape for her energetic show, Madonna trained several hours a day, running, biking, and weight lifting. This muscular development prompted her lawyer to tease, "You've lost weight, my daughter's going to be so upset. You finally gave girls who are voluptuous a new lease on life. Don't get any skinnier, okay?"

Marlene Stewart created the show's costumes, including the peep-show *bustier* from "Open Your Heart," a retro fifties dress for the "True Blue" numbers, and a leather jacket for "Papa Don't Preach." For "Dress You Up" Madonna wore a psychotic dress dripping with funny plastic toys, beads, dice, buttons, and other goodies. She looked like the collision of Dame Edna Everidge and Minnie Pearl. Ultimately she donned a flame-red flamenco-style dress with matching brocaded jacket. Stewart worked closely with Madonna and reported, "She pays 1001 percent attention to everything!"

The first show, slated for Tokyo's Korakuen Stadium, had to be canceled when a minityphoon brought torrential rains and gale-force winds to town. Madonna was devastated but not nearly as heartbroken as thirty-five thousand fans, many of whom refused to leave. They chanted prayers to stop the rain and called Madonna's name, as if to conjure her through sheer willpower. That night three hundred fans camped beneath her hotel window.

Why is Madonna's popularity second only to Mickey Mouse's in Japan?

I think I stand for a lot of things in their minds. . . . a lot of kinds of stereotypes, like the whole sex-goddess image and the blond thing. But mainly I think they feel that most of my music is really positive, and I think they appreciate that, particularly the women. I stand for everything that they're really taught to *not* be, so maybe I provide them with a little bit of encouragement."

The following day the weather cleared enough to allow the concert to proceed. And what a show! It was the first time fans encountered Madonna's Broadway musical sensibilities combined with good old-fashioned pop music, channeled through a philosophy promoting dignity and self-respect.

The stage was an elaborate three-tier construction with a conveyor belt along the middle level. The band came in twos—two percussionists, two pianos, etc. Sensual, stylized dancing accentuated Madonna's lean form, and the black corset ignited libidinous urges. She worked with three backup singers, including Niki Harris and Donna DeLory. Madonna also brought along thirteen-year-old dancer Chris Finch. "He's the ideal man," she joked. "He does everything I ask him to do and never complains."

Throughout the performance eight huge screens beamed visual messages, including a church door, the Pope, and Ronald Reagan during "Papa Don't Preach," followed by the words *safe sex*. "White Heat" began with a clip from the Cagney film. Later the *New York Post* headline from 1985, "I'm Not Ashamed," flashed on-screen.

During the ballad "Live to Tell," a glamour shot of Madonna's face appeared. Near the song's end Madonna crashed to the stage, defeated, and the picture went black. Then she slowly rose, like a phoenix, to finish the song in triumph. That projected image proved as powerful for Madonna as for her audience:

I say, "Oh God, what have I done? What have I created? Is that me, or is this me, this small person standing down here on the stage?" That's why I call the tour Who's That Girl?— because I play a lot of characters, and every time I do a video or a song, people go, "Oh, that's what she's like." And I'm not like any of them. I'm all of them. I'm none of them.

Performers make themselves very vulnerable, she insists. "You're saying, 'This is me. And here I am for all you people.'... I have mixed feelings... In one sense I want to go out and personally thank everyone.... On the other hand it's scary to think of yourself as larger than life."

Stateside, *USA Today* announced the world tour on its front page. According to their statistics, the tour had a $500,000 ad campaign and most tickets went for $22.50. The elaborate stage sets traveled in twenty-three trucks, and required both a 747 and DC-7 to be flown from Japan to Miami, the first American stop. Setting up the stage took three days of work on the part of a fifty-person tech crew.

Madonna and Sean spoke nightly via long distance, but husband and wife weren't reunited until she arrived in Florida. To all appearances they were a cozy pair, loving and close. But when he left, Sean was headed for his second thirty-day jail term.

In New York, Madonna designated proceeds from her July 13 Madison Square Garden concert to the American Foundation for AIDS Research (AMFAR). David Geffen, one of the organizers, said:

> She volunteered her whole show. She not only provided us with her lights and her set and her musicians and everything that goes into a production the size of hers, but she also donated all the merchandising profits from the programs and the posters and the souvenirs. The woman is not only a consummate professional, she's also got a big heart."

Unlike Donna Summer, whose infamous homophobic comments alienated her staunchest fans, Madonna has never been ashamed that a large proportion of her fans are gay, black, and Latino, three communities being decimated by AIDS. She's "gay-positive," one of the first pop superstars to address the epidemic head-on:

> I want to do anything I can to promote AIDS education, awareness, prevention... because I am a celebrity, a public person, I have a responsibility to be a spokesperson. Next to Hitler, AIDS is the worst thing to happen in the twentieth century. The sad thing is that it makes people even more bigoted. It gives people a reason to vent their true feelings about homosexuality.

> Rather than just lay a gob of money on AMFAR, I felt it would be better to do a show that was directed at bringing attention to the organization. And since I have a very young following, I thought it would be a good chance to educate my audience, because at this point, it's the only way to fight AIDS. At the concert, we're handing out a free comic book... that gives the facts about how you can and cannot get AIDS. I want it to be an education event as well as a concert.

For the record, she has also made several large, private donations to AMFAR. This concert raised $400,000. Proceeds from her 1990 Blond Ambition concert would total over $300,000, while money from the *Truth or Dare* premiere brought in $100,000.

> *"She's a very noisy girl."*—Griffin Dunne

Charity or no, the *New York Times* trashed Madonna's performance, prompting her comment, "There are still those people who, no matter what I do, will always think of me as a little disco tart."

The concert was deeply personal. Martin Burgoyne's death the previous year was a loss she'd never really gotten over. That night she dedicated "Live to Tell" to his memory. "I am trying to think of something eloquent to say, but I don't want this to be a morbid event. Hopefully your presence and our help together will help us find a cure for this thing together."

On August 6, 1987, New Yorkers literally rolled out the red carpet for the world premiere of *Who's That Girl?* Over ten thousand fans mobbed Times Square, and one hundred and fifty cops were specially assigned to the opening. Broadway was closed to traffic. Madonna arrived at the Armed Forces building in a shimmering silver-beaded sheath. After greeting the crowd and giving deejay Scott Shannon of Z100 a brief interview to be broadcast worldwide, Madonna moved down a red carpet to the National Theater.

The private post screening party took over the Cadillac Bar on West Twenty-first Street, where Madonna, according to a hilarious, anonymous report in *The New Yorker*, "spent the evening holding court on the restaurant's balcony." When she finally descended to walk among mortals, the writer's teenage niece asked for an autograph:

"I love you, Madonna. Will you sign my poster?"

"Hey, what's this? No autographs," said Madonna.

"But, Madonna, I came all the way from Italy."

"That's nice, kid. So did my ancestors."

Critical reaction to the film was scathing. One reviewer suggested that instead of trying to suppress the 1979 nudes, Madonna should have fought to suppress this film, adding, "the plot's as thin as one of Madonna's teddies." Most agreed that the movie—which had been designed as her showcase—actually diminished Madonna. And David Denby's vitriolic review asked, "Will the people endlessly hyping Madonna shut up now? . . . She's not only a terrifyingly bad actress; she barely seems a human being."

Madonna found the critics "pretty unforgiving," but took solace in the knowledge that *Who's That Girl?* became a critical and popular hit in Europe. "I think the movie did badly in America because I upstaged it with my tour. I also think that there are people who don't want me to do well in both fields. I had to really fight to get any respect from the music business, and now I guess there are some people who feel that I ought to be grateful for that respect and stick with music."

At some level, Madonna had come to terms with reporters' need to say horrible things about her:

> [They] used to think that I had no talent and would drop off the edge of the earth in a couple of months. That didn't happen. . . . People thought I was unhappily married the week after the wedding, but who isn't unhappily married on alternate days? . . . I think the press is a little afraid of me because they don't know quite what to think of me.

Just after her birthday Madonna brought the tour to England. There the papers concocted Madonna fashion spreads, diet sheets, and anything else they could think of to sell as many papers as she'd sold tickets. Nearly

Solo and stunning!

Photo courtesy of Ron Galella

150,000 seats for two shows sold out in eighteen hours, prompting Madonna to schedule extra dates.

Reviewing the show, *Melody Maker* said: "Madonna works so hard, prostrates herself like a nubile waif gladly offering herself up as a human sacrifice to the cult of efficiency, of relentless sexuality, of power through exercise." When some enthusiastic rowdies in the audience shouted, "Get your tits out for the boys," Madonna retorted, "Forget my tits, they belong to me!"

Madonna's next stop was Italy, where they hailed her arrival like a second coming. One newspaper established a special "Who's That Girl?" header, devoting pages a day to her every utterance. An estimated 61,000 tickets had been sold.

In Turin, Madonna met with her second cousin's family. Amelia Vitucci gave Madonna a painting of the original Ciccone home in Pacentro. Madonna asked Amelia's eleven-year-old son, Giuseppe, "Do you want to dance with me?" He shyly replied, "I don't know how."

Her grandmother, Bambina de Guilio, was too frail at eighty-two to accompany the Pacentro delegation when it delivered a scroll proclaiming Madonna an honorary citizen. Reporters who cornered the elderly lady asked her opinion of Madonna. Bambina replied, "Of course I'd like to see her and hug her. After all, it's an honor to have such a famous relation." When pressed for grander remarks she retorted, "What do you want from me? The girl is a singer, just a singer. In my times we didn't behave like that." Another Pacentro local commented, "That girl sings, dances, and shows her thighs, so the old people of Pacentro consider her a *malafemmina* [slut]. No Madonna she! The devil is more like it!"

Amid all the hero worship, at least one Italian reviewer hated her: "If Madonna should be considered the queen of anything, it's of this new universe where values and things to say have been drastically reduced to zero."

On the gossip front, Italian papers reported that Madonna took a tumble while jogging, that her hotel was struck by lightning, and that young Chris Finch fell down and needed six stitches. When Madonna ran, hundreds of kids followed on scooters. Hundreds more camped outside her hotel. In Rome, Madonna supposedly declined an audience with the Pope, commenting, "If His Holiness wants to see me, he can come to my show." The papers also reported secret plans to meet Sean for a second honeymoon in the Eternal City.

Even *Pravda* had something to say about Madonna, though her tour didn't go near Moscow. The Soviet paper called her an artificial product of the entertainment industry, attributing her popularity to commercialism. The combination of insatiable egoism and a passion for work and music were, in their estimation, the qualities that made Madonna a superstar.

Madonna felt her stardom reflected people's dreams and the importance of holding on to ideals. "I think I represent hope to people who come from nowhere and have no show business connections but want to be performers, because I basically came from nowhere and scratched and clawed my way to the top." She denied that

> Loudon: *"You're lying."*
>
> Nikki: *"How do you know?"*
>
> Loudon: *"Your lips are moving."*

she was ruthless, if that meant she was uncaring, but freely admitted to being "absolutely focused, and people who don't understand that kind of focus—and not that many people have it—can feel hurt by it even though there's absolutely no reason for them to."

By the tour's end Madonna was sick of herself. "I don't ever want to hear any of my songs ever again," she announced. Clever Patrick Leonard cured her ennui with a visit to his brand-new recording studio. Within an hour the two old friends had written a terrific new song.

September of 1987 saw the arrival of *You Can Dance*, a compilation of seven previously released tunes remixed by such hot deejays as Shep Pettibone and Jellybean Benitez as extended dance versions. The songs were "Spotlight," "Holiday," "Everybody," "Physical Attraction," "Over and Over," "Into the Groove," and "Where's the Party."

In December, *Time* magazine announced that "pouty actress" Madonna was seeking a divorce from "pugnacious actor" Sean Penn. A week later *People* ran the divorce on its cover. At the same time divorce news made headlines in the *National Enquirer* and the *Star*. The *Enquirer* said Madonna often woke up in the middle of the night to find Sean missing not only from their bed, but from the house. When he returned, he wouldn't say where he'd been.

And this was the year of the Thanksgiving debacle. Supposedly the couple planned to rendezvous at their New York apartment. Instead of showing up, Sean disappeared for three days, only to reappear mysteriously, wondering why there was no turkey left. One version of this story claims Sean was in New York the whole time, drinking the days away at Columbus, a favorite local hangout. Madonna spent the holiday with her sister Paula, in Brooklyn.

That divorce papers were truly drawn up was confirmed by Madonna's trusted publicist, Liz Rosenberg, who admitted they'd been ready for some time. Rosenberg said, "There were so many moments in their marriage when it was shaky that Madonna was finally forced to face the reality of the situation—that they weren't happy together."

But they didn't divorce. Madonna withdrew the papers and the couple vowed to give the marriage another try. "Love is the ultimate escape," said Madonna. "It's better to focus on a positive escape like love than to concentrate on all the terrible things in the world."

MADONNA
SEPTEMBER '87

WE LOVE YOU!

During the Who's That Girl? tour, the Italians poured out their love.
Memorabilia courtesy the Bill Ryan Archives

wea Italiana

"Who's that girl?"

La più grande festa del rock si è celebrata senza incidenti gravi (soltanto qualche decina di contusi nella ressa dello stadio). Prima del concerto Madonna ha voluto incontrare i suoi parenti abruzzesi

Qui sotto, Madonna fotografata nel pomeriggio di ieri assieme ai suoi parenti italiani e, accanto, la cantante durante il concerto di Torino

Eccola: miracolo a Torino

dal nostro inviato

TORINO — Si spengono le luci e si accendono i riflettori della Rai e quelli dello show; nello stadio Comunale un boato, quasi 70 mila persone applaudono l'apparizione. Madonna indossa il famoso body di raso nero, quello delle fotografie che i giornali non cessano di pubblicare da giorni. Non è una sorpresa neanche il primo brano della scaletta «Open Your Heart» e in questo show di sorprese ce ne sono davvero poche. «Aprimi il tuo cuore baby, io ho la serratura e tu hai la chiave» canta.

Non c'è neanche bisogno di chiederlo, accidenti; migliaia di cuori sono aperti, spalancati, alla divina del rock. C'è il cuore del ragazzino che ha dormito sotto le stelle, c'è quello di chi arriva dal sud per vederla al debutto italiano, c'è il cuore di chi verso le sei del pomeriggio ha cercato di guastare la festa distribuendo volantini contro il capitalismo americano, contro l'organizzazione di Zard.

Nulla da fare, i fans di Madonna sono i più pacifici che abbiamo mai visto ad un concerto; alla fine qualche contuso c'è stato, una dozzina di persone è finita in ospedale, nessuno in gravi condizioni e sono pochissimi se si pensa alla folla oceanica che il concerto è riuscito a radunare. Poche ore prima del debutto italiano la cantante aveva ricevuto nel suo camerino i quattro parenti giunti da Pacentro, un paese dell'Abruzzo, proprio per incontrarla. La cugina Amelia, suo marito e due bambini, Giuseppe e Annalisa, le hanno regalato un quadro che raffigura il loro e il suo paese. Madonna è sembrata molto contenta, ha canticchiato una canzone ed ha chiesto al cuginetto Giuseppe, 11 anni, che le assomiglia molto, se avrebbe avuto piacere a ballare con lei. «Non saccio balla'» è stata la risposta del piccolo.

Dopo mezz'ora i parenti se ne sono andati e Madonna ha iniziato a prepararsi nell'orrendo camerino arredato con mobili autentici del barocco torinese. Una vera pacchianata. Poi alle 21,15 l'ha accolta una atmosfera distesa e tranquilla e lei a fine concerto sembrava felice. Fuori dallo stadio la macchina era già pronta per portarla via. Nessun volo verso la Costa Azzurra; il suo aereo privato la stava già portando verso Firenze. (l.pu.)

Dietro le quinte solo una ragazzina formato mignon

dal nostro inviato

TORINO — Ma è davvero Madonna quella ragazzina bionda seduta tutta sola sui gradini del palcoscenico? E' una diva piccina piccina silenziosa, in scarpe da ginnastica e body bianco sul quale indossa una camiciona blu. Sono le 3 del pomeriggio, nello stadio la squadra è in piedi per iniziare le prove dello spettacolo. Arrivare fin qui è stata dura: il servizio d'ordine di Zard è difficile da depistare. Ma ora il grande palco ci è di fronte siede in tutti i modi, si allunga sulla sedia, ma un body bianco di lycra non è proprio come uno di raso nero dal quale non spunta certo un reggiseno antiestetico. No, le gambe non sono granché, i polpaccetti tozzi, possono dare un'idea di grande energia, non certo di sensualità.

Gli elicotteri continuano a volteggiare sulla sua testa, lei sembra non farci caso. Inizia a cantare «Kausing a commotion» allegro, saltellante brano

Io, Veronica pazza di lei

dal nostro inviato LAURA PUTTI

TORINO — Veronica va fiera del nome che porta «anche lei si chiama così» dice «ma fa bene a farsi chiamare Madonna, le sta meglio». Veronica è toscana, di Scarperia, un paese appena fuori Firenze, ma non ce l'ha fatta ad aspettare il concerto fiorentino di domenica sera. E' qui da giovedì, è arrivata col treno ed ha dormito nel Palasport. Dormito, si fa per dire, anche se erano più di trenta. «Stamattina sono uscita molto presto, non mi sono neanche lavata».

Occhi cisposi, spettinata e un tantino fuori moda, con le sue crocette appuntate dappertutto cucite anche sulle scarpe di stoffa, la minigonna nera, spille da balia e i capelli legati con un nastro di voile. Una Madonnina old fashioned. Porta i suoi quindici anni con quella grassezza indecisa dell'età, la stessa che Madonna aveva qualche anno fa.

Lo sa Veronica che la sua diva ha cambiato look? «Lo so, certo che lo so» risponde quasi offesa dalla domanda «ora gioca ad essere una Marilyn sbarazzina e felice. Solo che è dimagrita troppo: io quei vestiti attillati non me li posso mica

lungo con le parrucche bianche». E' quasi mezzogiorno, il sole è fosco, ma caldo, abbiamo intorno un capannello di ragazzi, età media anni quindici. Facce pulite. Ognuno una storia, molti sono del Sud e hanno parenti a Torino, qualcuno ha dormito in stazione molti attorno allo stadio, vicino al sagrato della cattedrale nel quale si sta per celebrare il rito. La città più austera d'Italia è stata tollerante, nessuno ha preso a calci i sacchi a pelo.

Caldo, sete. Con Veronica ci avviciniamo ad uno dei tanti banchetti del mercato improvvisato di ogni cantante sulla magliettta ufficiale del tour. L'atmosfera è allegra, si aspetta la diva, l'unica grande diva del rock.

Se i fans dei Duran e degli Spandau deliravano per i loro beniamini, quelli di Madonna sembrano allegri e distesi, senza concitazione e con una gran voglia di divertirsi. «Chi urla sono le ragazzine» spiega Veronica con tono saccente «Spandau e Duran sono bei ragazzi, lei è una donna e il richiamo sessuale non c'entra, o meglio dovrebbero averlo i maschi, ma loro non si scompongono mai...». «Ma chi te l'ha detto» sbotta un romano «noi

stopoli qualcuno ha una radio trasmittente che gracchia forte. L'aereo di Madonna sta per atterrare a Caselle; tra poco più di mezz'ora lei sarà qui. La città è mobilitata. Torino l'austera ha messo la cantante in quasi tutte le sue vetrine del centro; cartolerie vendono portapenne con la sua faccia, negozi di jeans espongono magliette stampate con decine di fotografie diverse, negozi di dischi cercano di vendere il primo Lp di Madonna come fosse un cimelio, un pezzo raro. Ed invece lei nel corso del suo concerto non canta neanche una canzone di quell'album. La signorina Ciccone va venduta e comprata, come del resto accade a qualsiasi prodotto commerciale.

Ma Veronica non è d'accordo. «Lei ha un cuore, è donna fino in fondo, ha scritto in faccia quanto le è costato arrivare a questo punto». Nel frattempo giunge voce che Madonna entrerà da un altro cancello; mai vista tanta calma, qualcuno si alza in piedi e si avvia all'altro ingresso, senza fretta, senza allarmismi. Veronica resta con noi. «Ho il biglietto e il binocolo. La vedrò da

---

They called it the "Miracle at Turin" when Madonna hit town. Here she is with her Italian relations.

Memorabilia courtesy the Bill Ryan Archives

EIGHT: **SINK OR SWIM**

"People have this idea that if you're sexual and beautiful and provocative, then there's nothing else you could possibly offer."—Madonna

"It's not her habit to lie. Her habit is to be truthful. And that is the essence of being an actor—to tell the truth in imaginary circumstances. . . . I love her straightforwardness."—Gregory Mosher, director, Speed-the-Plow

Madonna's healthy box-office and nonstop record sales earned her a slot on *Forbes*'s Top 40, their annual announcement of the year's highest-paid entertainers. Not content to rest on these moneybags, Madonna chose 1988 to concentrate on serious acting. It was also a year she'd spend largely apart from her temperamental husband, become embroiled in an outlandish lesbian rumor she'd start herself, and ultimately face some hard home truths.

"There have been times when I've thought, 'If I'd known it was going to be like this, I wouldn't have tried so hard,'" she told an interviewer in 1987, little guessing that by 1988 she'd be wondering, "What's it all about?" and confronting her darkest fears: "The truth scares me. Being alone scares me. Failure scares me. Dying scares me. I don't think in that sense I'm different from anyone else."

Hitting thirty is traumatic for most and it was especially unsettling for Madonna. "My memories of my mother drift in and out. When I turned thirty, which was the age [she] was when she died, I just flipped out because I kept thinking I'm now outliving my mother. I thought something horrible was going to happen to me. Like this is it, my time is up." Like Elvis Presley, who vowed not to live longer than his mother had—and didn't—Madonna worried that her number was up.

Small wonder the tabloids went crazy in March when word leaked that she had discovered a lump in her breast. By the time it made news, Madonna had undergone a biopsy to discover the lump was benign. But the weeks of uncertainty must have brought back nightmares of her mother's agonizing illness. Luckily Sean was on his best behavior, providing the support Madonna needed to stare down her fears.

In 1988, Penn traveled to Thailand to film *Casualties of War* with Michael J. Fox. Madonna also found an acting job that would occupy her for most of the year. "The more unpredictable you are the more misjudged you are," Madonna said, and proceeded to defy everyone's expectations by tackling a Broadway play written by no less a talent than Pulitzer Prize winner David Mamet.

After seeing the movie *House of Games*, Madonna's admiration of Mamet escalated into virtual worship, so when news got around that Elizabeth Perkins had dropped out of his new play, Madonna says she "pursued the role like a motherfucker."

"I was at lunch with some people and Mike

Nichols mentioned that David Mamet had written a new play. I was a fan of his so I just started bugging my agents and people I knew. I met the director and the writer and it finally came to a reading."

Madonna was one of hundreds of high-powered actresses considered for the role of Karen, an office temp who nearly drives a wedge between two Hollywood manipulators played by Ron Silver and Joe Mantegna. She performed at two multihour auditions, but Mamet and director Gregory Mosher say they "knew" after the first reading. Mamet made "small but significant" rewrites to accommodate Madonna's personality.

Speed-the-Plow is a scathing critique of Hollywood. The play examines commercialism, asking whether art can ever emerge from a community obsessed with bottom-line profits.

Ron Silver plays Charlie Fox, a producer; Joe Mantegna is Bobby Gould, head of production at a huge studio. Madonna is Karen, an extremely unbusinesslike temporary secretary who tries to convince Gould to back a movie based on an allegorical novel about technology. At the same time Gould tries to seduce Karen and win a five-hundred-dollar bet with Fox. Gould briefly swoons over Karen and even considers her project. He comes to his senses rapidly, however, and the killer instinct takes over. "[The play's] a metaphor," Madonna explained. "It's not just about Hollywood. It's about life."

Madonna hoped acting a nonshowy role would prove her talents weren't limited to pop star identities. "People kept on saying, 'She's just playing herself,' so I said, 'Okay, for six months I'm not going to play myself.'"

David Mamet's plays aren't easy or fluffy so Madonna had to work hard to master the part. Mamet favors profanity. Characters talk rapidly and all at once. Staging Mamet is the closest thing to choreography.

Her role was always ambiguous. Mosher said, "Madonna brings a backbone of steel [to it]. Mamet made the character, rather than a poor soul . . . someone about whom there is an element of doubt. . . . The audience is meant to go out asking one another: 'Is she an angel? Is she a whore?'"

Didn't she want to play against type?

Before long she was as disillusioned as Karen. Part of Madonna's funk was undoubtedly in making the transition from boss to worker bee. On top of that, she told *Rolling Stone:*

> It was a real mind-fuck of a script. Brilliant but confusing. My part ended up being a plot manipulation. But at first I saw her as an angel of mercy who was coming down to save everybody. Little did I know that David Mamet and Greg Mosher and everybody else . . . saw me as a vixen, a dark, evil spirit. That didn't dawn on me till halfway through rehearsals, when David kept changing my lines to make me more and more a bitch. . . . So in the middle of this process I was devastated that my idea of the character wasn't what she was at all. . . . It was like getting trampled on every night. Mamet is a stubborn man—he is not interested in collaborating.

On that point, costar Ron Silver agreed. Unlike Mantegna, Silver had never played Mamet before. Settling into Mamet's style took some adjustments. When the *New York Times* interviewed the cast, Silver remarked, "I don't think David finds discussion valuable for the process. And he may be right. I don't know."

History, as we know, plays on an endless loop. It wasn't long before the buzz around town called this "the Madonna play." Many reckoned she'd been hired solely for her marquee value. Madonna's involvement pushed advance sales over $1million, forcing producers to hire a bigger theater than originally planned. If her fame unnerved or annoyed Madonna's coworkers, her devotion to hard work won their respect. Silver commented, "She's funny, feisty, and the first one to know her lines." Mantegna said, "The girl does not lack confidence. She's strong."

Mosher, a friend since *Goose and Tom-Tom*, had only wonderful things to say about his leading lady:

Madonna could have made a spectacle of herself, thrown her weight around or even tried to capitalize on her sexy image, but she didn't. She was a real actress.

On the night of the first public performance, thirty beautiful floral arrangements arrived backstage. They were from Madonna to everyone. Not just the actors, but the dressers, the crew, the doorman. That kind of courtesy has nothing to do with whether you can run that stuff up on your Amex card, but whether it would occur to you to do that.

The play opened on May 3, followed by a cast party at Tavern on the Green. Reporters trailing Madonna dwelled on her dark tresses, her tailored, distinctly unflamboyant costumes, and sensible shoes. "Everything I do in this play is different from how I am in real life," she said.

Did it matter whether Madonna could act? Mamet traditionally gives the good stuff, the important messages, to male characters. She wasn't the star of the evening, but when she entered, fifteen minutes into the show, audiences gasped. It seemed what really mattered was her *presence*.

Opening night people didn't ask "How was it?" but "How was she?" prompting the *Daily News*'s banner headline, "No, she can't act!" *News* drama critic Howard Kissel offered a fun interpretation of viewers' reactions: "They're not in Mamet's play anymore. They're in Madonna's. They're asking themselves: 'Can she act? Is this what she's *supposed* to be doing?' They're nervous for her."

Clive Barnes in the *New York Post* said Madonna was charming, but not good enough. *Time* called the play a "foulmouthed and ferociously funny slice of Hollywood life." *Newsweek* thought the play brilliant and Madonna gutsy: "She has a lot to learn, but she's a serious actress. . . . She doesn't yet have the vocal horsepower . . . to drive Mamet's syncopated dialogue. But she has the seductive ambiguity that makes Karen the play's catalytic force."

The *Wall Street Journal* considered Madonna hardworking, but "out of her depth." Their reviewer found Madonna's role "so underwritten it's impossible to know where she is coming from, or even whether or not she is for real." In *New York* magazine, John Simon initially found Madonna's work inadequate. Upon reflection, days later, he found the entire play lacking and Madonna the least of its problems.

> *"Being there for other people, showing up on time, and making a go of it when you're exhausted—I've done that all my life."*
> — *Madonna*

All smiles on opening night—before the reviews.

Photo courtesy of Ron Galella

***Speed the Plow*'s cast party at Tavern on the Green**

Photo courtesy of Ron Galella

Frank Rich, eminent critic for the *New York Times*, declared the play hilarious and chilling. He hailed Madonna's performance as "intelligent, scrupulously discreet comic acting," adding that she needed to relax and project more confidence when onstage.

This review so outraged CBS television's critic Dennis Cunningham that he publicly attacked his colleague's judgment. Cunningham declared he'd meet with Mosher and Mamet to contest Madonna's casting.

Madonna remained philosophical. "I expected [to be attacked] because I get it with everything I do. There are people who are violently opposed to the fact that I exist on this earth, so I was just thankful that there were people who liked it and also who reviewed the play as objectively as possible and didn't let who I am, my persona . . . get in the way."

It was a long, hot summer—too hot, as far as Madonna was concerned. Fans swarmed the stage door nightly, but she resolutely refused to stop. Instead she hustled into a limo pointed toward her West Side apartment. Madonna was depressed. "It's the monotony," she told Harry Crews. "It's having to do the same thing every night. . . . I've never felt so stationary in my life."

The role demoralized her:

I hated to love it and I loved to hate it. . . . I didn't have a glamorous or flamboyant part; I was the scapegoat. . . . Still, night after night, that character failed in the context of the play. To continue to fail each night and to walk off that stage crying, with my heart wrenched. . . . It just got to me after a while. I was becoming as miserable as the character I played.

Still, she meant to stick it out, challenging all the Madonna bashers hoping she'd fail or at the very least, throw a tantrum.

They thought they would wake up one day and I'd go away. They keep waking up and I keep not going away . . . they thought that I was the flavor of the month. . . . But slowly as the years go by I've been showing a little bit more of myself. . . . And every time they think they have me understood, I do something else. It took them forever to accept the fact that I could write music and that I have something to contribute. . . . Now I'm going through the same thing with acting and movies. To be accepted as an actress, I'm just going to have to work very hard. . . . That's the way it has always worked.

Madonna was lonely and cultivated her friendship with comic Sandra Bernhard. Sandra's one woman show, *Without You I'm Nothing*, was at the height of its successful downtown run. Madonna loved it, especially a segment about the two of them surviving a nuclear holocaust. Sandra had been using material about Madonna before they were pals. In her book, *Confessions of a Pretty Girl*, she wrote of a dream in which Madonna turned up singing in her backyard and then they became best friends. Like Madonna's fantasy about Sean, this dream quickly became a reality.

Madonna and Sandra spent a lot of time together. "Sandra was just what I needed. We became really good friends." Bernhard added, "Our friendship is real kooky, real fucking kooky. I never had any idea what she'd be like, so I was more than pleasantly surprised." Another friend that summer was Jennifer Grey, of *Dirty Dancing* fame, who would work with Madonna in *Bloodhounds of Broadway*. The three were core members of an all-girl clique dubbed The Snatch Pack, a spoof on the mostly male Brat Pack, which Sean belonged to.

On June 5, Madonna appeared at the Tony Awards wearing a black turtleneck tube festooned with 3-D fuchsia flowers and a matching boa. The evening began with a press conference at Sardi's followed by a dinner/dance at the New York Hilton. Madonna skipped rehearsal and subsequently messed up her lines during the telecast. June also marked Bernhard's birthday. Her party was held at The World, a downtown nightclub. Madonna and Jennifer Grey wore identical denim cutoffs, and the three ladies danced nonstop.

On June 27th, Madonna attended the world heavyweight championship fight between Mike Tyson and Michael Spinks as a guest of Donald Trump. Madonna said she's attracted to boxing because "it's primal and savage. It's one-on-one." Sean was home and they took writer Harry Crews as their guest. The night was a three-ring circus, thanks to Madonna's popularity.

Crews described the evening for *Fame* magazine, noting that of all the celebrities on hand, including Warren Beatty and Jack Nicholson, Madonna was the only one mobbed. Fans cheered her introduction and booed Sean's. Madonna wouldn't give autographs to her fans, but later she gladly scribbled her name for the kitchen staff. Why? Because she felt sorry for them, and because they asked humbly.

Crews wrote:

> *"I may not be appreciated here now, but I'm going to be appreciated. And I'm not going to stop until I am."* —Madonna

Hovering in the air about her every act and utterance is the proposition, never articulated but always present: Show me the goddamn wall I have to get through to get to the place I want to be and I'll take the wall down with my teeth and fingernails if necessary. It is not always a lovely thing to see.

He decided that she wasn't conventionally pretty, but exuded "the sweet musk of sex."

In July, Madonna made an unscheduled appearance on *Late Night with David Letterman* with Sandra Bernhard, thereby launching the rumor they were lesbian lovers.

"When I did the Letterman show, it was toward the end of the show's run, and I really was marking off days on the calendar," she said, explaining the aggravated state of mind that led to some extended silliness between the two close friends. Dressed alike, they giggled, hugged, and kissed like schoolgirls and announced that they spent their spare time at the Cubby Hole, a lesbian bar in the Village. Sandra told Letterman she'd slept with both Sean and Madonna, though not simultaneously. Letterman sat back and let them rip.

"Sandra and I decided to tease everybody. Then, of course, it got out of hand and I didn't want to do it anymore, because it was more important for me to have a friendship. But we had our fun with that and it sort of worked itself to death."

After *Speed-the-Plow*, Madonna acted in *Bloodhounds of Broadway*. The film aired on public

Photo courtesy of Ron Galella

No autographs, please!

Madonna finds the perfect ensemble for navigating the Great White Way.

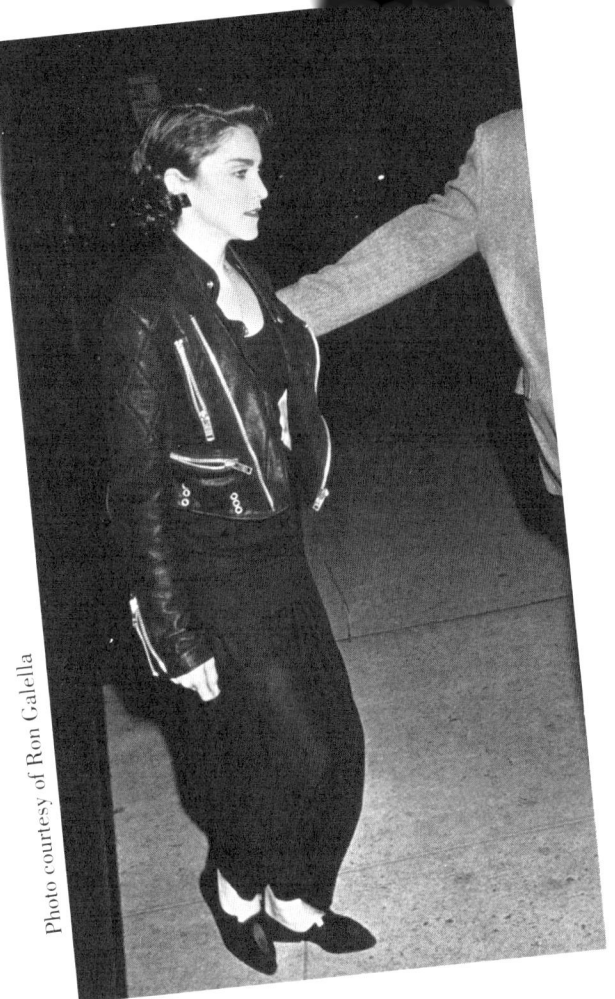

It's dark hair for David Mamet's dark horse.

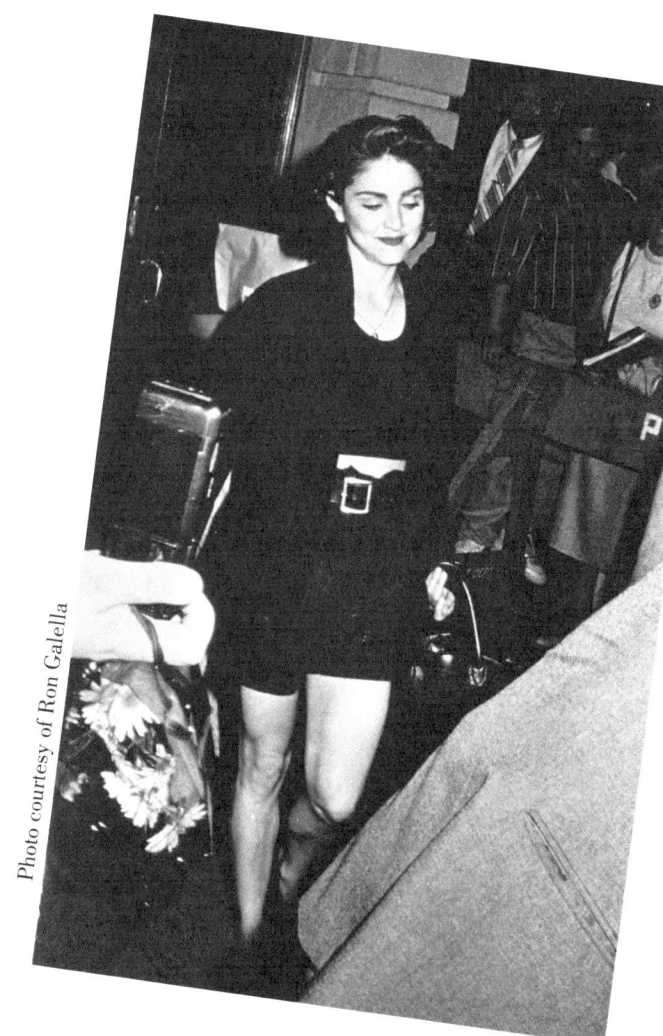

Heading home after a performance.

Keeping it cool, classy, and chic.

Taking pointers from Tyson and Spinks?
Photo courtesy of Ron Galella

Moments later, he shoved a cameraman.
Photo courtesy of Ron Galella

Broadway's brightest bloom.
Photo courtesy of Ron Galella

Setting the trend for long denim cutoffs.
Photo courtesy of Ron Galella

Marking days until the show's over.
Photo courtesy of Ron Galella

Partying with her manager and buddy Sandra Bernhard.
Photo courtesy of Ron Galella

Nearing the end of her *Speed the Plow* run.
Photo courtesy of Ron Galella

Perfecting the man-tailored Baby Dietrich look.
Photo courtesy of Ron Galella

Sandra Bernhard and a friend muscle Madonna into a Christmas bash.
Photo courtesy of Ron Galella

television then went directly to video, bypassing movie theaters. *Bloodhounds* was a series of interlocked stories based on the work of Damon Runyon. Screenwriter/director Howard Brookner assembled a talented cast including Randy Quaid, Rutger Hauer, Jennifer Grey, and Matt Dillon. In Madonna's story line, she's chorus girl Hortense Hathaway, adored from afar by Feet Samuels (Quaid).

Samuels sells his monstrous appendages to an unscrupulous doctor in order to buy Hortense a lavish gift. But the doctor wants his merchandise ASAP, so Feet's days are numbered. Though she *has* a beau, played by Tony Longo, Hortense is secretly smitten with Feet. Together they scheme to outsmart the doctor.

During the shoot, Madonna befriended Tony Longo, a six-foot-six, 280-pound actor best known for playing Mad Dog on HBO's sitcom "First and Ten." The media inflated this to a romance and later reported—at the height of her relationship with Beatty—that Madonna was pregnant with Longo's child.

Unfortunately Howard Brookner's health was deteriorating. In 1989 he died of AIDS. Writer Brad Gooch described Madonna's loyalty during the final days: "She was incredibly supportive. . . . She not only visited Howard, but all the other patients on the AIDS ward. It was like Judy Garland visiting another sort of Oz."

Year's end found Madonna back in Los Angeles where Sean was acting in David Rabe's *Hurlyburly* at the Westwood Playhouse. She regularly attended rehearsals and called Sean frequently, yet on opening night she arrived late—with Sandra Bernhard in tow. This sparked another of Penn's public outbursts—complete with unquotable expletives. It was painfully apparent that their marriage had become more row than romance. The union was zooming toward its final hour.

That hour—more like nine according to the tabloids—continues to be the subject of intense speculation. The story goes that on December 28, 1988, Sean, who was living elsewhere, broke into the couple's Malibu home where he bound, beat, and sexually assaulted his wife. The alleged incident sold a lot of copies of the *National Enquirer*, but Madonna has denied it. It *is* true she filed a complaint against Penn with the Los Angeles County sheriff's office and later withdrew the charges. In *Rolling Stone*, Madonna denounced the story. She maintained that as with most marriages, no one thing drove the couple apart.

> I'm a *very* old-fashioned girl. Marriage is a great thing when it's right. And I did celebrate it and embrace it, and I wanted the whole world to know that this is the man I loved more than anything. . . . Ever since I was in high school, when I was madly in love with someone, I was so proud of this person, I wanted the world to know. . . . But once you reveal it to the world—and you're in the public eye—you give it up, and it's not your own anymore. I began to realize how important it is to hold on to privacy and keep things to yourself as much as possible.

Nevertheless, on January 5, 1989, Madonna filed for divorce. Penn got the Malibu house and Madonna bought out his half of the Manhattan apartment, which amounted to nearly half a million dollars.

Madonna went shopping for a home. Back in 1985 when asked if she'd ever relocate to California, she'd answered no, not permanently, then added, "But I'd like to get a house in the hills—a real Hollywood house. There's one that belonged to either Anna Pavlova or Isadora Duncan. I want that house! It's on top of a hill and it's very dramatic."

With the help of her brother Christopher, she found a modest hilltop home that appeared unremarkable from the front, but offered Madonna the Hollywood panorama of her dreams. The three-bedroom ranch set her back $2,950,000. Christopher filled it with art, antique Italian furniture, and exercise equipment.

Madonna had turned a corner. From 1989 on, her work would be more personal, more provocative, more political than ever.

NINE: SHIFTING FOR HERSELF

"I talk to my mother often. I tell her things that a girl can only say to her mother. Private things."—Madonna

"It's something of a cliché, but you can have all the success in the world, and if you don't have someone to love, it's certainly not as rewarding. The fulfillment you get from another human being—a child in particular—will always dwarf people recognizing you on the street."—Madonna

Divorce was not an easy option. Catholics believe marriage is a sacrament. Madonna felt she'd failed. "I was raised to believe that when you marry someone, you marry him for life. You never give up." Until now, everything Madonna had fought for she won. "I'm not depressed about getting divorced. I'm sad about it. *Very* sad. You can't be married to somebody for three and a half years and then just forget him."

Never a sound sleeper, Madonna sometimes awoke in the middle of the night and thought, "My God! I was married once. I was married and he was the love of my life." Coping with divorce was like dealing with death, a loss so all-encompassing it was difficult to fathom, much less accept. Madonna was restrained; she avoided the Hollywood tendency to hit the talk show circuit dishing up her side of the split.

I never slammed him publicly. But I went through a hostile period. My heart was really broken. You can be a bitch until your heart's broken, and when your heart's broken, you're a superbitch about everything except that. . . . Then we went through a period where I never would have known I was even married to the guy. It was like that part of my life did not exist. Four years.

The first year was good—sort of.

Characteristically, Madonna threw herself into work, juggling several projects at once. By the end of 1988 she'd already discussed *Dick Tracy* with Warren Beatty; now contracts were signed. Madonna would play vixen Breathless Mahoney to Beatty's square-jawed hero. This year Madonna recorded the songs written during 1988 and released her most personal album, *Like a Prayer*.

At the end of January Madonna made headlines—and followed in Michael Jackson's footsteps once more—by signing to endorse Pepsi for a year. Few people realize Madonna once made a commercial for Mitsubishi that aired only in Japan.

The Pepsi ads were designed to tie in with her upcoming album, so the commercial, called "Make a Wish," featured the title cut, "Like a Prayer." In the ad, Madonna's watching a home movie of her eighth birthday. She jumps into the film, trading places with the little girl. At the end, with order restored, she urges the child, "Go ahead—make a wish!"

BBDO Worldwide produced the commercial, which was directed by Joe Pytka. Pepsi bought two minutes of prime time in forty countries, and the commercial debuted on March 2. In the States it was seen on "The Cosby Show."

Depending upon the newspaper you read, Madonna's fee was $2 million, $3 million, $5 million, or $10 million. When the dust settled, most accounts agreed on the $5-million figure. Meanwhile, Coke prepared to retaliate with commercials starring George Michael. Madonna must have been amused by her sudden marketability, since early on she tried, but failed, to interest Revlon in sponsoring her. Someone at the top, unwilling to gamble, asked, "Madonna who?"

The *Wall Street Journal* reported that Marketing Evaluations TVQ Inc., a firm that ranks the popularity of celebrities, said Madonna was recognized by 88 percent of teens but liked by only 25 percent. George Michael, they discovered, was liked by a full 40 percent of teens who recognized him. The company president called Madonna "a turn-off personality," lumping her with such unbeloved stars as Howard Cosell, Donny Osmond, and Charo. One wonders whom they polled, since Madonna's fans have traditionally been young and devoted.

Pepsi responded, "The reality of her image is a string of record-breaking albums, millions of adoring fans, and a series of sold-out concerts. That's what we're tying into."

Why did Madonna do it? "I like the challenge of merging art and commerce. As far as I'm concerned, making a video is also a commercial. The Pepsi spot is a great and different way to expose the record. Record companies just don't have the money to finance that kind of publicity. . . . The can of Pepsi is positioned very subliminally. The camera pans by it, so it's not a hard-sell commercial." In essence, Pepsi paid handsomely to promote Madonna.

Around this time Madonna said, "People have certain notions about me, and it is time for a change." She disturbed those notions on March 3, one day after the Pepsi commercial aired, with the release of her video for "Like a Prayer."

In the video Madonna plays a woman who flees the scene of a crime by ducking inside a church. There she has an erotic dream about a black saint, gets stigmata, and dances in front of a field of burning crosses. Within a week the video was MTV's most-requested clip.

But this was the era of Terry Rakolta, the Chicago housewife who spearheaded a boycott against advertisers on the ribald Fox TV show "Married with Children." Following her lead, the American Family Association, led by executive director Donald Wildmon, announced it was preparing a one-year boycott of Pepsi. They were offended by Madonna's video and outraged Pepsi had chosen her as a spokesperson. They called for Pepsi to cancel their advertising contract with Madonna.

Initially Pepsi pulled the ad from U.S. television and MTV. On April 5, Pepsi announced they'd cancel all U.S. broadcasts permanently, though the ad would be seen overseas. They also canceled plans to sponsor Madonna's tour. The action was not a result of Wildmon's threats, they insisted, but because viewers were confusing Madonna's video with their commercial.

The laws of physics dictate that every action has an equal and opposite reaction. On April 12 the *Wall Street Journal* reported that a group called Fundamentalists Anonymous decided to boycott Pepsi *because* they canceled Madonna's ads!

Madonna kept her millions. Which is not to say the ads didn't cost her anything—she told *Vogue* she lost a valuable pair of French eighteenth-century platinum and diamond drop earrings during the shoot.

Did Madonna pull one over on Pepsi? Why did she time the video's debut for just twenty-four hours after the commercial's? Madonna has repeated over and over that she told Pepsi what was in her video, though she didn't allow them to preview it. In fact Warner didn't even send out the usual advance review copies of the album; they made critics attend a special listening session on their turf.

One Pepsi insider said, "We knew she was making a video in a church with a choir. We didn't know about burning crosses, priests, and religious figures." Roger Mosconi of BBDO Worldwide told a reporter, "One day Madonna, who liked to joke with me, came up and said, 'Hey, Roger, are you going to have the burning cross reflecting in the Pepsi can?' And I said, 'What burning cross?' And she smiled and said, 'You'll see.'"

Prior to the video's release Madonna told *Interview* magazine, "My treatment for the video is a lot more controversial. It's probably going to touch a lot of nerves in a lot of people. And the treatment for the commercial is . . . It's very, very sweet. It's very sentimental."

While it's easy to paint Madonna as a gold digger who bilked Pepsi out of millions, the commercial—which Madonna herself loved—continued airing outside the United States. So Madonna actually fulfilled her end of the bargain, albeit unorthodoxly. There's a moral here, somewhere.

It's flattering to me that people take the time to analyze me and that I've so infiltrated their psyches that they have to intellectualize my very being. I'd rather be on their minds than off. I guess I just have a sense of mischievousness. I never want to hit something on the head. . . . I don't want to be pigeonholed.

Like a Prayer was released in mid-March, and Madonna celebrated at L.A.'s Park Plaza Hotel along with her brother Christopher, Warren Beatty, and Sandra Bernhard. The new Madonna was a serious brunette singing about pain and heartache. She cleverly took her own outdated image—the seductive navel—and upended it. The cover of *Like a Prayer* featured a close-up of her middle all right, but not festooned in Boy Toy buckles and lace, rather covered in strings of beads, rings, gold chains, and other ornamentation evoking the 1960s. Instead of leggings, she wore jeans. The records were scented with patchouli.

Each of the 5 million units shipped to stores contained a one-page sheet called "The Facts About AIDS" reminding listeners that anyone—male, female, gay, or straight—can get AIDS and advocating condom use.

Like a Prayer zipped to the top of *Billboard*'s pop album chart in three weeks, and the song quickly hit number one on the pop singles chart. It had taken *True Blue* five weeks to make number one and *Like a Virgin* eleven weeks.

In addition to the title track, *Like a Prayer* contains "Express Yourself," "Love Song" (cowritten with Prince), "Till Death Do Us Part," "Promise to Try,"

"Cherish," "Dear Jessie," "Oh Father," "Keep it Together," and "Spanish Eyes." There were no covers, no outside authors. Every song was penned by Madonna and her collaborators. The album was dedicated to Madonna's mother.

"*With Like a Prayer,* Madonna doesn't just ask to be taken seriously, she insists on it," wrote *Rolling Stone*'s J.D. Considine, echoing the prevailing sentiment. Critics liked the album and applauded its integrity. They praised Madonna's willingness to defy the "disco tart" label and delve into more complex musical themes better suited to her increasingly grown-up concerns. This was the first album she recorded with live musicians on hand when singing her vocal tracks. The vocals themselves have a raw, unpolished quality far removed from the glossy production values of her early work.

Most songs on *Prayer,* which *New York Times* critic John Rockwell dubbed a "mature confessional album," deal with uneasy relationships. "Till Death Do Us Part" is a fictionalized account of her troubled marriage. "Oh Father" and "Promise to Try" address Madonna's feelings toward her parents. "Keep It Together" talks about the strains and rewards of family life and concludes "your family is gold." "Like a Prayer" itself explores familiar Madonna territory, walking the wire between spiritual and carnal ecstasy.

"Cherish" is a deliriously upbeat love song, and "Dear Jessie" a giggly tribute to childhood—reminiscent of Prince's "Starfish and Coffee." Jessie is Pat Leonard's daughter and proudly tells everyone, "It's my song."

For once Madonna let the world see her vulnerability. And her anger. "My first couple of albums I would say came from the little girl in me, who is interested only in having people like me, in being entertaining and charming and frivolous and sweet. And this new one is the adult side of me, which is concerned with being brutally honest."

"I haven't overcome any big obstacles," she said in 1988. "All my obstacles are still there. And ultimately, my big demons will always be there. . . . One of the hardest things I've faced in life was the death of my mother, and that's something I really haven't gotten over to this day. Inside, I carry many deep wounds, and they're obvious in the way that I deal with people."

Stereo Review was impressed by the new outlook. "Without being maudlin or bitter, Madonna announces that the party's over and it's time to look into the mirror and commit to the things that have lasting value in this life: honoring family ties, pursuing a higher ideal of love, possibly even placing faith in a higher power." *Newsday* called *Prayer* a "meticulously crafted pop album, a deeply personal record that shows a wide emotional range." *USA Today* called the album "a confessional feast, with Madonna's Catholic upbringing as the main course."

It was probably inevitable that Madonna would collaborate with that other God-and-sex-obsessed wonder, Prince, whose work combines Christianity and orgasm in a beat-crazy cosmic squeal. Madonna visited Prince's Minneapolis studio in the hopes of pulling together a full-fledged musical, but they only finished pieces of songs. Later, Prince came to see *Speed-the-Plow* and brought her a rough mix of one fragment. After that, "we sent tapes to each other back and forth between L.A. and Minnesota. Then we would talk on the phone, and he would play stuff for me over the line. I loved working that way."

Celebrating the release of "Like a Prayer."
Photo courtesy of Ron Galella

Carrying her flirtation with sacrilege to the extreme, Madonna promoted "Like a Prayer" with this mock altarpiece and votive candle.

Memorabilia courtesy the Bill Ryan Archives
Photos by David Palmore

Madonna grabs her crotch throughout the video, so it's only appropriate that her single slips into a pair of jeans . . .

Memorabilia courtesy the Bill Ryan Archives.
Photo by David Palmore.

Much has been made of "Till Death Do Us Part," which describes a crumbling marriage complete with alcohol abuse, violence, flying crockery, harsh words, and a husband who can't love his wife because he's never learned to love himself. While she clearly drew from the well of experience, as writers do, the song can't be read as a day-by-day account of Madonna's marriage. "People don't see that you can take some of your experiences from real life and use part of them in your art. They try to make everything an absolute truth."

She told *Rolling Stone*:

[It's] about a destructive relationship that is powerful and painful. In this song, however, it's a cycle that you can't get out of until you die. . . . I wanted the song to be very shocking. . . . It's about a dysfunctional relationship, a sadomasochistic relationship that can't end. Now that's where the truth stops, because I would never want to continue a terrible relationship forever and ever and ever until I die.

Because it was the first single and because of Pepsi and because it was so unlike anything she'd ever created, the "Like a Prayer" video attracted tremendous attention. It was debated in the popular press and in papers like the *National Catholic Reporter*. People asked, "What does it mean?" "Is this sacred or profane?" Italy sided with profanity and banned it.

Madonna said the video is about a girl who witnesses a crime and sees the police unjustly arrest an innocent black man. But one of the criminals sees her and his threatening look frightens the girl away. She runs into a church where a statue of St. Martin de Porres reminds her of the black man. She says a prayer to help her decide what to do.

The girl falls asleep and dreams that she's falling, only to be caught by a woman representing earth and emotional strength, who tosses her back up, telling her to do the right thing. The saint comes to life and they embrace passionately. She touches a knife and gets stigmata. As the choir sings, she reaches an orgasmic crescendo of sexual fulfillment intertwined with her love of God. When the girl wakes up, she goes to the authorities and gets the man exonerated, certain that God will protect her for following her conscience. "It's a song of a passionate young girl so in love with God that it is almost as though He were the male figure in her life."

Her original notion of the video was even more off-center and tragic:

I kept imagining this story about a girl who was madly in love with a black man, set in the South, with this forbidden interracial love affair. And the guy she's in love with sings in a choir. So . . . she goes to church all the time. . . . I wanted to put something in about the Ku Klux Klan. . . .
Then Mary Lambert got involved as the director, and she came up with a story that incorporated more of the religious symbolism I originally wrote into the song. . . . I mean, I had these ideas about me running away with the black guy and both of us getting shot in the back by the KKK. Completely insane. So Mary made it more palatable.

> *"I hope someday [Sean and I] can be friends again. Time heals everything. . . . But there was that year when every time you turn the radio on or see a color or experience a smell it reminds you. . . . and you just crumble."*
> —Madonna

But no less controversial. Singer Niki Harris couldn't or wouldn't perform on the video. When Geraldo Rivera asked why, she said:

First of all, I had a prior engagement. . . But I'm a woman of color. Burning crosses do mean something different to me than they mean to Madonna. . . . It was not right for me to do that video, but not because she was dancing in church 'cause in my church, we dance and we praise Him. But burning crosses do mean something to me. I couldn't dance in front of a burning cross . . . . That doesn't mean that I'm against Madonna if it might be right for her. Go for it. She's got to do what she's got to do.

Father Andrew Greeley, a Catholic priest best known as a sociologist and novelist, lauded Madonna and the video. His article "Like a Catholic: Madonna's Challenge to Her Church" ran in the May 1989 issue of *America*. Greeley found the video "utterly harmless, a PG-13 at the worst, and by the standards of rock video, charming and chaste." Perhaps he was remembering Billy Idol's "Hot in the City" video, which featured a woman tied to a crucifix.

Greeley called the video a morality play, since Madonna awakens to realize "that in the power of God's love she can run the risk of doing right." It is not blasphemous, he said, suggesting *that* notion held true "only for the prurient and the sick who come to the video determined to read their own twisted sexual hang-ups into it."

Greeley reminded his readers that Christianity is filled with people who used sexual passion as a metaphor for religious ecstasy—Josea, Jesus, St. Paul, St. Teresa of Avila. Greeley denounced the Pepsi boycotters and argued for keeping an open mind. Remember, he wrote, "one person's blasphemy may be another person's sacramentality."

Madonna had tackled the issue of "imprisoning Catholic guilt"—and its flip side, "a liberating sense of God's love." But the biggest problem, he concluded, is that Madonna is a "sexually attractive woman who dares to link her sexuality with God." A problem for others, that is. Greeley said, "Madonna is . . . preaching effectively a component of our tradition of which we are afraid—the sacramentality of human eroticism."

Finally, he argued, Madonna was part of the tradition of venerable artists—painters, writers, sculptors—who made God accessible to their peers by creating art that spoke the language of their generation. Instead of mocking Christ, Madonna suggested we follow his example to lead better lives.

Though she doesn't practice her religion, Madonna doesn't ridicule it. She does, however, reserve the right to take issue with its doctrines. "I don't make fun of Catholicism. I deeply respect Catholicism—its mystery and fear and oppressiveness, its passion and its discipline and its obsession with guilt."

Madonna cleverly deduced that Wildmon and other fundamentalist Christians were more offended by her power, freedom, and control of the video per se. "For them to go around banning records and books and trying to get people arrested, it's a pretty clear statement about their own obsessions. Obviously I'm tapping into something in their unconscious that they're very ashamed of. . . . It's like Hitler; they want to purify your thoughts."

Like a Prayer came out at the height of the

Salman Rushdie crisis, and England's *Hot Press* wrote that Madonna's life was threatened by the London-based Islamic Media-Monitoring Committee. They felt the video was blasphemous and depicted their "revered black prophet in a heretical and mortally insulting way." Of course the saint was clearly identified as Martin de Porres so the argument carries no weight. There are no reports of any assassination attempts at this time.

Anyway Madonna nearly did the job for them when she threw herself off a forty-foot-high diving board for a scene that was later cut from the video. "When I got to the top, I looked down and went, 'Oh God, it's really far.' Then I figured, 'What the hell.'"

An alternate interpretation of the video came out of a *Washington Post* editorial by Brooke Masters. To Masters, the "Prayer" video was nothing less than "a feminist fairy tale. Sleeping Beauty and Snow White waited for their princes to come along. Madonna finds her own man and wakes him up."

Madonna entered her most exciting era as an image maker. For "Cherish," she and Herb Ritts hit the beach with a fleet of hunky mermen to capture the gleeful joy of her exuberant ditty—a song that unapologetically borrowed riffs from every pop classic ever written about true love.

"Oh Father" was Madonna's musical tribute to Simon and Garfunkel, and the haunting lyrics reminded listeners "there's a side of me I'm finding less and less inhibited about expressing, and that's a side that has to do with a real pain and sadness that I feel." The video packs a punch—it's an indelible story about lost childhood and misplaced love. Madonna developed the autobiographical plot, then hired David Fincher to execute the video. Its theme, she said, "is about how you marry your father."

Here are the familiar milestones from Madonna's life—her mother's death, childhood confusion, piety, a sad, abusive father/lover, redemption, joy. The images are striking. One powerful moment comes when the child approaches her mother laid out for burial and we clearly see stitches where her lips were sewn shut by the embalmer. In another shot Madonna walks into the frame, but the shadow she throws is the child's.

The video frequently returns to the image of a snowy graveyard; in the last frames the child dances on the grave. "The end of the video, where I'm dancing on my mother's grave, is an attempt to embrace and accept my mother's death. I had to deal with the loss of my mother and then I had to deal with the guilt of her being gone, and then I had to deal with the loss of my father when he married my stepmother. So I was just one angry, abandoned little girl."

Though the lyrics to "Oh Father" might suggest otherwise, Madonna insists, "I have a million different feelings about my father, but mostly I love him to death. . . . Whenever I need him, he's there for me."

"Art should be controversial," says Madonna. "It should make people think about what they do and don't believe in. It's good to get people to question their beliefs, their values. So much music and entertainment today just puts people in a trance. They're asleep and you've got to do what you can to wake them up."

> *"Everything you've read about Madonna has been wrong."*—Publicist Liz Rosenberg

"Express Yourself" is Madonna's million-dollar alarm clock. Madonna financed the video personally in order to, well, express herself. Since she's a working-class hero, it's not surprising that Madonna chooses to channel her millions into videos as well as extravagant possessions. "My manager gets insane about what I spend. But it placates me to put my energy into that work. I could be buying a Ferrari, but I'd rather spend it this way."

Many call "Express Yourself" the antidote to "Material Girl." This is a woman's song for other women—it begins, "Hey, ladies!" Madonna says the theme is:

People should always say what it is they want. The reason relationships don't work is because [people] are afraid. That's been my problem in all my relationships. I'm sure people see me as an outspoken person. . . . But sometimes you feel that if you ask for too much or ask for the wrong thing from someone you care about that that person won't like you. And so you censor yourself. I've been guilty of that in every meaningful relationship I've ever had. The time I learn how not to edit myself will be the time I consider myself a complete adult.

People separate things. They have someone they idolize, and they idolize them so much they put them on a pedestal and see them as holy. And then they have to find people they can get low-down and dirty with. I think you have to put the two together, let them both surface. It has to do with being honest with yourself and the people you love; to say, "This is me and this is what I need and what I want"

The action occurs in a factory patterned after Fritz Lang's silent film *Metropolis* complete with sweaty, sexy, half-dressed male toilers. It's a visual masterpiece that rips through a slew of borrowed images, including the paintings of Tamara de Lempicka, which Madonna's collected for years. (She used a de Lempicka nude in "Open Your Heart," too.)

"I oversaw everything," Madonna said, "the building of the sets, everyone's costume. I had meetings with makeup and hair and the cinematographer, casting . . . the ultimate thing behind the song is that if you don't say what you want, then you're not going to get it. And in effect you are chained down by your inability to say what you feel or go after what you want."

She used this chain metaphor literally. After stalking through the factory grabbing her crotch and bossing everyone around, Madonna appears nude except for a thick steel collar chaining her to a bed, where a glistening hard-hat lover eventually tracks her down for a passionate embrace.

Feminists had aneurysms.

Why a chain? "It's just an image I thought was powerful. . . . It showed an extreme. Extreme images of women: one is in charge, in control, dominating; the other is chained to a bed, taking care of the procreation responsibilities." But don't get the wrong idea, she said. "The sexuality in my videos is all consented to. No one's taking advantage of each other." The video ends with the motto "Without the heart there can be no understanding between the hand and the mind."

It's precisely this head-on collision between sexuality and power that endears Madonna to women like writer Brooke Masters, who calls Madonna a yuppie goddess, "strong, self-reliant, and above all, sexy." A Princeton grad student told Masters: "Madonna embodies things we would like to be in our wildest dreams but would never be in real life."

Author Judith Viorst hailed Madonna as one of the new Hollywood sex symbols personifying ways women have changed since the heyday of brainless blond bombshells. "The eighties and nineties are giving us a panoply of strong, smart, savvy sirens who don't intend to be *anybody's* victim." With the very definition of sexiness at stake, said Viorst, Madonna helps us establish new criteria by retaining her right to strength and intelligence.

Madonna once said, "You want it, you find a way to get it." She advocates choice, advocates holding out for what's right and feels good instead of settling. Throughout 1989, Madonna startled fans with vibrant, controversial images. She set little fires and watched them burn. Listen, she seemed to say, we women have tremendous sexual power, but we've been afraid to seize it. Seize it.

Plenty of women heard the message: "You can do this, too."

Music is the most accessible art form. . . . It's completely universal and the most powerful way I know of telling the truth about what goes on in people's hearts and minds. My songs deal more and more with issues that mean a lot to me, the assimilation of experiences I've had in my life and relationships. They're about the ties that bind us all together, about growing up and letting go. But even in the most personal songs I write and sing, people tell me they recognize themselves.

Through artist Kenny Scharf, Madonna learned about the threat to South America's rain forest and its devastating effect on world ecology. In June the two organized a benefit called Don't Bungle the Jungle, to raise money to buy land there that would be protected from development. The benefit played for 2,100 people at the Brooklyn Academy of Music and featured performances by the B-52's and Bob Weir. The highlight of the evening came when Madonna and Sandra Bernhard took the stage in matching Keith Haring-decorated shorts and flashy sequin bras for a bump-and-grind version of the Sonny & Cher hit "I Got You Babe."

"Don't believe those stories you hear about us," said Madonna.

"Believe them!" countered Bernhard with a grin.

After the concert, celebrities like Calvin Klein, Glenn Close, Meryl Streep, Iman, Debi M., and Billy Joel munched a midnight supper at Indochine on Lafayette Street. At dinner Bernhard told a reporter, "Madonna and I have a heart-and-soul friendship. Beyond that it's nobody's business. The way we act together is a political statement. It's a way to say to the world, 'Get past the judgments. Accept people for what they are.' The rain forest is dying. What do you care more about, the rain forest or our sexuality?'"

The joke was out of hand. Since Sandra Bernhard's made no secret of her lesbian relationships and Madonna was fresh from a fiery, possibly abusive marriage, people found it easy to imagine them in the throes of passion. While the rumors couldn't harm Madonna's career—what could?—Bernhard may have worried.

She told another reporter:

We're friends and that's it. The press just can't be happy when two cool girls like us are tight buddies.... Did anyone ever accuse Dean Martin and Jerry Lewis of getting it on? No. The press have to turn it into some freaky, sordid scandal when they *should* be highlighting the fact that maybe for once, two strong women are setting a positive example for the rest of the gals—it's fine to be supportive of your girlfriends, like not all women are back stabbing, vicious nightmares.

Madonna treated the whole thing as a giant goof until 1991, when she spoke out:

Sandy and I have always been great friends. I think in the very beginning there was a flirtation, but I realized I could have a really good friend in Sandra, and I wanted to maintain the friendship.... The fact is that Sandra sleeps with men, too, and I think maybe she's trying to find happiness in her life. Maybe she was just thinking, "Can everybody just shut up so I can find somebody to have a decent relationship with?" Sandra's one of the most open people I know.... I think it's ludicrous that people are accusing her of being in the closet or ashamed of being gay.

Whether I'm gay or not is irrelevant. Whether I slept with her or not is irrelevant. I'm perfectly willing to have people think that I did.

That September, Madonna appeared at the MTV music awards to sing "Express Yourself" with Niki Harris and Donna DeLory. She later emerged smoking a cigarette and talking tough—still in her pinstripe suit—to present the Video Vanguard award to George Michael. "I'd rather be getting an award than giving one away," she cracked.

Though she lost Best Video to Neil Young, "Express Yourself" picked up a few awards: David Fincher for Best Director, Holgar Gross and Vance Lorezini for Best Art Direction, and Mark Plummer for Best Cinematography. The Viewers' Choice Award went to Madonna's "Like a Prayer," beating out Michael Jackson's "Leave Me Alone." Accepting it, Madonna satirized Sally Field's infamous Oscar idiocy, gulping, "You really like me." After thanking her family, Warner Bros., Freddy DeMann, and Mary Lambert, she thanked Pepsi—"for causing so much controversy." What cheek! Pepsi sponsored the awards telecast!

In October she hosted the premiere of *It Had to Be You*, a comedy starring husband and wife Renee Taylor and Joe Bologna at the Samuel Goldwyn Theater in Beverly Hills. It was a benefit for Hollywood Helps, an AIDS foundation.

Rounding off 1989, Madonna was named one of *People* magazine's twenty-five most intriguing people of the year. But it wasn't only the editors of *People* who found her intriguing. True to form, lothario Warren Beatty had fallen for his leading lady—not Tess Trueheart, played by Glenne Headley, but sexy Breathless Mahoney, played by Madonna Louise Veronica Ciccone.

TEN: LUCK AND PLUCK

"Do anything you want, just never make a film with Warren Beatty."—Sean Penn

"They used to say I was a slut, a pig, an easy lay, a sex bomb, Minnie Mouse, or even Marlene Dietrich's daughter, but I'd rather say that I'm just a hyperactive adult."—Madonna

Throughout her life Madonna has gravitated toward women like Anne Sexton, Frida Khalo, and Georgia O'Keeffe, women who endured pain and suffering—often in the shadow of a great man—who nevertheless survived, creating art out of their challenges. "I tend to be attracted to things that are about the sadness of living, the ultimate loneliness of living," she explains.

That darkness may have been one of the qualities she found appealing about Breathless Mahoney. Breathless was a villain and a manipulator, but she was also trapped and frightened. "She's a seductress in a lot of pain," Madonna told an interviewer, joking that she'd been "preparing for the role all my life."

Madonna perceived the demimondaine as an abused woman, "as a person with a lot of pain who's never really been loved. . . . And that's what she sees when she sees Dick Tracy. Because [he] treats her with respect for the first time. No other man has, so that's why she falls madly in love with him."

Earlier, Madonna turned down the Michelle Pfeiffer role in *The Fabulous Baker Boys* to work with Beatty instead. Seeing the other film later, she said she had no regrets. "I hated it. It was too mushy. Such a Wonder-bread cast. I think of all these people as being California people—blond and boring." That may be so or it may be a smoke screen. In 1987, when the eternal question of *Evita* arose, Madonna told *American Film*, "I'd love to do a movie someday where I sing, but it's hard to make a transition if I do movies about singers." If that's true, why Breathless?

Was it Warren Beatty's seductive promise to "light you better than anyone's ever lit you," or the failure of her previous films that convinced Madonna to greenlight this project? Asked if she thought *Dick Tracy* would make her a movie star, Madonna replied, "Uh-huh. And if it doesn't, something else will. Just give me some time."

Dick Tracy was a hot package. "I was attracted to a good part in a good movie. A chance to work with a lot of great talent. This movie looks like nothing anyone's ever seen." Here was an opportunity to establish a relationship with the powerful Disney studio, work alongside great actors like Al Pacino, Paul Sorvino, and Dustin Hoffman, and appear in a story with built-in audience appeal. The Chester Gould comic strip, which originated in the 1930s, remains syndicated throughout the country, beloved of millions. Beatty himself is a lifelong fan of the stoic detective and dreamed of making this film for years.

The hardest, most frightening aspect of

Madonna's role was performing three original Stephen Sondheim songs. "Sondheim writes in a kind of chromatic wildness. They're very difficult songs to learn. I mean, one song is written with five sharps. They're brilliant, but really complex." Madonna and Sondheim both worried she couldn't do his songs justice, but he soon became a fan. "It was her dancing that convinced me. I was really knocked out the moment she started to move—that's when you immediately know why she's a star." Madonna trained with voice coach Seth Riggs to master the Sondheim style.

Though they argued, Madonna ultimately capitulated to Beatty and dyed her hair blond. She'd done two screen tests, one as a brunette, another in a blond wig, and cinematographer Vittorio Storaro went gaga over the way light haloed around blond. Madonna spent "more time figuring out Breathless's character in terms of the way she looked than anything else." She endured lengthy costume fittings that took longer than actually delivering her lines on camera.

Which is saying something, since Warren Beatty is famous for ordering take after take after take. "His favorite thing is to do so many takes that you forget everything you planned on doing, and you're completely broken down," Madonna said. "And then you just do it without thinking, and that's usually your best stuff."

When two people have completely opposite working styles, there's bound to be frustration. After all, Madonna's the kind of hyperactive who stands in front of a microwave oven shouting, "Hurry up!" She's a perfectionist, but impatience is her greatest failing.

So how did she cope with Beatty's style? She toed the line: "There was a scene where Al [Pacino, playing Big Boy] kept smacking me in the stomach. It would sting, and what made me cry was not so much the hit, but that Warren wouldn't shout 'Cut.' Al just kept going and I was humiliated. And of course that was what they intended—they wanted me to show the right emotion as Breathless."

Pacino won a richly deserved Oscar for his wildly manic performance as Big Boy, but working with the great actor wasn't always easy on Madonna. "When Al put his prosthetics on, his suit, he was a gross pig. And he's not that way in real life. . . . As Big Boy . . . he was always smacking my butt and my face. I hated him, I loathed him, I was disgusted with him." Offscreen Pacino would stay in character and chase Madonna around, behaving like an obnoxious lout with itchy fingers. Madonna tensed, and the tension between them inspired both performances.

Madonna's eight gowns were designed by Milena Canonero, who won Best Costume Oscars for *Barry Lyndon* and *Chariots of Fire*. In this highly stylized film every character had his or her signature color. Breathless signified the night, the moon, sex, and her palate was midnight blue, silver, black. Storaro called her "a creature lighted by the color of blood and the light of the moon."

Though Madonna itched to get through her fittings lickety-split, she cultivated patience during the many hours of pinning and cutting, thanks to a little stroking and a supply of air-popped popcorn. Milena Canonero praised Madonna: "Here she was, the actress all the way! She was not making her video or working on her stage act. She left me to decide. She just wanted the clothes to fit well and to be able to feel the tightness of

Breathless dolls were just one part of Disney's relentless push to get the public excited about *Dick Tracy*.

Memorabilia courtesy the Bill Ryan Archives
Photos by David Palmore

Ironically, Madonna can't read or write music.

Memorabilia courtesy the Bill Ryan Archives
Photo by David Palmore

This cardboard display capitalizes on Madonna's likeness to draw fans to the film.
Memorabilia courtesy the Bill Ryan Archives
Photo by David Palmore

the dress on her body."

The costumes were cut to fit each of her carefully sculpted curves like second skin. As Beatty understated, "She's dressed in a way that accentuates her good health." Canonero said Beatty gave her carte blanche with the men's costumes, but had definite ideas about how his women should look.

"Breathless is larger than life," said Madonna. "She doesn't go anywhere unless she's wearing an evening gown." Canonero's ultimate challenge was creating skintight gowns that allowed freedom of movement for the nightclub scenes. One dress was so low-cut that Madonna's breasts popped loose every time she flung her arms overhead for the song's finale. The makeup men worried Beatty would ask them to glue her into the dress. According to makeup maestro John Caglione, "We felt it was too dangerous. It was like if the Museum of Natural History had asked us to watch the Star of India for the weekend."

Newspapers reported Madonna's wages for *Dick Tracy* were actor's scale—a minimum of $1,440 a week. That's true, but she negotiated to earn far more over the long haul. Madonna received points on the film's profits, as well as on video and merchandising revenues, dollar values that could ultimately total millions when one tallies the revenue from such items as *Dick Tracy* watches, shower curtains, T-shirts, and Crimestopper games at McDonald's.

Plus, Madonna decided to ignore the "confusion" she claimed sabotaged the movie *Who's That Girl?* by releasing *I'm Breathless*, an album of songs inspired by the film. She tied it all up with her Blond Ambition tour, featuring chorus boys decked out in canary trench coats and G-strings.

More dollars in the bank. Though touring is an expensive proposition for Madonna, HBO paid her $1 million up front to televise one concert. The show, beamed by tape delay from France, became the highest-rated nonsports event they've ever shown. In light of all this merchandising, *Harper's Bazaar* quipped, "Everything connects to something else. Madonna may be the only woman who networks with herself."

I'm Breathless featured the three Sondheim tunes "More," "Sooner or Later," and "What Can You Lose," a duet with Mandy Patinkin. The rest of the album consisted of "Hanky Panky" (a sanitized version, thanks to Disney censors), "Something to Remember," "Now I'm Following You" parts I and II (written by Andy Paley, Jonathan Paley, Jeff Lass, and Ned Claflin, and sung with Beatty), and the supersuccessful Shep Pettibone collaboration "Vogue," released well in advance of the film.

> *"I know how you feel. You don't know whether you want to hit me or kiss me. I get a lot of that."*—Breathless Mahoney

Though Breathless didn't get her man, it wasn't long before Madonna and Beatty were a hot romance. On August 12, 1989 they were snapped leaving photographer Herb Ritts's birthday party at an exclusive Hollywood club. Though Madonna joked that probably 75 percent of Hollywood had slept with Beatty, she admitted she found his sexual history intimidating. "I'd be a liar if I said it didn't bother me. Sometimes I think, 'He's been with the world's most beautiful, most glamorous, talented women.' . . . I mean, how can I ever be as fabulous as Brigitte

It's official! They're an item.
Photo courtesy of Ron Galella

Looks like leather-clad Beatty's getting fashion tips from Madonna.
Photo courtesy of Ron Galella

Trying to sneak out of an L.A. eatery.

Bardot when she was twenty-five? Or Natalie Wood? . . . Then there is the other side of me that says I'm better than all of them."

Madonna says she's drawn to men who are in touch with their sexuality and *work* it, men who acknowledge their feminine side instead of playing it macho. Beatty had these qualities in spades, but the price was his "hyperactive" reputation. She reasoned, "You can either be threatened by it or flattered by it. I choose to be flattered. . . . At least for today."

Beatty reminded Madonna of Dick Tracy—a quiet loner who's very smart and very probing. "Warren should have been a psychiatrist or a district attorney. When he wants to know somebody, he goes out of his way to investigate. You feel like you're under a microscope. . . . But it's admirable. Everybody ought to examine the people they're going to work with as intensely as he does."

Best of all, Madonna didn't have to apologize for being famous. "Warren understands the bullshit. He's been an icon for years. He's had a lot more practice at it than I have. . . . You can't understand being hugely famous until it happens, and then it's too late to decide if you want it or not. Warren's been a sex symbol for so long he's just not surprised by anything."

Plenty of people thought the "romance" was another publicity maneuver to promote *Dick Tracy*. Or to promote Beatty, who at fifty-plus was losing touch with the younger set and still smarting from *Ishtar*. One writer said by loving Beatty, "Madonna makes him more famous than he was before." The two certainly conducted their affair publicly. They cuddled on the set, in restaurants, and during interviews. Madonna especially enjoyed crawling into Beatty's lap for a snuggle. Does the phrase *father figure* come to mind?

Would their romance outlast *Dick Tracy?* Madonna speculated: "Sometimes I'm cynical and pragmatic and think it will last as long as it lasts. Then I have moments when I'm really romantic and I think, 'We're just perfect together.'"

He called her Buzzbomb and she nicknamed him Old Man. He showered her with exquisite, expensive antique jewelry. He was complimentary in print: "She's no accident. . . . Madonna is simultaneously touching and more fun than a barrel of monkeys. She's funny and she's gifted in so many areas and has the kind of energy as a performer that can't help but make you engaged. . . . She's a wonderful comedienne."

Beatty's friend and collaborator on *Bugsy*, writer/director James Tobak, met Madonna during *Dick Tracy* and offered his assessment to *Movieline* magazine: "She makes her audience feel, 'If she can do it, I can do it.' . . . She's incredibly shrewd and cunning. One of the great marketing geniuses of the last fifteen years. Her product is herself."

In May the marketing maven descended on "Arsenio Hall," resplendent in a white double-breasted trouser suit and bobbing blond curls, her face lit by a devilish megawatt smile. "Vogue" was a huge hit on radio and MTV, so Arsenio's people surprised her with a fun homemade video of audience members and other "real" people vogueing in synch to the tune.

Arsenio played straight man to Madonna's wisecracking, profane moll. Talking about "Vogue," he asked, "What do you mean, gives good face?" She replied, "Well, it's not exactly like giving good BLEEP."

Though she begged off from singing that night, Madonna plugged her Blond Ambition tour—already in rehearsal—and praised her inventive dancers. But the real reason for the appearance was to plug *Dick Tracy*. Which led Arsenio to inquire about her other hit, "Hanky Panky," in which Madonna/Breathless sings about the thrills of being spanked.

Arsenio asked, "How do you interpret that?"

"Interpret it? I wrote it. It's about a girl who likes a good spanking. I'm talking about the spanking you get when you're not bad. I'm talking about the spanking you get when you're good." Madonna joked that personally, she liked a little stinging but not a hard wallop.

Not until 1991 did Madonna confront the absurdity of this conversation and remind fans that the silly little tune was written for *Breathless:*

> It's a joke. It started because I believed that my character in *Dick Tracy* liked to get smacked around. . . . I despise being spanked. I was just playing with Arsenio. . . . I certainly punish myself in lots of ways but not by having people hit me. . . . I thought it would be obvious—because of my image as a person who wants to be domineering and take charge—that there was no way I would actually want someone to spank me.

Arsenio was dying to dish about Warren Beatty, but Madonna played it cool, outfoxing him at every juncture. When he teased that Joan Collins called Beatty insatiable, she just laughed. "He was *twenty* at the time. Aren't all twenty-year-olds?"

And nowadays? "I would say he's satiable," she said, grinning madly.

Dick Tracy came out in June to predominantly good reviews and a $23-million box office its first weekend. The overhyped film might have imploded like a dense soufflé. Disney spent millions promoting the film ahead of time and spent their money so effectively that a survey of moviegoers showed fully 100 percent were aware of its existence. Yet that kind of buildup has been known to backfire badly. Think of *Days of Thunder* or *The Two Jakes*.

Unlike *Shanghai Surprise*, viewers definitely felt the sizzle between Breathless and Dick Tracy. But did Madonna get enough screen time? Canada's weekly news magazine, *Macleans*, thought not, suggesting Beatty had squandered his most valuable asset.

Madonna's scenes are more like tableaux vivant than cinema. She called Breathless a poseur and that attitude permeates her performance. She makes an entrance, hits her mark, arranges her glorious self, then delivers saucy lines in a slow, stagy manner that seems to expect immediate applause. Still, she's just perfect for the film, which comes off as a series of vignettes spooled out to tell a story.

Madonna claimed she never saw the entire film, only enough to resent the way her musical numbers were cut up. By 1991 she was telling reporters, "I learned a lot about filmmaking from Warren, but obviously [*Dick Tracy*] didn't make me a big box-office star, did it?"

Naturally writers compared *Dick Tracy* to *Batman*. Both films relied heavily on style over substance and drew on comic strips for inspiration. *Macleans* agreed with Madonna that the film "looks quite unlike any movie that has ever been made. . . . Visually [it's] a stunning achievement: it has the quality of a remarkably sustained optical illusion." *Time* called it "the best comic-strip movie yet." They also praised Madonna, calling her "sexy and wily, a bracing blend of Marilyn Monroe and Jessica Rabbit." *Newsweek* raved, "Madonna is smashingly unsubtle as the femme fatale."

David Denby despised Madonna, of course. He deemed the movie "charming and beautifully designed," but said: "Madonna's triumph is that she projects beauty without having it. . . . Her singing, with gloved arms extended, is neo-Marilyn. . . . But I've seen bishops who projected more sexual warmth than Madonna. . . . She's an awful actress, but she's adequate as a masochistic, two-dimensional floozy."

At the very least, working on *Dick Tracy* endeared Madonna to one of Hollywood's most powerful men, Disney chairman Jeffrey Katzenberg. He told *Vanity Fair:*

> She has a very secure sense of her life and her business. As far as I can tell, she's always had a vision of exactly who she is—whether as an actress or a performer or a lyricist or a music producer or a businesswoman. . . . She's always evolving; she never stands still. Every two years she comes up with a new look, a new way of presenting herself, a new attitude. And every time it's successful. . . . When something like that happens once, okay, maybe it's luck. Twice is a coincidence. Three times it's just remarkable talent. A kind of genius. And Madonna's on her fifth or sixth time.

Since it's not Madonna's style to sit around waiting for reviews, she jumped into her next project. It was time to unveil Blond Ambition—the concert tour to end all concert tours.

Photo courtesy of Ron Galella

ELEVEN: THE WORLD BEFORE HER

"You can't affect people in a large, grand way without being scrutinized and judged and put under a microscope, and I accept that. If it ever gets too much . . . or I'm not enjoying it anymore, then I won't do it."—Madonna

"I don't want to be pedantic. For me it's more interesting to inject humor into all the messages. That way people get what you're saying but get it laughing."—Madonna

Was it only five years ago that the world recoiled at the thought of nude photos of Madonna? By 1990, she was gleefully baring her breasts (well, one at any rate) for *Vanity Fair*, and dishing up stylish videos like "Vogue," featuring a see-through black lace shirt that left no questions of Madonna's anatomy unanswered. Had the world become less skittish because of her? Perhaps not, but as usual, she capitalized on our changing mores and leapt to the vanguard to barge forward.

Madonna began conceptualizing Blond Ambition in September of 1989 and rehearsing on a Disney soundstage late January for two intense months. The tour would play twenty-five cities on three continents, starting with Tokyo on April 24 and ending in Nice on August 5. *Amusement Business Magazine* reported that 400,000 Madonna tickets sold in two hours. Four Los Angeles arena dates sold out in sixty-eight minutes.

The advance word was excitement. "I've created five different worlds, and the set is all based on hydraulics. . . . The world changes completely. I think of it more as a musical than as a rock concert." The worlds included a *Metropolis* set like the "Express Yourself" video, a church, a bedroom, a fifties-musical set, and a *Clockwork Orange*-inspired cabaret set.

Madonna needed separate universes to encompass her many moods. "I don't try to candy-coat anything or make it palatable for mass consumption. I sing what I feel, who I am. And I guess you could say there are a lot of different sides to that identity. I'm constantly inventing scenarios that are a combination of something I know and something I imagine. Different parts come at different times."

The tour's art director, Christopher Ciccone, explained, "Madonna has always approached her material on a slightly theatrical level." Madonna's audience was raised on television. They expect rapid-fire scenarios—they can't focus on anything that takes too long—and Madonna's own attention span moves at the speed of light. Blond Ambition was calculated to keep both audience and performer amused.

Touring employs a lot of people. Madonna placed an ad for "fierce male dancers . . . wimps and wannabes need not apply!" "I was hanging around a lot of clubs—watching different styles, looking for dancers. . . . I was looking for some street dancers . . . I chose José and Luis because I thought they were the strongest performers. I invited them to come to the auditions. Luis came, Luis will try anything . . . and I loved him for that. José wouldn't do a goddamned thing. . . . So of course I loved him for that." Luis Camacho said, "Once you walked into the audition you knew who was the boss. She just radiates power."

She radiated something else to Oliver Crumes, the only heterosexual dancer, and before long there was talk. . . . "I was carrying on an Oedipal relationship, a mother and son. It wasn't fully realized. He played Little Boy to my Mother. I took him under my wing. . .He got attached." Madonna was an unorthodox mom. According to Kevin Stea, "She was always worried about us. There were always condoms in our per diem."

Besides dancers, Madonna needed some backup singers, and the Blond Ambition tour reunited her with Niki Harris and Donna DeLory. She hired eight musicians and "about a zillion tech guys just to take care of the musicians, and then all the crew guys underneath the stage working everything. . . . Probably seventy-five to a hundred [people]. And a lot of trucks."

She fired people, too, usually in jest, and once got so exasperated she fired herself! "It's a running joke. I fire someone every day. . . . I fire Lenny every day. He's the guy who opens the trapdoors, and he's always doing it at the wrong time and almost killing me."

Someone who stayed fired was Madonna's friend choreographer Karole Armitage. Armitage said: "Our parting was amicable. It's disappointing, but Madonna's vision is so strong there was no room for me." In her place, Madonna hired Vince Paterson, another of Michael Jackson's former employees.

Paterson had just eighteen days to choreograph the show, which largely aped Madonna's videos. She told him: "I want you to break every rule you can think of, and when you're done with that, we'll make up some more and break them." He was impressed by Madonna's chutzpah. When she asked if she could grab her crotch the way Jackson does, he said, "Go ahead. You have more balls than anyone."

Originally Madonna refused to be lifted by any of her dancers. She protested, "I really don't like the idea of being manipulated by men on the stage—it goes against what I believe." Paterson argued, "I'm not talking about male manipulation—I'm talking about great dramatic moments."

"Whether you like her or not," he concluded, "you must be jealous of the girl—[she's] one of the few artists in America who can do whatever they want."

Madonna may be ruthlessly efficient, but she's also loyal. Niki Harris sprained her ankle rehearsing the "Keep It Together" dance routine. "I thought Madonna would have to fire me, but she kept me on," marveled Harris. Madonna brought a physician on the road who gave Harris ultrasound and electro therapy and advised her to wrap the ankle every night after the show. On top of this, Madonna had special shoes made for Niki.

Madonna's younger brother, Christopher, who "art directed" both her homes, was artistic director for this tour. "It took a while for the people I'm working with to get past the fact that I'm Madonna's brother and to accept that I know what I'm doing. But once that happened, everything was fine."

Of the five universes, Christopher felt special affinity for the church setting. "If there's something that's distinctly mine, it's the central, religious section of the show." The elaborate set boasted columns, banks of votive candles, a stained-glass window of the original Madonna, and a velvet-covered altar. The expenditure for sets ran upwards of $2 million.

For costumes, Madonna turned to her friend Jean-Paul Gaultier, the eccentric French designer who once created a line of skirts for men. Madonna's long admired and worn Gaultier's work; as early as 1985 she named him among her favorite designers. Gaultier has always been fascinated and inspired by corsets and lingerie, so their sensibilities dovetailed. Gaultier prepared nearly fifteen hundred sketches and Madonna flew to Paris during Christmas of 1989 to undergo fittings, prompting Gaultier's assistants to stock up on aspirins.

As usual, Madonna knew just what *she* wanted. Said Gaultier:

Madonna's very easy to get along with. I don't have to speak to twenty-five people before I can reach her on the phone. She doesn't change her mind like other people I've worked with. She doesn't suddenly think, "Oh my God, I look like Liza Minelli!" But you can't just tell her what to wear. When I proposed my designs she said "yes, no"—very simple. I saw her with black hair and I told her it was great, but she prefers to be blond. Madonna definitely knows what she wants.

She wanted a pinstripe suit slit at the breasts to expose a pointy corset and garters worn *outside* her pants. She wanted glittering bodysuits that turned her breasts into sharp weapons. She wanted a monogrammed chenille bathrobe and curlers. She wanted church vestments. She wanted filmy negligees and a hot-pink blazer. She wanted a calypso shirt and bell-bottomed hip huggers. And she wanted black leather cages worn as vests. All this, combined with the battery pack and head mike she wore for many numbers gave Madonna a not-of-this-earth demeanor. Instead of inviting caresses, the look said keep your distance, I'm armed and dangerous! Her body was her weapon.

Madonna totally reshaped that body for the tour. "We wanted to go for a sleeker, more defined look," said Robert Parr, Madonna's personal trainer since the late eighties. On the Virgin tour Madonna had a protruding tummy; the Blond Ambition Valkyrie had become a walking advertisement for decathlon training. She hadn't an ounce of spare flesh and somehow lost another twelve pounds during the grueling tour.

Parr helped Madonna build stamina in order to maintain the high energy level required to survive the show over four months. They ran seven to nine miles daily, used a Versa Climber, and rode a stationary bike. He said, "No one ever talks about the changes in her cardiac output, her respiratory system, the fact that her cholesterol and blood pressure are low. We're looking for health in fitness—which is in the image of this gorgeous body."

Madonna topped her strong, sinewy physique with a clip-on blond ponytail. Most fans thought immediately of Barbara Eden romping through "I Dream of Jeannie." If that was the allusion, Madonna tipped the bottle on its pointy little stopper. Jeannie was the epitome of submissive femininity. Madonna, the antithesis. During dance routines Madonna worked the ponytail for all it was worth—swishing it, flicking it, thrashing it. But by the time she hit Europe the ponytail was history. Niki Harris said it was partly "because she's Madonna and she

Photo courtesy of Ron Galella

Madonna flashes her foundation.
Photo courtesy of Ron Galella

Causing a commotion with Donna DeLory and Niki Harris.
Photo courtesy of Ron Galella

The infamous Gaultier corset. Don't mess with Madonna! Our Lady of Perpetual Motion.
Photo courtesy of Ron Galella

Choreographer Paterson admits she has more balls than anyone he knows.
Photo courtesy of Ron Galella

wanted to," but added that the ponytail was damaging her real hair, causing it to break off.

One of the tour's sponsors was Pioneer Electronics. In exchange for rights to an exclusive laser disc of the show plus additional footage, Madonna promised not to release a competing video version of the tour for at least one year. This was shrewder than it initially seems, since a video of Blond Ambition would have competed with her May 1991 film *Truth or Dare*. Few people own laser-disc hardware, so she sacrificed little in return for much needed financial backing.

And as usual fans could shop at the well-stocked concession stand bursting with T-shirts, posters, watches, scarves, and jigsaw puzzles bearing Blond Ambition images.

Trust Madonna to capitalize on contradiction. If Breathless was a cinematic study in failure and sexual abuse, Madonna live personified power, strength, and control. For all the overt sexuality of her act, she remained aloof, distinctly unerotic. American fans could see the film and the show at the same time—and that opposition didn't faze her. Either she no longer worried about confusion or she trusted *Dick Tracy* was a stronger box-office draw than *Who's That Girl?*

Reactions to the Blond Ambition tour ranged from dizzy hero worship to moral outrage—what else? Eyebrows jackknifed during Madonna's simulated masturbation. Ears burned with the sizzle of four-letter words. Jaws unhinged over huge pointy bras strapped to *male* dancers. Hearts fluttered when Madonna straddled an altar and got intimate with an incense burner.

Macleans said the show "unfolds like a kaleidoscope of sexual decadence. The references range from Berlin cabarets to New York leather bars." *Rolling Stone* called it "a nifty summation of the spectacle that is Madonna." A *New York Times* critic felt the vignettes were designed to go right to videotape: "Madonna is so stylized she wears her current images like armor." Another *Times* critic, Jon Pareles, thought Madonna hugely entertaining and innovative: "Through the metamorphoses, she has taken up old roles only to reveal their limitations, and she has insisted that pleasure and sexuality are positive, liberating forces, not to be constrained by anyone's unexamined stereotypes. And with the whole world watching, she has only gotten bolder."

Once again Madonna hit Japan during the rainy season—on Friday the thirteenth to boot! This time she didn't cancel any shows at the Chiba Marine Stadium, but the look was modified to accommodate high winds and a slick stage. At one point she fell and refused to continue until men came out to wipe down the stage. The dancers wore layers of protective clothing to stay dry and safe. Madonna slid across the floor. She joked, "You didn't know you were here for an ice-skating show. Well, I'm Dorothy Hamill."

Immediately following the first show for thirty-five thousand fans, Madonna invited Kurt Loder and the MTV crew into her hotel to film "Breakfast With Madonna." Still in stage makeup, she was husky voiced but spirited and funny, despite the weather and her fatigue. She talked about being a lapsed Catholic and said she didn't know whether her dad had ever seen the disturbing video for "Oh Father." They bantered about Beatty and babies. They discussed vogueing: "Vogueing was going to be big but didn't take off. Because they

Building stamina for the Blond Ambition tour.
Photo courtesy of Ron Galella

didn't have a spokesperson like me!"

When Loder asked about the Pepsi controversy, she replied, "They just said they didn't like it, afraid the whole thing would blow up. I was surprised. There's a fable in the video. It's about standing up for somebody and telling the truth. I was shocked that they couldn't see that. I told them about the video. I told them everything."

In Los Angeles by mid-May, she found time to dine with Warren Beatty. She still considered him her exclusive boyfriend. Warren gave the show an enthusiastic review: "I really defy anyone not to succumb to it. Nonstop energy! It fulfills my name for her. Buzzbomb." On June 6, Madonna backed out of an appearance at the Orlando, Florida, celebration for *Dick Tracy*. She claimed a scheduling conflict, but the press attributed it to a lovers' quarrel. At any rate, the two were together later that month in New York.

Madonna reached Detroit in time for her dad's birthday. She invited him onstage and sang a rousing version of "Happy Birthday." As he left, she genuflected and said, "I worship the ground he walks on."

The tour nearly cost Madonna her voice. By the time she rolled into New York in June, she was practically hoarse. Being Madonna, she refused to cut back on her strenuous workouts, but she was forced to cancel a show. Altogether she canceled only four dates on the tour—one in Chicago, another in Worcester, Massachusetts, one in Philadelphia, and the New York show slated for the Brendan Byrne arena.

Proceeds from the final New York show were donated to AMFAR and totaled more than $300,000. The money was earmarked for community-based clinical trial centers to test experimental AIDS treatments. Later, Madonna and Beatty arrived at the nightclub La Palace de Beauté for a party honoring her road crew.

Every night Madonna advocated safe sex. In Toronto she teased Canadians with, "Don't be silly, put a rubber on your willy." The Toronto police received complaints that Madonna's act was lewd, especially the masturbation sequence. They arrived before her final show threatening to raid the performance and haul her off to jail. Madonna staunchly refused to censor herself and defied the police to cancel her show. "I would rather have canceled the show than let anyone dictate how I can or can't express myself as an artist," she announced. Madonna was nervous enough to "get out of Dodge." The entourage made a speedy exit immediately after the show.

> *"I admire her drive. I don't have it."—Kelly McGillis*

As early as July the papers reported that Italy's Roman Catholic establishment had mounted a campaign to ban Madonna's concerts, calling her "an offense to good taste." When she arrived in Italy, Madonna found things were radically different from 1987. Three years earlier the press deified her and thousands flocked to her shows. This time she faced empty seats and lots of bad press linking her to the devil and a worldwide decline in morality. The state-run TV network, RAI, canceled plans to broadcast the show. Hoping to do some damage control, Madonna read a prepared statement to the press in Rome. (see box page 186).

In an interview with *La Repubblica*, Madonna talked about her reception:

Glamorously made-up for a rendezvous with Beatty.

Photo courtesy of Ron Galella

I don't understand what was scandalous. I wanted to give a message of love—love, sensuality—instead, it has all been misunderstood. When I say love, I mean for and with others and yourself. Even masturbation. I've heard that the scene that throws everybody is when I'm on my red velvet bed and touch myself. But it's only about a woman who discovers sensuality while alone.

Madonna viewed the show as an "emotional journey on the theme of a woman's place in the world."

I start out very aggressive and hostile, dressed in a man's suit, saying "Express Yourself," and if you don't like it, get out of my face. Then I delve deeper into my sexuality and live out the fantasy of being worshiped and adored.

Later I try to bring together sexual passion with the passion of religion, but . . . a priest stops me and says they don't mix. I end up pushing off the male authority figures and running away. . . . Finally, right when you think it'll end on a happy note, I come out with my family to do a Bob Fosse meets *Clockwork Orange* rendition of "Keep it Together." It's the show's ultimate statement about the family, because we're absolutely brutalizing with each other, while there's also no mistaking that we love each other deeply.

It's a show in which I have tried to change roles—the woman is the protagonist and the man assumes the exterior roles, but always with a vein of humor, which has been misunderstood.

One thing that *is* easy to misunderstand is Madonna's take on violence. She's often said, "I will not be attracted to making violent films. I'm attracted to roles where women are strong and aren't victimized. Everything I do has to be some kind of celebration of life." Yet her "Material Girl" video, and the stage rendition of "Causing a Commotion," employ the choreography of violence. In the video she decks a dancer, then stands over him like a hunter posed for a trophy photo. In "Commotion" she stages a mock fight with her backup singers, complete with shoving, kicking, punching, and insults. She bellows, "I know people say I'm ruthless, violent, and manipulative. . . . When people get in your face, when they stab you in the back, you got to show them who's boss, right?" The paradoxes never end.

For months Madonna had been negotiating an endorsement deal with Reebok, but by July 1990 the contract fell apart, this time before any commercials were filmed. The deal would have garnered her $6 million, but Reebok shied away, partly because she was still in litigation with Nike over a previous contract for $4.25 million. Officially, Reebok announced they simply couldn't come to terms with Madonna on "timing or schedules."

At some point, her relationship with Beatty also fell apart. Some said it was a "you're fired—I quit" scenario. Madonna said, "I should have known better. I was unrealistic, but then, you always think you're going to be the one."

This naïveté is surprising coming from the woman who cautions friends, "Don't assume anything. It's a way of protecting yourself from being hurt. And it's a way of allowing yourself to go on if you are hurt. . . .It's a way of keeping yourself from being too devastated."

Madonna claims she allows herself a twenty-four-hour mourning period when anything bad happens, then snaps out of it—at least on the surface.

What went wrong with Warren? Was it her jealousy? Her independence? Or merely that *Dick Tracy* had run its course? Madonna said:

It's a really hard thing to accept in life that no matter what you do you can't change a person. If you say, 'I don't want you looking at that woman,' they're going to do it anyway.... You want to think that if this person is in love with you, you have control over them. But you don't. And to accept that in life is next to impossible.... Then again, I want to be a fly on the wall for all of Warren's conversations, but I wouldn't want the reverse.

It's extremely ironic how often Madonna mentions her desire to have children. *Both* Beatty and Penn moved on to romances with costars—Beatty with Annette Bening, Penn with Robin Wright—and had children with them. Tabloid gossips said Madonna told Penn if he'd given her a child, they'd still be together. *During* the marriage, they claimed Madonna refused to have kids.

In this vein, 1991 began with the *National Enquirer* headline: PREGNANT MADONNA LOSES HER BABY. It said Madonna discovered herself pregnant on December 10, 1990, and "was forced to terminate the pregnancy due to complications" on the fourteenth. Later, Madonna's publicist called the story a lie, but during subsequent interviews Madonna complained that the *Enquirer* illegally purchases her medical records and tells the whole world every time she has an abortion. Where there's smoke...?

In August, HBO aired Madonna's show semilive from France (it was delayed by several hours). It ran during prime time, which outraged *Chicago Tribune* columnist Bob Greene, who felt that her obscene language and lewd behavior should not have been available to underage viewers. "What is most troubling is that her product appeared in America's homes during prime time on a Sunday, and people seemed to think it was no big deal."

For her birthday in August, brother Mario "gave" Madonna male model Tony Ward, and the two began an affair that was nothing if not unorthodox. Ward married another woman shortly after meeting Madonna, but claimed it was a marriage of convenience. He was also a reputed cross-dresser with a fascination for S&M. Ward has the sultry Latin looks Madonna's always loved. Early in his career he, too, posed nude for male skin magazines. Madonna felt a "sort of camaraderie... I finally felt like, 'God, somebody can understand how I felt.'"

When September's MTV awards rolled around, the night belonged to Madonna, Paula Abdul, and Janet Jackson, who had dominated the charts throughout the previous year. "Vogue" was nominated for Best Choreography in a Video and Best Dance Video, as well as Best Video of the Year.

Madonna performed live and truly outdid herself. She and her dancers were decked out like the doomed courtiers of Louis XVI or the cast of *Dangerous Liaisons*. In a powdered wig, her bosom elevated nearly to her ears, she navigated the stage in a pannier skirt nearly four feet wide. Madonna vogued and vamped like mad. She tore the house down, prompting columnist Steven Saban's comment: "Madonna, just when you think you've had quite enough, thank you, does something to top, to amaze. The noise in the [press] tent fell to a manic hubbub as we watched her, slack-jawed." The next night she repeated the spectacle at a benefit for AIDS Project Los Angeles (APLA) at the Wiltern Theater.

At the start of October, Madonna was back in New York with Tony Ward for the opening night of the Martha Graham Dance Company's sixty-fourth anniversary. She appeared in a spot for MTV's "Rock the Vote" wearing a red bikini, black biker boots, and the American flag. "Rock the Vote" encouraged young adults to exercise their political voice. Madonna rapped her message: "Dr. King, Malcolm X. Freedom of speech is as good as sex." Then she threatened to spank anyone who didn't vote.

On the sixteenth of October, Madonna, Christopher, Tony Ward, Sandra Bernhard, and Debi Mazar arrived in Paris to attend the Gaultier and Thierry Mugler fashion shows. Both Tony and Debi were modeling. Afterward, Madonna and the gang went to Gaultier's private party at a gay club called Boy. There she met Amanda Cazalet, who'd appear—kissing Madonna—in the "Justify My Love" video.

That Friday, the nineteenth, Madonna posed for the "Justify" cover shot with photographer Patrick Demarchelier in a studio just south of Paris. By now she'd had collagen injections and looked like a whole hive had stung her lips. On the twentieth she dined, appropriately enough, at Le Vingt, then danced the night away at Les Bains Douches. The next day she returned to New York.

In October, *Harper's Bazaar* voted Madonna one of the one hundred most-talked-about women of all time. Some of the other women included Cher, Barbie, Helen of Troy, Cleopatra, Ingrid Bergman, Garbo, Queen Victoria, and Anne Frank. And that was the month she unwillingly became the *Forbes* cover girl when the magazine proclaimed her America's top-earning female performer. *Forbes* reckoned the financially secretive singer earned "at least $125 million over the past five years" (see box p. 200).

On a sadder note, October 27 marked mentor Christopher Flynn's death from AIDS at Hernandez Hospice in Los Angeles.

By November 9, Madonna and Tony Ward were back in Paris to film "Justify My Love." She reserved the entire sixth floor of the Royal Monceau Hotel for three days and filmed the video in utter secrecy. Even the hotel staff were mystified. She remained in Paris until the eighteenth, then flew back to Los Angeles.

Madonna was gearing up to release *The Immaculate Collection* in time for Christmas gift-giving. The deluxe edition, called *The Royal Box*, contained the CD of greatest hits along with a compilation of her videos. *Immaculate's* seventeen tracks gathered all fifteen of her top-twenty tunes in chronological order, plus two new songs, "Justify My Love" and "Rescue Me." Some songs were remixed by Shep Pettibone.

But let's face it. Even though she masterminded a supersuccessful international tour of startling energy and drama; even though she starred in one of the summer's hottest movies; even though her face graced the covers of more magazines than Elizabeth Taylor's; even though she dated Warren Beatty; even though *Alive and Well* magazine gave her a "Broccoli" award for promoting vegetarian good health—1990 will always be remembered as the year Madonna made the video that was banned from MTV.

Of course it wasn't Madonna's first confrontation with the network:

> Every time I do a video they say they're not going to show it. When I did "Oh Father," they said, "We're not going to show the scene with the lips sewn up." And I said, "Fuck you." And then they showed it. In "Express Yourself," they weren't going to show me with a chain around my neck. I don't get their rules. I don't know what they find offensive.

The *Washington Post*'s Richard Harrington wrote, "For those who weren't aware MTV *had* standards, they prohibit not only nudity but also profanity, portraying violence against women or groups identified by racial, sexual, or religious characteristics, and product placement."

"Justify My Love" is a slow, silly moan about carnal love penned by Lenny Kravitz and Ingrid Chavez. Robert Goldberg, in the *Wall Street Journal*, put it best when he said, "You'll wait a long time for any kind of tune to start. It's like one of those lengthy spoken introductions before the song kicks into gear, except in this case, no tune follows."

The black-and-white video was directed by Jean-Baptiste Mondino, who locked everyone in Paris's Royal Monceau Hotel for days then shot most of his footage at the last minute. Blond, lithe, and lippy, Madonna comes writhing down the hallway wearing a wispy black dress over sexy black underwear. Snaking past hotel rooms, she whispers her fantasies—"I wanna kiss you in Paris / I wanna hold your hand in Rome"—to a lover played by her real-life fella, Tony Ward.

Before you can say "Helmut Newton," they're joined by a cast straight out of *The Night Porter*, and the video explores some of Madonna's favorite themes: homosexuality, voyeurism, cross-dressing, multiple partners, and sadomasochism. Madonna makes love to her boyfriend. Madonna also kisses model Amanda Cazalet, and for a fleeting moment Cazalet's naked nipple flashes on-screen. The video ends with the motto, "Poor is the man whose pleasures depend on the permission of another." The whole clip would be rated R if it were part of a motion picture.

> *"You can look at it two ways: wanting to wear your underwear outside your clothes or wanting to have your tits be inside tinfoil. They're both just the externalized passion of the moment."—Jack Nicholson*

Mondino said his goal was to put the paparazzi out of work:

> How can a picture of Madonna and Tony together be surprising when you've already seen them together half-naked in the video? I said, "Let's lock ourselves in a hotel for two days and one night without going out and just see what happens." So we did. It was very cheap, very easy. It's very real—that's what's so shocking about it. And maybe her kissing a woman . . . but it's part of our society. And with AIDS, shouldn't we celebrate kissing as a beautiful thing?

Madonna's motives may have been cheekier. She told the *Advocate*:

> Every straight guy should have a man's tongue in

Photo courtesy of Ron Galella

Celebrating Martha Graham's 64th Anniversary Gala shortly before the dancer's death.

Photo courtesy of Ron Galella

Exiting the Michael Jackson concert with John "Jellybean" Benitez.

Photos courtesy of Ron Galella

Portrait of a winner.

Strutting her stuff on the Like a Virgin tour.

Memorabilia courtesy the Bill Ryan Archives.

Greeting Corey Hart, who's not wearing sunglasses at night!

Photos courtesy of Ron Galella.

"I ain't taking *shit* off!"

Through the looking glass—the Penns sup at Columbus Cafe.

Sean practices the Vulcan mind probe.

Madonna's appearance surprised—and delighted—everyone.

Heading home after a performance.

Building stamina for the Blond Ambition tour.

Madonna flashes her foundation.

The infamous Gaultier corset.

It's official! They're an item.

Making the scene at La Palace de Beaute.

Photos courtesy of Ron Galella

Call the beautician! Sunglasses can't hide those dark roots.

Photos courtesy of Ron Galella

Leaving the Muse restaurant with Alek Keshisian.

Dancing at the Third Annual APLA benefit for AIDS.

Tres sheik!

Sporting an industrial strength bra, Madonna arrives at Love Ball 2.

Posing with dancer Jose Gutierez.

At the New York premiere with Niki Harris and Donna DeLory.

Photos courtesy of Ron Galella

Those lips! Madonna's plumped for "Justify My Love."

Sneaking a word with new beau Tony Ward at the *GoodFellas* premiere.

his mouth at least once. . . .

The sexual themes in it, it wasn't just about me. It's about life, about human nature. I think everybody has a bisexual nature. That's my theory, I could be wrong. . . .

I'm incensed by the prejudices in the world, and if I can do something with my celebrity to make people see things that ordinarily they may not pay attention to, then I feel responsible to do it. But I want to have fun while I'm doing it.

On November 28, 1990, MTV rejected the video and excised it from their weekend-long "Madonnathon" featuring videos, interviews, performance and film clips. Spokesperson Carole Robinson said, "We respect her work as an artist and think she makes great videos. This one is not for us."

"Justify" made the first cut of MTV's acquisitions committee, but didn't get past the standards committee. Allegedly they were upset by "graphic scenes depicting bisexuality, cross-dressing, sadomasochism, and other sexual fantasies." Rumor had it the pesky peekaboo nipple tipped the scales. Madonna, who expected her see-through shirt to get "Vogue" banned earlier that year, really thought she'd get away with this.

She took the ban in stride. "MTV has been good to me and they know their audience. If it's too strong for them, I understand that. . . . This is my interpretation of the song. I'm practicing freedom of speech and expression."

Asked to justify her video, Madonna explained, "It's the interior of a human being's mind. These fantasies and thoughts exist in every person. Why is it that people are willing to go to a movie and watch someone get blown to bits for no reason, and nobody wants to see two girls kissing or two men snuggling? I think the video is romantic and loving and has humor in it."

The Gay and Lesbian Alliance Against Defamation (GLAAD) despised MTV's decision. They issued a statement saying, "MTV's rejection of Madonna's latest video, apparently because of its gay and lesbian imagery, is hypocritical and smacks of censorship." MTV countered by pointing out that they give Madonna's work for AIDS plenty of coverage.

On the twenty-ninth, 112 seconds of the video had their world premiere on CNN's "Showbiz Today" program. "Saturday Night Live" showed ninety seconds, "Entertainment Tonight" aired sixty seconds, "The Howard Stern Show" showed it relatively uncut, with some censoring. Fox showed the video on the news but electronically distorted portions they thought might offend. NBC's "Friday Night Videos" showed excerpts while hosts Tom Arnold and Roseanne Barr offered a blow-by-blow description of the bits viewers were missing.

Warner Bros. cleverly packaged the video for sale at $9.98 a copy and shipped it to stores on December 11. It was the first single video release ever and at that price, broke down to about $2 a minute for five minutes of fun.

On December 4, 1990, ABC's late-night news show, "Nightline," played the uncut video and interviewed Madonna. The show's ratings peaked, second only to their interview with Tammy Faye Bakker for all-time-high numbers. Madonna sparred clumsily with Forrest Sawyer, who said, "In the end you're going to wind up making even more money than you would have." "Yeah. So lucky me," she countered.

When Sawyer brought up the disturbing manacle from "Express Yourself," Madonna said, "But I have chained *myself*. I may be dressing like the traditional bimbo, but I'm in charge. And isn't that what feminism is all about, you know, equality for men and women? And aren't I in charge of my life, doing the things I want to do?" Well, he wondered, where does she draw the line at what's acceptable? "Violence, humiliation and degradation."

Madonna's been justifying her sexuality ever since the "Virgin" album:

> It has nothing to do with whether I'm a man or a woman. I think I am a sexual threat, and I think there is a prejudice against that. I think that it is easier for people to accept people who don't frighten them and poke at their insides and make them think about their own sexuality.
>
> Kim Basinger showing her breasts isn't threatening. . . . I'm assertive. I'm not embarrassed or shameful or inhibited. I'm not just showing a breast. There's something defiant about what I do. I'm challenging the mores and ripping open the taboos and turning up the underbelly of our society—all the things American culture tries to keep hidden.
>
> I'm saying I have a pussy and I'm dealing with my sexuality and you can deal with yours if you want to, I'm encouraging that. But I'm not saying go out and fuck randomly. You can have sex, but you have to practice safe sex. There's no way around it. . . . Use your imagination. Be *creative*.

Camille Paglia penned an editorial for the *New York Times* hailing Madonna as the future of feminism. Invoking Baudelaire and Oscar Wilde, she reminded Madonna that art and artists have "no moral responsibility to liberal social causes." Nevertheless, Madonna insisted the video bear a parental advisory warning when it went on sale.

Paul Grein, the *Billboard* columnist who years earlier predicted Madonna's swift demise, saw this controversy as one of a series of successful marketing ploys. "If you look at Madonna's career, every year there are a couple of big events. Her career events are as carefully choreographed as the GOP convention—down to the minute. . . . It's no coincidence this happened when her album is in its second week on the charts."

The movie survived the hype—their romance didn't.

Memorabilia courtesy the Bill Ryan Archives.
Photo by David Palmore.

TWELVE: DO AND DARE

"People who don't think the controversies and the press affect her are wrong. She doesn't work up a strategy for all this attention. It's just who she is and what she does. And there's definitely a cost."—Christopher Ciccone

"Madonna is a movie star without a movie. . . . I'd say she's got a good ten years to find the right movie to prove it. . . . She's incapable of doing anything that's not interesting. If she's in a photograph, it's interesting. If she sings a song, it's interesting. Her videos—all interesting."—Barry Diller

The new year started with a bang January 4 when Rabbi Abraham Cooper, associate dean of the Simon Wiesenthal Center for Holocaust Studies, accused Madonna of anti-Semitism. On a mix of "Justify My Love," called "The Beast Within," Madonna read from the book of Revelations: "I know your tribulation and your poverty and the slander of those who say that they are Jews, but they are not, they are a synagogue of Satan."

"Who would have ever thought she'd get into trouble for reading the Bible?" asked the *Los Angeles Times*. Cooper sent an angry letter to Freddy DeMann in which he protested, "The imagery of 'Jew as Devil' has led to untold violence against the Jewish people over the course of the last two thousand years." Cooper asked that Madonna remove the offensive lines. "The text is incredibly insensitive and potentially dangerous. Anti-Semitism is a real problem in America today, and an entertainer as big of a blockbuster as Madonna should show some responsibility to such social issues."

Madonna replied immediately. "I certainly did not have any anti-Semitic intent when I included a passage from the Bible on my record. It was a commentary on evil in general. My message, if any, is pro-tolerance and antihate. The song is, after all, about love." Cooper was mollified by the speed and content of Madonna's reply.

On January 13, 1991, Madonna attended the New York Film Critics Circle awards dinner at the Rainbow Room with director Alek Keshishian, the young filmmaker behind her upcoming release, *Truth or Dare*. Over the next few months they'd often be photographed together, as they were undoubtedly putting the finishing touches on *Truth or Dare* and preparing for the publicity onslaught ahead.

Madonna was also wrapping up a small part as a circus acrobat for Woody Allen's film, *Shadows and Fog*. The cast included Mia Farrow, John Malkovich, Fred Gwynne, and Jodie Foster. Madonna was brunette for the film. As usual, when acting, Madonna rose at dawn for her workout, then reported to the set when most people are contemplating breakfast.

Working with Allen was an education. "I'll never learn patience. But I've learned, watching Woody, how a real artist works. Woody is a master of getting things out of people in a really gentle way. He's not a tyrant, and that's good for me to learn because I can be something of a tyrant. In a working situation . . . in a living situation, too."

Never one to run from a challenge, Madonna again followed her pattern of going from boss to peon almost overnight. Still, she found it a strain:

> The whole process of being a brushstroke in someone else's painting is a little difficult. I'm used to being in charge of everything . . . it's hard for me to shut up and do my job. . . . I have a stupid little part and I have to sit around on the set and wait all day and then say a few lines. . . . I can feel the grips and electricians looking at me—I'm painfully aware of it. They don't see me as an actress, they see me as an icon, and it makes me extremely exhausted.

On March 25, Madonna appeared on the 63rd Annual Academy Awards to sing "Sooner or Later," nominated as best song from the film *Dick Tracy*. She wore $20 million worth of diamonds loaned by Harry Winston and a strapless, white-beaded Bob Mackie gown with elbow-length gloves and an ermine stole. Her hair was shoulder length and blond. Her date was Michael Jackson.

America gaped—we didn't even realize they knew each other! But there was the proof, propped in adjoining front-row seats. Speculation ran the gamut from "She's having his love child" to "It's a promotional gimmick." Michael Jackson had just signed the world's biggest music deal with Sony, promising six albums in return for a figure that's bound to hit $6 billion when his accountants have finished toting up advance payments plus a whopping 25 percent royalty.

Madonna said it was simply a matter of two dateless bachelors opting to attend together instead of solo. "He goes, 'Are you going with somebody?' I said, 'No, I'm not. I don't have a date.' He said, 'Well, I'll be your date.'"

She was visibly tense onstage—as any perfectionist playing for 3 billion might be. The unforgiving camera caught her hand shaking as it clutched the microphone. Madonna shimmied and she stripped; she twitched her bottom and tossed her wrap. It was a far cry from Rob Lowe and Snow White.

After the Oscars, Madonna and Jackson went to Swifty Lazar's famous Spago fete. She ditched Jackson and ran to curl up in Warren Beatty's lap, but like any good girl, Madonna left the party with her original date. The pair turned up at the Ivy restaurant a week later, fueling speculation that they planned to make beautiful music together. Not this time.

Madonna itched to retire Jackson's effete look and replace it with something up-to-date. "This man is a genius in his own right, but only in terms of music. He has lived his life with blinders on. And it's hard for me to conceive of anybody who's an artist living that way. I know this sounds trite, but I wanted to get him to love himself." She also wanted to get him a haircut.

For the self-proclaimed Michael Jackson wannabe, this newfound alliance must have been immensely gratifying. In just a decade, she'd become her idol's equal. What a triumph for the woman who admitted:

> I have an iron will. And all of my will has always been to conquer some horrible feeling of inadequacy. . . . I push past one spell of it and

A strategy dinner with Keshishian gearing up for *Truth or Dare*'s premiere.
Photo courtesy of Ron Galella

The surprise date of the decade!
Photo courtesy of Ron Galella

discover myself as a special human being, and then I get to another stage and think I'm mediocre and uninteresting. And I find a way to get myself out of that. . . . My drive in life is from this horrible fear of being mediocre. . . . Because even though I've become Somebody, I still have to prove that I'm *Somebody*. My struggle has never ended and it probably never will.

April 21 marked the third annual AIDS Dance-A-Thon to benefit the APLA at the Los Angeles Sports Arena. Over five thousand dancers boogied for five hours and raised nearly a million dollars in pledges. Madonna attended in 1989 with Christopher Flynn and this year made a guest appearance to introduce Niki Harris performing her Jellybean-produced single, "What's It Gonna Be." After Niki sang, Madonna, Donna DeLory, Kevin Stea, Oliver Crumes, and some civilians leapt to the stage to dance. Later that month Madonna received a media award from the Gay and Lesbian Alliance Against Defamation for outspokenly championing the homosexual lifestyle.

I'm a high-visibility person, and I know [gays] know that I'm completely compassionate about their choice in life, their lifestyle, and I support it. To have a person like me saying that is helpful to them. They appreciate that. . . . A lot of the issues I deal with are sexual, and I'm constantly trying to challenge the accepted ways of behaving sexually. Maybe they appreciate that.

In May 1991, Madonna challenged the world to a game of *Truth or Dare*, and for a month she was as ubiquitous as the sun overhead. She gave countless interviews, landed on dozens of international magazine covers, turned up on nightly news, on entertainment shows, and in movie theaters across the nation.

With *Truth or Dare*, Madonna found the role that suited her best—Madonna. It was shot around the world during the Blond Ambition tour in 16-mm black-and-white offset by dramatic color concert footage. David Fincher, who did the "Vogue" video, was originally slated to film the tour, but he dropped out. Shortly before she left for Japan, Madonna asked Alek Keshishian to tag along with a film crew.

Once filming began, Keshishian and Madonna decided the *real* story was happening behind the scenes between Madonna and her troupe. Madonna told *The Advocate:*

Originally we were going to do a concert film because I was really proud of what I'd done on the stage, and I thought, "I wish I could capture this on film. But as I started working with the people, what really interested me were the relationships that were developing between me and the dancers and everybody around. We watched the footage of all the backstage stuff . . . and I said, "I couldn't give a shit about the live show. This is life! This is what I want to document.

Alek Keshishian said:

Many concert movies are unrevealing puff pieces pandering to the celebrity. I knew Madonna would not be happy with that, and I certainly wouldn't be either. So I asked for carte blanche: to be able to shoot anything and everything in an attempt to capture the essence of her life on that tour. My goal was to take you on a roller-coaster ride. Every time you feel comfortable about having a certain opinion about her, I wanted to challenge it. That's what I felt happened to me as I got to know her.

Who was the young man Madonna entrusted with nearly $5 million of her personal funds? Keshishian, then twenty-six, had had a privileged life. He attended private schools as a kid, then studied at the Sorbonne before going on to Harvard. A musician, dancer, and actor himself, Alek created a pop opera adaptation of Emily Bronte's *Wuthering Heights* as his senior thesis and used Madonna's music for the character of Cathy. He met Madonna when CAA agent Jane Berliner (who with Ron Meyer represents Madonna) showed her Keshishian's thesis. Prior to *Truth or Dare* he'd never tackled a full-length film, though he'd directed music videos for Vanessa Williams, Elton John, and Bobby Brown.

During the early days in Japan, Madonna was practically abusive to Alek, testing his mettle. When he fought back, he discovered she loved it. From then on Alek took a hard line with Madonna and the partnership thrived. When Madonna got really difficult, he'd turn to Christopher for advice.

Alek instructed his crew—two three-person units for backstage and up to twenty-two 35-mm cameras for the shows—to wear black and remain silent. Signs were posted explaining that entering certain areas equaled signing a release. Some backstage footage was shot behind a two-way mirror. Keshishian wound up with over 250 hours of film, sparking rumors that bootleg outtakes were selling in Hollywood for tens of thousands of dollars, a rumor Keshishian denied.

Before he agreed to take the job, Keshishian insisted on final cut. "As we watched the dailies, Madonna winced at everything," he recalled. "But she never said, 'Don't use this.'" Madonna admitted, "There were plenty of scenes I felt edgy about, but they're still in the film. Alek would debate with me and I eventually saw the light. Maybe all the moments aren't necessarily flattering, but they're the highs and the lows of the movie. And I realized that if I took one out, why didn't I take out all of them?"

Madonna had second thoughts in Detroit. She was afraid of hurting her family. Keshishian insisted they carry on as planned. He felt strongly about juxtaposing scenes with Madonna's real family against scenes of her with the road family of dancers. "Dealing with her father, her achievements, and fame no longer mattered. She was suddenly like every girl."

When she flashes her breasts for a photographer or masturbates onstage, Madonna always worries, "My God, what if my father sees this? . . . What I keep trying to impress upon my father is that he mustn't take what I do *personally*." Still, she bristles when advisers suggest she end the fretting by *not* being so bold. Self-censorship is not what this woman's about. (Tell her she curses too much—as the English papers did—and she'll use the F-word two hundred times during a brief BBC broadcast.)

It's a great moment when Madonna, wearing a shower cap and slurping soup, telephones her dad to find out how many people he's bringing to the show. "How many tickets can I get?" Tony asks. "As many as you like! You're my dad!"

That's the great thing about my dad. It still hasn't

> "It's kind of like Fellini meets The Boys in the Band."—Madonna describing Truth or Dare

really dawned on him who I am. Which is good because it keeps him from treating me any differently from all my brothers and sisters. He lives in his own world and generally the things that happen to me just pass right by him. I think that's good because he can have an okay life and not be bothered. The good thing is that I have all these rather insane brothers and sisters, so whatever happens to me is just another thing he has to deal with.

At home, nobody brings up the fact that I'm a star. Not one word. At first I thought, "Well, how come I'm not getting any special treatment?" But even though I had to sleep on the floor in a sleeping bag [at Christmas], even though I didn't know who else had slept in that sleeping bag, the trip was really such a joyous thing for my father.

Madonna was fascinated by her "kids." "The dancers are really funny," she said. "They keep me going. They're real pranksters. . . . I truly loved the dancers and my relationship with them. I just found them so inspiring and entertaining. Really, I would have been perfectly happy to make it about them. In my heart of hearts, I don't think it's just a movie about me. It's a movie about the life of a celebrity, but there's all these other parallel stories going on."

Keshishian called her entourage "real-life John Waters. A two-hundred-pound girl who calls herself Momma Makeup; six dancers who look like they came out of a Fellini movie set in Harlem. The absurdity of it on one level, and the emotion and pathos on another."

Some of the dancers panicked when the film came out. Would they have trouble finding other work? Madonna cracked up and offered this wisdom: "Are you kidding? In this country it works the other way around! The more notorious you are, the more you are going to work! *Don't you guys understand that?*"

The *New York Times* said Madonna "presides like a ringmaster and queen bee over a handpicked traveling circus where the emotional pitch falls just short of complete hysteria. . . . She is mother superior, impish playmate, bitch goddess, and peacemaker."

The film shows her running interference between the lone heterosexual—and homophobic—dancer and his flamboyant colleagues. She treats Moira, her childhood idol, as if the woman carried a deadly infectious disease. There's the cemetery scene (the *Daily News* accused her of vogueing on her mother's grave), and another with her father and stepmother backstage telling Madonna she went a little far for their tastes.

There's quite a contrast between Madonna's close relationship with Christopher and her problems with older brother Martin, whom the film exposes as an unreliable con man bouncing in and out of rehab. "Martin is a very hard person to get along with," said Madonna. "I adore him . . . but it's hard to be close to anybody in that situation because you never know what's real and what isn't. He's very tortured and I speak to him but . . . I find myself being very judgmental. . . . We have a strained relationship. I know he loves me and I love him but . . . it's difficult."

We don't see Madonna's preshow candlelight massages, but do watch her lead a prayer circle before each show. She stages an elaborate pajama party and drags everyone into bed with her separately, then as a group. She drops her top. She recites a self-penned poem honoring her personal assistant Melissa Crowe, and recalls a childhood ditty about farting. She pretends to vomit when Kevin Costner says the show is "neat."

Truth or Dare also shows Madonna leading her dancers on a shopping spree at Chanel, attending a party thrown by Pedro Almódovar (where she learns the one man she fancies in this world has a wife), and gossiping in an Italian hotel room with buddy Sandra Bernhard. And yes, during the eponymous game of Truth or Dare she's challenged to demonstrate fellatio on a bottle of mineral water and does so con brio.

Here, too, is her defiance of the Toronto police, her self-defensive speech at the Rome airport, and her dangerous performance on a rain-soaked stage in Tokyo. We see Madonna in full stage regalia and in her bathrobe. Most of the time she's munching some healthy fodder. An astonishing amount of film time is devoted to re-inking her exaggerated black eyebrows and rerouging lips.

Madonna was delighted with the finished product. "It's worth five years of psychoanalysis. There are some painful moments. I can see all of my extreme behavior, but I can also see my goodness. Certain people, like my agents, have seen it and said, 'I can't believe you're doing this. If I were you, I'd buy it back and put it in a closet.'"

More often than not, Madonna and Alek clashed because she wanted to leave too much *in*.

I don't feel raped or devastated. It would take a lot more than a two-hour movie to do that.

If I'm going to make a documentary and tell the director that I want to reveal truths, then I'm not going to say, "But this is where I draw the line". If you take all those parts out, what would you have? Life is about the highs and lows, and if you just present the mids, then what's the point? I chose to show that part of myself because I know that other people feel the same way. The only difference between this and other movies is that I don't have the safety net of saying, "This is fictional." These issues are dealt with in drama all the time, but I think the hard thing for people to take will be that there isn't someone playing the part of my life in the movie fifty years from now when I'm dead. I'm doing it myself. No one has ever done this before.

When Keshishian screened the movie for select Hollywood insiders, they got hysterical—laughing *and* screaming. "They couldn't understand why [she] would put something like this out. Stardom is based on an unspoken rule of maintaining a certain mystery. This movie throws that axiom out the window."

But where her career's concerned, Madonna's always been smarter than conventional wisdom. Defiance has served her well. What's ultimately striking about the film is not that it reveals any shockers, but all the things it *doesn't* tell us. The film obscures as much as it unveils because it observes from an extremely limited perspective. Watching it, you might think Madonna had no musicians on her tour. You never see her working out. She shuts the door on a business meeting. And you don't, as she pointed out, see her having sex.

During the early portion of the film—the early stages of the tour—she's still Beatty's girl. He's the only person who didn't sign a release for the film ("Ha! Do you

Every inch the glamour queen.
Photo courtesy of Ron Galella

Cozying up to heartthrob, Antonio Banderas—again! Regrettably for her, he's married.

Who's that boy? Looks like Spanish actor Antonio Banderas.

Photo courtesy of Ron Galella

think Warren is going to sign a release for a movie he hasn't seen!"), and Madonna had to excise a phone call they had. "It was a long, very loving conversation that portrayed him in a warm way, but it is illegal to tape someone's conversation without their knowing about it."

In an oft-discussed scene, Warren and Madonna are in the kitchen of her New York apartment at the height of her throat trouble. The doctor examining her asks if she wouldn't rather do it off camera, prompting Beatty to laugh. "She doesn't want to be seen off camera, much less talk," he snorted. "What would you say if it's off camera? What point is there in existing?"

Madonna countered: "I think Warren's statement that I don't want to live off camera is really a statement about himself. It's him saying, 'I don't want anyone to know anything about my life. I want it shrouded in mystery.' And I think Warren believed that if he kept saying to the camera, 'This whole thing is ridiculous!' that it would keep us from using the footage. . . . He's *always* underestimating me!"

Beatty hated being filmed, hated Madonna's exhibitionism, and couldn't believe Madonna and Keshishian weren't sleeping together. Regarding Alek, Madonna said she didn't want to have a crush on someone everyone else had a crush on. She told him afterward, "If we'd had a romance, we wouldn't be friends right now."

Warren Beatty was *not* at the *Truth or Dare* premieres.

During the film Madonna tells Niki and Donna, "I'm not the best singer or the best dancer. I'm more interested in pushing people's buttons, being provocative and political." Madonna's triumph is that people do listen. She's aware of her power and unafraid to use it. She hates shutting doors—she wants everything both ways. She'll insist she's a serious artist, but reserve the right to dismiss everything as a gigantic goof: "If I took my show seriously, I would hate it. But you only have to have half of a brain in your head to see that I'm quite often making fun of myself. I mean, how obvious can I be?"

Like the tour itself, the film was loved and hated. Celebrity-watcher Liz Smith found the film refreshing and admired Madonna's courage to take chances. She pooh-poohed the notion that any of it was shocking: "Someday we'll look back and find it 'quaint.' . . . Just watch, draw your own conclusions, accept Madonna on her own terms. She isn't you. You don't have to lead her life. She doesn't have to lead yours."

Us magazine decided *Truth or Dare* made a nice antidote to the Blond Ambition tour, where Madonna seemed incredibly inhuman and robotic: "She's human again—or, at least, she's pretending to be." The English magazine *Vox* said it was thoroughly entertaining and totally contrived, but offered "proof positive that Madonna *can* act."

Anticipating these reviews, Madonna told one interviewer, "People will say 'she's just acting,' but even if I *am* acting, there's a truth in my acting." That sounds a lot like the Barbra Streisand movie where she explains why she makes up dreams to tell her shrink: even though they're manufactured, they still reveal her mental process.

New York's David Denby made the interesting point that Madonna "is often lewd but she's never sexual. . . . When you see her up close . . . she had no reserve, no private self or sense of sin, no individual face offered to the people in front of her. . . . Celebrity has led to a kind of emptying out of her identity."

Sandra Bernhard offered a similar, insightful assessment of her friend: "I think she didn't understand what she was getting into. Her life is all about staying in the public eye and staying revered and needed and desired. Her addiction to attention is so intense that she'll go to any lengths to get it—to the detriment of her sanity, and of her soul, sometimes. . . . On some level she's bored; she has to do something to scare herself."

New York Paper found the film a little depressing. "The saddest thing of all is to see that all this work cannot really make her happy. . . . Madonna has no real friends, merely people she controls, who go through the motions."

The Advocate, on the other hand, applauded Madonna's frank treatment of her friendships with gays and lesbians. "Mainstream America has never seen anything like the easygoing straight-gay interplay on view in this film. And gay America has never seen its favor being courted with such enthusiasm by an established show-business figure." To the *Daily News*, these same antics show Madonna "more turned on by gay men as symbols of defiance than as people."

Madonna has spent her entire life enjoying the company of homosexuals. "It would be great to be both sexes. Effeminate men intrigue me more than anything in the world. I see them as my alter egos. I feel very drawn to them. I think like a guy, but I'm feminine." She admires the way some gay men boldly deal with their identities and finds they've the courage to display greater sensibility than macho straights. "I also feel that they're persecuted, and I can relate to that."

Because *every* review dwelled on Madonna's expert fellation of a bottle of mineral water, it was startling to read Carrie Fisher's 1991 *Rolling Stone* interview, where Madonna announced, "I don't like blow jobs." Boyfriends don't tell her she gives good head "because I don't give it." As for her sexual preferences, Madonna swears it's better to receive than to give. For the record, she also wishes she'd slept with Marlene Dietrich.

The film had two official openings, on May 6, 1991 in Los Angeles and two days later in New York. The L.A. premiere was at the Pacific Cinerama Dome on Sunset Boulevard and was followed by a party at The Arena. Proceeds from the premiere went to AIDS Project Los Angeles and AIDS Action Foundation, based in Washington, D.C.

Herb Ritts, Freddy DeMann, Barry Manilow, Mimi Rogers, Swifty Lazar, Laura Flynn Boyle, Teri Garr, Eddie Van Halen and Valerie Bertinelli, Steven Seagal, Gerardo, Rosanna Arquette, Vanilla Ice, k.d. lang, and Sandra Bernhard were some of the celebrities who turned out to toast Madonna, along with her sisters, Paula and Melanie. Madonna made a fashionably late entrance and stunned everyone with her dark brunette tresses. She wore a Gaultier catsuit, heavy-duty eyeshadow, and a crucifix. Madonna and her buddies snuck out before the film was finished to get a jump on the postscreening party.

The Arena rolled out the red carpet and presented guests with gift bags of Madonnarabilia such as a movie poster, a Blond Ambition T-shirt, an *Immaculate Collection* cassette, and copies of *Entertainment Weekly*

At the New York premiere with Niki Harris and Donna DeLory.

Photo courtesy of Ron Galella

Posing with dancer José Gutierez.
Photo courtesy of Ron Galella

Madonna plays the old-time movie queen—with an updated twist.
Photo courtesy of Ron Galella

featuring Madonna on the cover. Also in the bag were a safe sex kit and APLA newsletter.

Two nights later New York reenacted the opening, this time raising over $100,000 for Mathilde Krim's organization, AMFAR. Over 1,300 tickets were sold ranging in price from $50 to $500, depending upon the number of events one wanted to attend. The night began with a prescreening party at Laura Belle in the theater district. Madonna wowed the crowd in a skimpy Dolce & Gabbana bodysuit encrusted with jewels and trinkets.

Celebrity viewers at the Ziegfeld Theater included Tim Robbins and Susan Sarandon, Keenan Ivory Wayans and the Fly Girls, Debbie Harry, Jellybean Benitez, Mark Jacobs, Ron Silver, Kelly Klein, Steven Meisel, and Naomi Campbell. Christopher Ciccone was Madonna's date, but her entourage included Niki, Donna, and many of the dancers from Blond Ambition. Later, partygoers gathered at The Shelter where a factotum followed Madonna around with a huge bowl of popcorn.

Mid-May, Madonna traveled to Cannes for the forty-fourth annual film festival. She stayed in a sumptuous suite at L'Hôtel du Cap-Eden Roc—a favorite of the Windsors, Dietrich, Rita Hayworth, Picasso, and Charlie Chaplin. Her suite included a bedroom, living room, two bathrooms, and a huge terrace. Her entourage consisted of Christopher, four bodyguards, trainer Robert Parr, a makeup woman, and two or three unidentified buddies.

Cannes went wild for Madonna. Bakeries decorated cakes with her picture and the film's title. Journalists from around the world vied for an audience and an invitation to her exclusive party. Newspapers reported that Madonna single-handedly brought old-fashioned star quality back to a festival long regarded as a circus.

Truth or Dare, called *In Bed with Madonna* overseas, was shown at a special out-of-competition midnight screening at the Palais du Festival. Madonna arrived with Keshishian. They were picked up at her hotel by a boat, which delivered her to the Palais like Venus disgorged from the sea, swathed in a red satin cape, which she dropped to reveal a white satin cone bra and girdle that looked just like the ones Playtex sold to make you look five pounds thinner. Eddie Murphy and Spike Lee were two of the celebrities on hand for the showing, along with five thousand screaming fans, five hundred French police, and three thousand paparazzi and press.

Miramax threw her a party on David Bowie's yacht. Dino De Laurentiis, the film's distributor outside the U.S., threw another at the Cannes yacht club with over one thousand invitees. Black market tickets sold for hundreds of dollars.

It was probably inevitable. At a dinner party at Tetou restaurant, Madonna led the guests—including De Laurentiis, Gaultier, Roman Polanski, and Jack Valenti—in a game of Truth or Dare. When dared to French-kiss actress Anne Parillaud, star of *La Femme Nikita,* she did it—then dared Seymour Stein to French-kiss actor Rupert Everett for fifteen seconds.

One of Miramax's owners, Harvey Weinstein, was pressed into bodyguard service by Liz Rosenberg. He wrote about it for *Premiere* magazine's September 1991 issue, joking, "For once my 240 pounds and six-foot frame may come in handy."

Weinstein caught up with Madonna at the New York premiere and introduced her to some young fans who'd been camping out, hoping for a glimpse of their favorite star. But New York, he said, "was only the warm-up for the mother of them all: Cannes. Dino De Laurentiis . . . says he has rarely seen this much excitement for anybody. 'Not since Bardot.'"

According to Weinstein, the road to Madonna's heart is paved with candy. She admits her sugar addiction stems from childhood deprivation. When her boat arrived in the harbor and an attack of nerves gave Madonna the jitters, she begged for candy, but the ship had none. Weinstein impressed her by flagging down a yacht and bartering for their tin of chocolates in exchange for a snapshot of Madonna holding them aloft.

The tabloids were delirious when they realized Sean Penn would also be in Cannes with his girlfriend Robin Wright and their month-old daughter, Dylan. According to one account, Madonna had sent a congratulatory present of expensive baby clothes to Sean only, along with a note reading, "Silly boy. If you'd have given me a baby, we'd still be together." That story alluded to midnight calls to Penn's home and suggested he held off marrying Wright because of unresolved passion for his ex.

This theory was directly contradicted by a tabloid report that Madonna and Sean were guests at the same Cannes dinner party. When Madonna tried to sit on Sean's lap, the story goes, he humiliated her, shouting, "Get lost." Then he turned to a reporter and snarled, "I've never met that woman before."

Macleans asked Madonna how she felt about Penn's progeny. "I got over my initial state of shock. I can only hope for the best for him. Obviously there are those thoughts—'Oh, God, I was married to him and he wanted to have a baby with me.' But I'm not married to him anymore, so I have to be realistic."

Madonna still refers to Penn as the love of her life and even admitted she goes to his movies because that's the only way she can see him.

We had our problems. It's all over. But there's something to be said about people being the love of your life. Even if it doesn't work, there's always that person that you love. I did have a real connection with Sean and I still do. I feel close to him even though we're not physically close. Going through what we went through made us very close. . . . I mean, it really is amazing we didn't kill each other. But I don't feel like it was a waste of time. I still love him.

Throughout spring and early summer she was the subject of much scrutiny and editorialization. On May 3, the *New York Post* ran a huge headline, WHAT A TRAMP! alongside the cover photo from "Justify My Love." Ray Kerrison's column thoroughly vilified Madonna—he did everything but refer to the singer as Her Satanic Majesty—and prompted a flurry of reader responses that pretty much typified mail to magazines that summer. Most who applauded Kerrison agreed with the Brooklyn reader who called Madonna "that foulest of human cesspools."

Many more readers stood up for Madonna, reminding Kerrison that love her or hate her, the woman's entitled to freedom of expression. One reader pointed out that too few articles stress the millions she's raised and donated for AIDS research and her efforts to promote safe sex. Another suggested Kerrison's views were last heard in seventeenth-century Salem.

At the end of May, Madonna appeared at Love Ball 2: The Crowning Glory, a fashion and jewelry benefit for Design Industries Foundation for AIDS (DIFFA) held at Roseland Ballroom to raise money for AIDS. She came with Tony Ward and Alek Keshishian. The room was filled with celebrities, porn stars, and socialites who thrilled to a performance by Deelite's Lady Miss Kier.

Madonna hardly stood out amid the many drag queens competing for prizes in such classifications as Cross Dressing, Delusions of Grandeur, and Harlem Houses. Judges were Susan Sarandon, Queen Latifah, Robert Klein, Bob Mackie, and Jean-Paul Gaultier. The "crowns" were designed by architect Michael Graves. Cyndi Lauper was there with Sylvia Miles, both dressed as men. Sandra Bernhard flashed her bra. The evening raised more than $600,000.

Geraldo Rivera devoted his July 10 show to "Madonna Madness: The Maverick, the Movie Star, the Manipulator." His panel included Madonna employees Luis Camacho, José Guitierez, and Niki Harris, and Kurt Loder from MTV, pitted against Joseph Reilly, president of Morality in Media, and his colleague, Patty McEntee. Later, Madonna called in to thank her buddies for their support and dared Loder and Rivera to kiss on television.

Reilly and McEntee, representing an extreme position, called Madonna a pornographer who condones extramarital affairs, premarital sex, and perversion. "I think she's probably the premier scam artist of the century," said Joe Reilly, who additionally called her an anti-Catholic, antifamily bigot. He told her fans they were immature, which set the audience howling. Patty McEntee went even further. When someone asked why Madonna's so popular, she retorted, "Garbage attracts flies."

The audience came out in favor of free speech, and both sexes said they found Madonna's example inspiring and entertaining. Kurt Loder opined, "I think she's very talented. I also think that she's a very good role model for young women, that you can be in charge of your life . . . you can be entirely successful, you can express yourself in the way that you want, and you can be sort of on the cutting edge of art and I think what she does is art."

August 7, 1991, Madonna attended the West Coast premiere of *Paris Is Burning*, the award-winning Jennie Livingston film about real-life voguers and drag queens. Madonna brought Tony Ward and Alek Keshishian. The film documents drag balls like the DIFFA event, where groups called houses battle in dance, costume, and attitude categories. It was through this subculture that Madonna found José and Luis, both members of the House of Xtravaganza. They taught her how to vogue.

September meant the annual MTV Awards but Madonna didn't attend. She was nominated for Best Female Video for the *Truth or Dare* version of "Like a Virgin," for Best Choreography in a Video (same) and Best Long-Form Video for *Immaculate Collection*, which she won. *Truth or Dare* made it to home video in October, on the LIVE Home Video label, retailing for $92.95.

In November, readers of *Architectural Digest*

toured Madonna's Manhattan apartment, decorated by Christopher Ciccone. Alek Keshishian said of it, "Everything is the best but nothing is ostentatious." It has seven and a half rooms and features early French deco furniture and art. Here is the bulk of Madonna's Tamara de Lempicka collection, along with some cubist work by Léger and her Picasso, hung over her desk. In the living room hangs Dali's painting *The Veiled Heart*. There are photographs everywhere representing the world's pre-eminent talent.

The apartment, finished in the summer of 1990, features a huge, well-organized closet, a shower that pulses steam, a home gym, and an old-fashioned kitchen with all the trimmings. Madonna admits, "I don't cook, but other people do."

What's she cooking up for the future?

Angered by the release of her documentary, Ray Kerrison wrote a vituperative editorial linking Madonna to Satan.

Memorabilia courtesy the Bill Ryan Archives.
Photo by David Palmore.

Sporting an industrial strength bra, Madonna arrives at Love Ball 2.

Photo courtesy of Ron Galella

Reunited with Tony Ward at Love Ball 2, an AIDS benefit featuring Vogueing contests.

Photo courtesy of Ron Galella

THIRTEEN: MAKING HER WAY

"Power is the great aphrodisiac . . . and I'm a very powerful person!"—Madonna

"Everyone probably thinks I'm a raving nymphomaniac, that I have an insatiable sexual appetite, when the truth is I'd rather read a book."—Madonna

"I have tons of money and friends. What else do you need in life?"—Madonna

"She's become a repository for all our ideas about fame, money, sex, feminism, pop culture, even death."—Steve Anderson in the Village Voice

Madonna spent the summer of 1991 on location in Evansville, Illinois, filming *A League of Their Own*, about the first season of the All-American Girls Professional Baseball League in 1943. Debra Winger was originally slated to star, but she was involuntarily "removed from the cast" by Columbia Studios. Director Penny Marshall replaced Winger with Geena Davis, hot off the successful *Thelma and Louise*, to play opposite Tom Hanks.

Reports surfaced that Madonna demanded special treatment, asking that fences be erected to keep fans away from her trailer. They also said Tom Hanks can't stand her. They're enemies between takes. Whether or not these stories are true, Madonna worked hard to learn the finer points of the game. She trained with head baseball coach Joe Russo of St. John's University in Queens. And invited Oakland A's star Jose Canseco up for a midnight visit to her New York apartment. On the set, Madonna got her eye blacked by a stray ball, then wandered too close to batting practice and got beaned in the nose.

What else lies in Madonna's future? On the personal front, she'd like to find a good man, settle down (or her version of settling down), and start a family. Sometimes. Ask her when and she hesitates. Now. No, after the next project. A workaholic to the bone, Madonna's torn between her constant need to stay before the public and an urge toward domestication.

Recently, newspapers reported Madonna paid $8 million for a Bel Air mansion. The house wasn't for sale, but her offer convinced the owners to vacate. The report said Christopher decorated the house during the summer of 1991, while Madonna worked on *A League of Their Own*. Perhaps she wanted extra space for a brood of kids, or maybe she's found her dream house, owned by Pavlova or Duncan?

Madonna admits it's not easy being her mate. "I'm difficult on a lot of levels. Just my situation alone is pretty daunting and probably keeps a fair share of men away from me. You have to be prepared for your private life to be spilled to the world. . . . So they have to find that out and understand that their past is now public domain. I try to warn them, but you can never warn people completely."

Truth or Dare proved Madonna can be cold and bitchy. Even with her lovers she's often remote. "I give people a lot of room. Sometimes I give people far too much room, and . . . sometimes they're just begging me to come into the room."

Perhaps her shrink, recommended by buddy David Geffen, will help Madonna strike a balance instead of a pose. Madonna has specific goals: "I'm working towards knowing myself and I'm assuming that will bring me happiness. I'm slowly getting rid of the demons. I don't think you can truly be loved until you know and love yourself. Then, you can be truly loved and that's what I want."

Madonna's professional goals are more diverse and equally ambitious. She wants to rescue her acting career by putting time and effort into finding good material. "I simply haven't put a lot of thought into it. I haven't honored or respected a movie career the way I should have. I didn't approach it the way I approached my music career. . . . I underestimated the power of the medium. It's been a good lesson for me."

She has plans to produce and direct. She's pulling together a biographical film about Martha Graham that she hopes also to star in, and is working with writer Jerry Pikser on a screenplay about her idol Frida Kahlo. Rumor has it that Fellini wants her for the Anita Ekberg role in a remake of *La Dolce Vita* and she's thinking of producing that, too. Another tabloid suggested Madonna's searching for a steamy script to tackle with Mickey Rourke. *That* would be an eyeful since they're both known for going too far!

She's long talked of starring in *Leda and Swan*—a female cop/buddy movie—with Demi Moore and has said she'll be "making out with Uma Thurman" in Gus Van Sant's adaptation of *Even Cowgirls Get the Blues* by Tom Robbins.

Then there's always *Evita*. Disney said the movie's a definite go, but they've been saying that for years. Getting this movie before the cameras is a saga ten years in the making. Andrew Lloyd Webber finally sold his interest in the film. Madonna's involvement began eons ago—she wanted to do it as a straight drama—but she has said her interest is fading.

> "Someone like Madonna's gonna have to find something else to do, 'cause I don't care how pointy those bras are that she wears, they're gonna look a little odd when she's fifty-five!"
> —Bonnie Raitt

Madonna's list of dream projects includes ventures in theater and performance art, developing favorite books into screenplays, making movies about people who inspire her, writing a book of erotic short stories, and helping struggling artists. "Hopefully I'll have a movie career. There was a point when I wanted to be Peggy Guggenheim—be this patron of artists, have a gallery and a great art collection. When I'm really old, that's what I want to do. She had a wild life. I like that."

Can Madonna have a legitimate movie career? Some say she'll never be a true actress now that celebrity is her full-time job. Lee Grant said, "She once came in and read for me on a picture. . . . This was just after *Desperately Seeking Susan*. And she was wonderful—open, alive. She cried during that reading. These days she's so busy packaging herself that she's covering up whatever she had. She had talent, and she closed up like a clam."

There's always music. "As long as I can write songs, I'll make records," promises pop's reigning diva.

But Madonna's looking beyond albums. Her new seven-year, extendable deal with Time Warner essentially creates a Madonna media empire—complete with its own handpicked staff—and stands to earn her something near $80 million. Her Maverick record label will produce TV, film, merchandising, and book publishing projects in fifty-fifty partnership with Warner Bros./Sire. Madonna gets a $5 million advance for each of her own albums and at least a 20 percent royalty. It is reported that her first nonmusical project will be a coffee table collection of erotic photographs—featuring her blondness, natch!

Freddy DeMann says, "I think everybody loves to hate Madonna. But I think her frankness is very charming. She says things that people really want to say but are too inhibited to. That's the secret of her success."

Certainly the popular press can't decide whether to love or hate her. For every bad word printed they print something flattering. Skim the tabloids and discover she's sleeping with an army or acting like a brat on the set of her new movie. Turn the page and read that pranksters ordered dozens of pizzas in her name, and when they were delivered, Madonna not only paid the $250 bill but sent the pizzas to a homeless shelter. Or that she fired a Spanish bodyguard who couldn't match her running pace, but heard his child was very ill and sent him $25,000 with an offer of more. What's true, what's false?

Perhaps it doesn't matter. Madonna is a little kid tugging at daddy's sleeve. She needs attention, good or bad. It's reassurance. Her craving can't be satisfied, she's admitted as much. Still, if her relentless search for identity gives us the music and videos and films, if she keeps championing gays and women, if she keeps making us laugh—who's complaining?

Says Christopher Ciccone, " My sister is her own masterpiece. Is there any other way to do it right?"

Photo:©1979 Martin Hugo Maximillian Schreiber

EXCLUSIVE INTERVIEW WITH NORRIS BURROUGHS

In 1979, when she'd been in New York City less than a year, Madonna dated artist and musician Norris Burroughs. Through Norris she met Dan Gilroy, the man most biographers credit with starting her music career. In this exclusive interview, Norris describes Madonna at twenty as a savvy street urchin and comments on her transformation into a "contemporary goddess."

* * * * * *

In the winter of 1979 a dancer friend invited me to a party. When we got there, Madonna commanded the middle of the room, spinning around in a circle like a whirling dervish in leopard-skin tights. It looked like a ritual, like she was dancing in a ring of fire. Madonna didn't wear any makeup; she had lots of really messy hair, stringy and weird looking, really animalistic. She looked interesting, exciting. This was a room full of dancers yet she stood out; it looked like everyone was dancing around her. She was so obviously an exhibitionist. I think the tune was "YMCA" and my friend and I started dancing around her, too, bellowing out the lyrics and acting like complete fools.

After that party she dated my buddy briefly, but his steady girlfriend got jealous so he was a little nervous. Madonna had already noticed me. One day they called and Madonna got on the phone with a line like, "Get your gorgeous Brando body over here," so I suggested they stop by and we ended up dating. It lasted about three to four months, but I saw her on a friendly basis off and on while she was in The Breakfast Club. All told, our influence over one another spanned roughly a

(continued)

year. I lost touch with Madonna around 1980-81. By 1982 she'd made her move.

In those days Madonna studied with Pearl Lang. She lived in Morningside Heights but never stayed anywhere long. She'd room with people for a month or so, something would go wrong, and she'd move on. During our friendship she moved up to 125th Street near Riverside Drive to live with a bunch of people.

I was fascinated when the whole Material Girl thing erupted because the girl I remember didn't care at all about her looks. Sure, all dancers are narcissistic about being in shape and being attractive, but Madonna didn't try to look conventionally pretty. I gave her a pair of jeans with a thirty-two inch or thirty-four inch waist—way too big for her—and she wore them. She'd wear whatever she found, like sweaters with holes in the sleeves, and then she'd stick her thumbs through the holes. I used to describe her as an angelic Dead End Kid. She was a ragamuffin, almost androgynous. But she always looked cool.

And she didn't have bracelets and stuff dripping from her the way she did later on. Maybe a pair of fingerless gloves now and then, but more often the ragged sweaters.

Madonna had an incredible sweet tooth. I remember taking her out to lunch once. She ordered a sundae with ice cream, bananas, and chocolate syrup, then poured maple syrup over the whole thing. I was getting sick watching her. And she licked the bowl clean. Even so, she wasn't at all fat. I don't understand what people are getting at when they say she was. If anything I think she's a little *too* lean now, but that's part of that gender-bending stuff she's into.

Madonna is a very sensual person. As I recall, she enjoyed sex, but that was a long time ago. I think she has an ambivalence toward men, yet *most* feminists and egocentrics share that emotion, since implicit in the standard male/female relationship is a

Photos courtesy of Ron Galella

submission thing. I can't see Madonna settling down with a man and obeying what he says.

Studying dance was something of a means to an end. I think she didn't quite know what she wanted to be, only that it was performance oriented. The more she got into dancing the more she realized how much work she'd have to do and how little glory she'd actually have, even as the member of a prestigious dance company.

By the time we met she was moving out of dance, leaning more towards music. And I was a musician. She always sang and had a good voice. We'd sing together, walking down the street. This was at the height of New Wave, and the hippest stuff was Blondie, the Pretenders. Plus a lot of good disco. Madonna really liked Gloria Gaynor's "I Will Survive."

Madonna was a lot like her character in *Desperately Seeking Susan*. There was a freedom about her, a kind of "I don't give a fuck" freedom, as if she felt, "I'm myself and I'm wonderful and don't really have to live up to any standards other than my own." Madonna had a really well developed sense of self and who she thought she should be, who she didn't want to be. She was always very bold, very hungry, very direct. She was contemptuous of things she didn't approve of and very supportive of things she did. Need I say she was very outspoken?

Even then, Madonna had a natural instinct for what was genuine and life affirming. She hated pompous, phony, self-important things. She was self-centered and selfish, but utterly charming about it. I think she got away with a lot because there was an innocence to her. She came off like, "I'm not pretending to be anything other than I am." She really *is* a total Leo—along with Napoleon, Mick Jagger, and Arnold Schwarzenegger. There's a sense of destiny about these people.

In 1979, Madonna was broke. She posed for art classes a lot. I remember drawing her on Greene Street a couple of times. And she was a waitress for a while, but she never kept those jobs very long. She had a job later on when she was seeing Danny, with a textile company that he and I worked at for roughly six years. Madonna lasted about two weeks. A total disaster. We were creating hand-painted silk fabric and put her on the runs to paint, filling in colors. She simply could not deal with any sort of menial work that detracted from what she had to do. Totally unemployable!

A lot of our dates were spent just walking the streets; it was one of our favorite pastimes. I remember we'd go to churches to look around. Of course I wasn't as smart then as I am now, not as aware of certain things. She certainly seemed to be rebelling against all of her religious upbringing. It's fairly obvious now that most of her behavior relates to reacting to her family and her mother's death. You definitely sensed that she didn't trust people and overcompensated massively to fill a loss that was impossible to fill. Still, Madonna was always self-reliant—to the point of denying that she felt any pain. Madonna competed for her father's attention, but also rebelled against it. She rebelled against her stepmother. It's all too obvious to miss: losing her mother, the Catholicism, her name.

Now I think she's over thirty and starting to realize what it's all about. I think she used to move on instinct, maybe even destiny. For instance she was basically a bubble-gum creature in the eighties because it was the era of bubble-gum creatures. It was the height of Reagan and Apollonian denial: "There's no problem. There's no deficit. We're rich, we can indulge ourselves." Today we need to stand up for something.

Madonna knew about a lot of stuff— she's a very smart person. But when you're twenty years old, how bright can you be? And you're full of yourself. She's much more

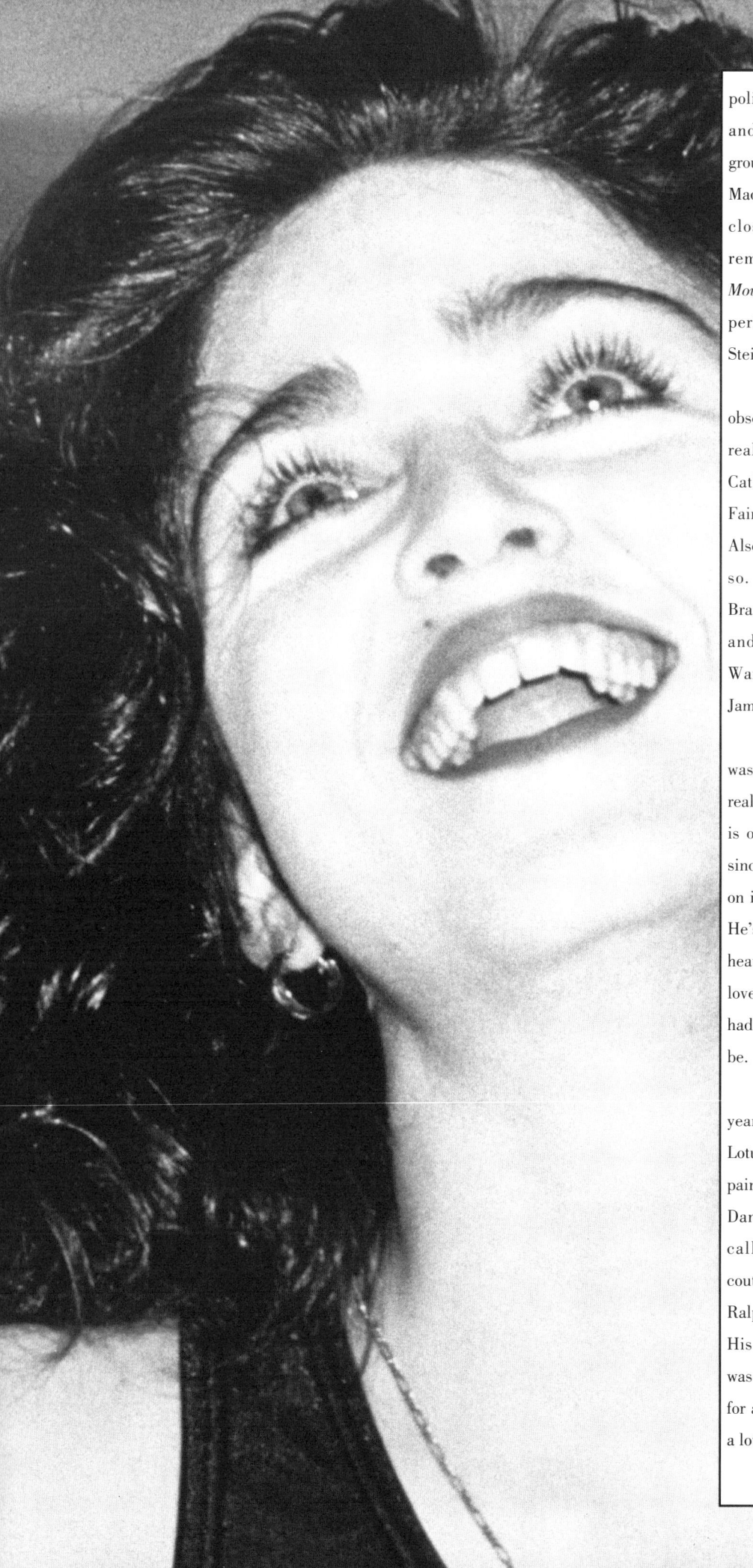

political now, she's developing a conscience and I see a really big change in her. It's grounded in seeing people she's close to die. Madonna was always close to gay men, always close to artists and actors and dancers. I remember she gave me Hemingway's *The Moveable Feast* and was really into that whole period, Paris in the twenties, the Gertrude Stein salon.

More than Marilyn, Madonna was obsessed by James Dean when I knew her. She really identified with him, with growing up Catholic in a very Catholic city. He's from Fairmount, Indiana, more or less the Midwest. Also Dean's mother died when he was nine or so. She was attracted to the whole Dean-Brando school of acting, beatniks, early rock and roll. I'm amused that she got to date Warren Beatty since he was one of the first James Dean replacements.

One thing I noticed when we met was that her attitude was "I like you and we really get along but I'm going places and this is only temporary." It was never spoken, but since I'm that kind of person also, I picked up on it immediately. Dan Gilroy is that way, too. He's not the type of person who usually invests heavily in relationships, but I'm sure he was in love with her as well. You always sensed they had some kind of love but it wasn't meant to be.

Dan and I have known each other for years. We met in 1974 at a place called the Lotus Shop, the first company creating hand-painted T-shirts. When the Lotus Shop folded, Dan, his partners, and I started a company called Gossamer Wings, which was more couture. We designed for Mary McFadden and Ralph Lauren. Dan was also a rock and roller. His band was called the Acme band, then I was in a band with Dan and his brother Eddie for a while. We were cronies and hung around a lot.

Every year on or about May 1 we

threw a rites-of-spring party. I wasn't dating Madonna by then. I ran into her on Thirty-four Street—literally bumped into her—and invited her to the party. I guess she met Dan there. That stuff about my "passing her along to him" is a bunch of shit. It's not like I broke up with her, we just drifted apart because we were both so egocentric that it was getting in the way of what we had. We'd have fights about what to do together.

I think Dan was hooked up with Patrick Hernandez first. Dan and Eddie had a duo called the Bill and Gill Show that was part of a show called Voidville—sort of a vaudeville revue with a bunch of different performers. Voidville came to the attention of the two producers working with Hernandez, and I'm pretty sure they met Madonna through Danny. So she went to Paris, and when she got back, joined The Breakfast Club.

Breakfast Club had a girl named Angie Smits on bass. Angie couldn't play bass to save her life, but she was interesting to look at. After she left they were joined by two guys that played in the Acme band, Mike Monahan (drums) and Gary Burke (bass). Then, essentially, Madonna wanted more attention and they split up. Madonna took Mike and Gary with her—guys who'd been with Dan ten years! It was a scene, but everyone got over it. Madonna's rehearsal schedule burnt Mike out. He had a career in banking or something that was just taking off, and they were rehearsing too hard. At that moment, very propitiously, Steve Bray moved to town from Detroit. Then when Madonna got her demo, she ditched everybody, but I don't know exactly how it happened.

Was she using people? Madonna is an elemental force; it's vital to understand that. She's the most unstoppable person I've ever seen. I've never seen or heard about anyone who made it to the top as quickly, totally disregarding obstacles. Madonna never

denied or hid anything. She wasn't trying to keep secrets about herself. Her basic attitude was "Accept me for what I am or go fuck yourself."

Madonna is a contemporary goddess, a contemporary Diana.

Diana, or Artemis, was goddess of the forest, fertility, the hunt, animals, and in particular the late summer. Her festival is celebrated on August 13—Madonna's birthday is the sixteenth. Diana carried a torch in her right hand. She's also goddess of the hearth, associated with vestal virgins, who keep the fire burning. And she helps young girls, especially during childbirth.

Nowadays we need myths, and some performers have become representative of more than just their art. They're bigger than life. Another example is Jim Morrison and the cult of Dionysus. Even being dead doesn't pose a problem there!

What Madonna has done for women is turn around stereotypes. She's a strong role model by doing whatever the fuck she pleases and having power and not conforming to expectations. She shows us something different, that you don't have to be a slave. You don't have to be man-directed. You can use sexuality. You can be a woman and still be powerful. Women have so much power and yet they've been so oppressed. In terms of creative power, who has more power over you than your mother? And who has more power over a man? Men are slaves of their sex drives, but don't want to admit it. As soon as women realize how much power they have, they can be Madonna or whatever else they want.

Very few people can be as outspoken as Madonna and survive. She's not next year's model. She's not disposable. People are excited by that. Almost no one who grew up in the seventies or eighties is proud of that fact. They always apologize for it and say they haven't any important heroes from these eras. Now they have Madonna.

Concert-going fans buy T-shirts like this one at a rate of one per minute.
Memorabilia courtesy the Bill Ryan Archives.
Photos by David Palmore.

VENUS ENVY

For years we publicly giggled over (and privately believed) Wallis Simpson's motto, "You can never be too rich or too thin." In the eighties, infected with fitness mania, the chant became, "You can never be too ripped or too shredded."

Back in 1986, *Women's Sports & Fitness* ran a story linking rock music and aerobics that asked, "Could aerobic dance be making at least a subliminal impression on the pop-rock psyche?" Madonna said, "My first album was a total aerobics record. I make records with aerobics in mind. That's because when I'm mad or have a fight with someone . . . I work out."

Every trend has its backlash. *Glamour*'s April 1990 editorial, entitled "Kiss Health Terrorism Good-bye," points out that too much of a good thing can be brutal on our bodies and our psyches when genetics prohibit boyish hips, flat tummies and bulging biceps. Who's to blame for this obsession, asked the editor, before providing her own response: "It's Madonna's fault."

Part of Madonna's appeal has always been the boost she gives fans, who think, "If she can do it, I can do it!" But bodywise, at least, it just doesn't translate to real life.

In the first place Madonna isn't juggling a nine-to-five job and family responsibilities. She works phenomenally hard, but the schedule's of her own devising. She's not the victim of health-club accessibility or even health-club hours. Madonna maintains state-of-the-art home gyms on two coasts. She employs a chef and personal trainer, both of whom travel with her. If she wants to work out at four A.M., nothing's stopping her.

Madonna's measurements are 33 (34 when premenstrual), 24, 34. She contours her body—now soft-shouldered for Breathless, now Olympian for Blond Ambition—to suit her

(continued)

Can Tony go the distance?

Photos courtesy of Ron Galella

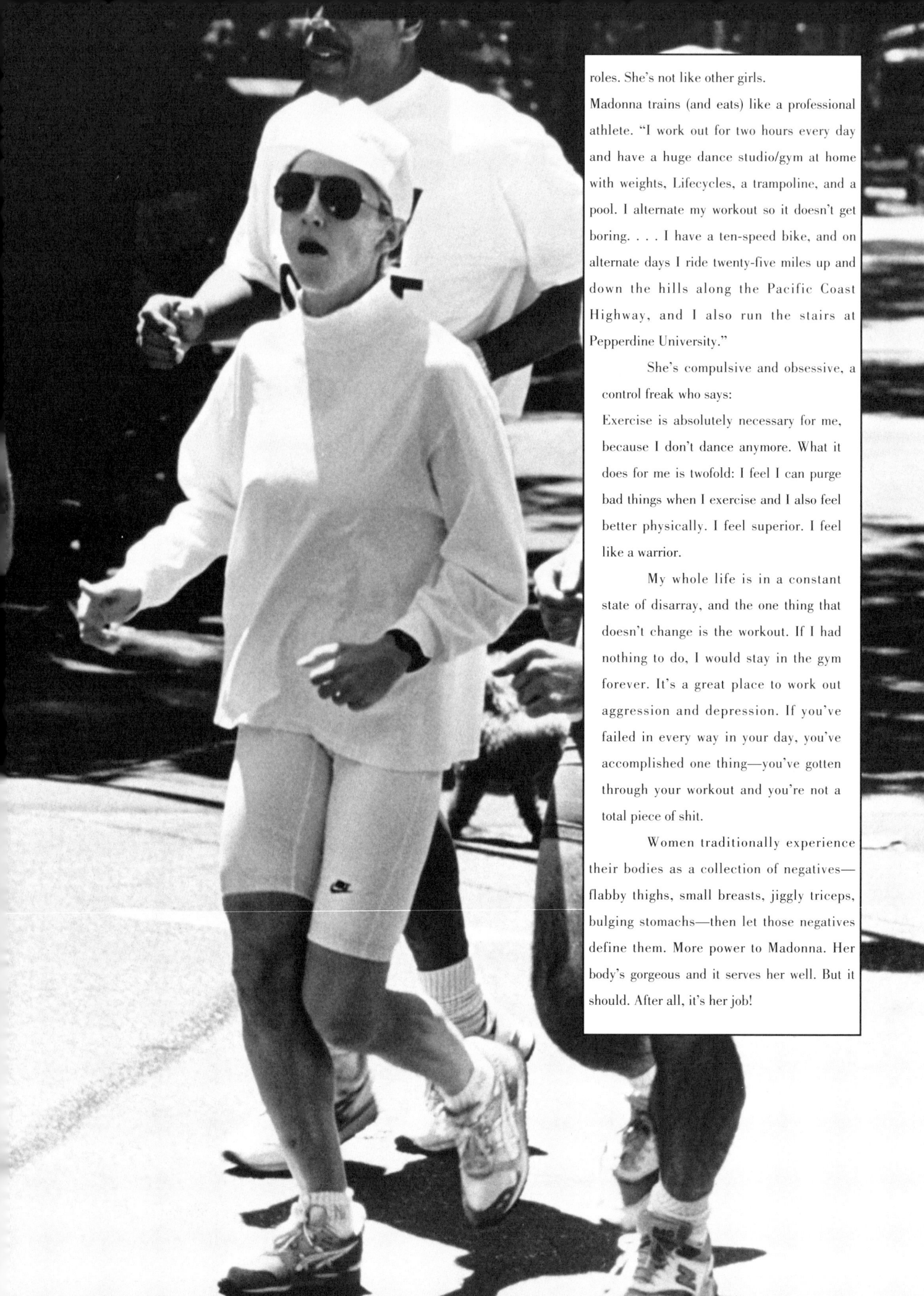

roles. She's not like other girls.

Madonna trains (and eats) like a professional athlete. "I work out for two hours every day and have a huge dance studio/gym at home with weights, Lifecycles, a trampoline, and a pool. I alternate my workout so it doesn't get boring. . . . I have a ten-speed bike, and on alternate days I ride twenty-five miles up and down the hills along the Pacific Coast Highway, and I also run the stairs at Pepperdine University."

She's compulsive and obsessive, a control freak who says:

Exercise is absolutely necessary for me, because I don't dance anymore. What it does for me is twofold: I feel I can purge bad things when I exercise and I also feel better physically. I feel superior. I feel like a warrior.

My whole life is in a constant state of disarray, and the one thing that doesn't change is the workout. If I had nothing to do, I would stay in the gym forever. It's a great place to work out aggression and depression. If you've failed in every way in your day, you've accomplished one thing—you've gotten through your workout and you're not a total piece of shit.

Women traditionally experience their bodies as a collection of negatives—flabby thighs, small breasts, jiggly triceps, bulging stomachs—then let those negatives define them. More power to Madonna. Her body's gorgeous and it serves her well. But it should. After all, it's her job!

Part of the intense regimen that keeps her svelte.

Photos courtesy of Ron Galella

Spettacoli

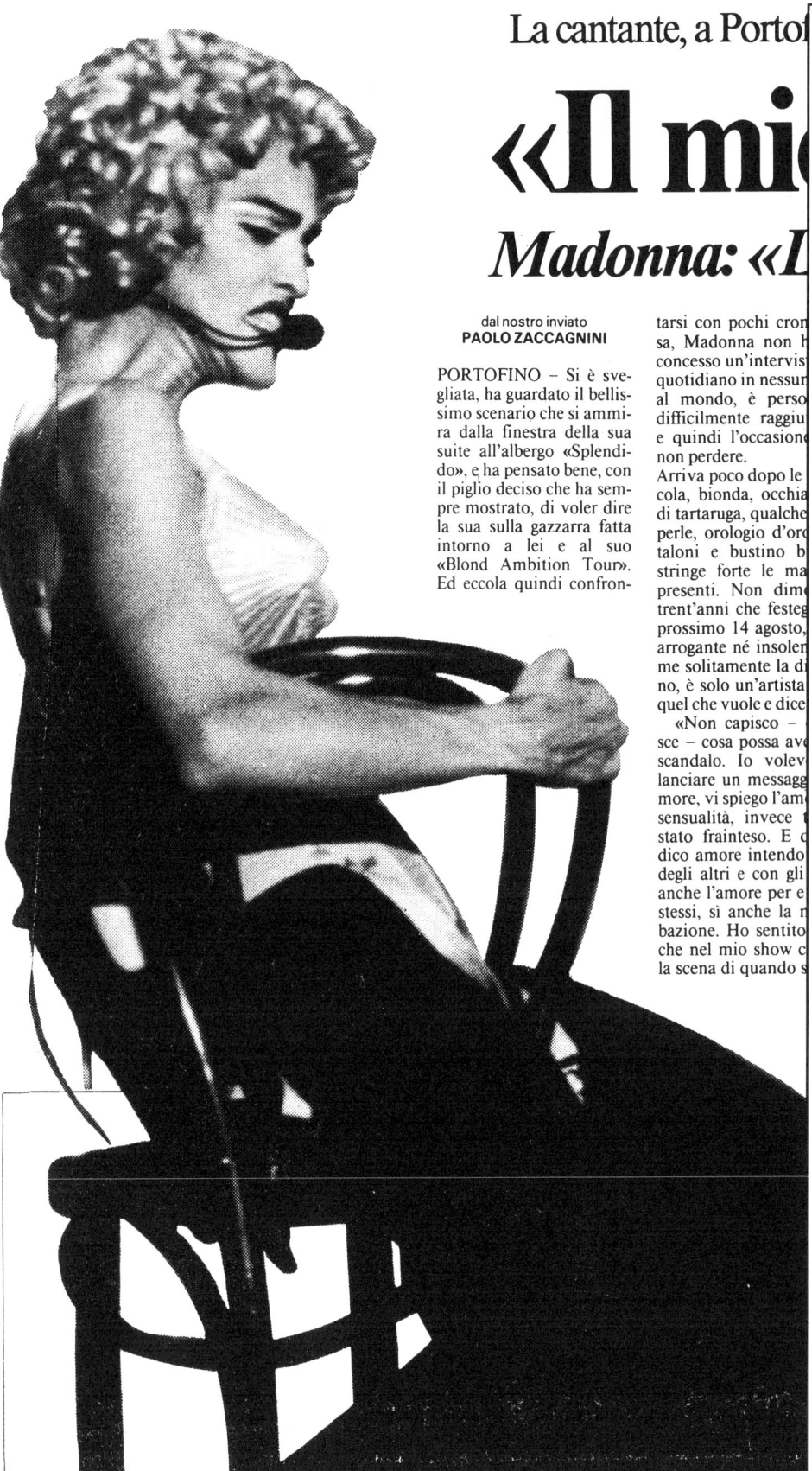

La cantante, a Portofino... volta ne...

«Il mi...

Madonna: «... paese...

dal nostro inviato
PAOLO ZACCAGNINI

PORTOFINO – Si è svegliata, ha guardato il bellissimo scenario che si ammira dalla finestra della sua suite all'albergo «Splendido», e ha pensato bene, con il piglio deciso che ha sempre mostrato, di voler dire la sua sulla gazzarra fatta intorno a lei e al suo «Blond Ambition Tour». Ed eccola quindi confrontarsi con pochi cro... sa, Madonna non h... concesso un'intervis... quotidiano in nessun... al mondo, è perso... difficilmente raggiu... e quindi l'occasione... non perdere.

Arriva poco dopo le... cola, bionda, occhia... di tartaruga, qualche... perle, orologio d'oro... taloni e bustino b... stringe forte le ma... presenti. Non dim... trent'anni che festeg... prossimo 14 agosto, ... arrogante né insolen... me solitamente la d... no, è solo un'artista... quel che vuole e dice...

«Non capisco – ... sce – cosa possa ave... scandalo. Io volev... lanciare un messagg... more, vi spiego l'am... sensualità, invece t... stato frainteso. E d... dico amore intendo... degli altri e con gli... anche l'amore per ... stessi, sì anche la ... bazione. Ho sentito... che nel mio show c... la scena di quando s...

MADONNA'S SPEECH AT THE ROME AIRPORT, 1990

I am Italian American and I'm proud of it. Proud of being an American because it's the country I grew up in, the country that gave me the opportunities to be who I am today—and a country that believes in freedom of speech and artistic expression.

I am also proud of being an Italian because it is my father's heritage and because it is the reason that I am passionate about the things I believe. It is also the reason my blood boils when I am misunderstood or unfairly judged for those beliefs.

I am aware that the Vatican and certain Catholic communities are accusing my show of being sinful and blasphemous. That they are trying to keep people from seeing it.

If you are sure that I am a sinner—then let he who has not sinned cast the first stone.

If you are not sure, then I beg of you as righteous men and women of the Catholic Church that worship a God who loves unconditionally to see my show and then judge.

My show is not a conventional rock show but a theatrical presentation of my music—and like the theater it asks questions, provokes thoughts, and takes you on an emotional journey.

Portraying good and bad, light and dark, joy and sorrow, redemption and salvation. I do not endorse a way of life but describe one, and the audience is left to make its own decisions and judgments. This is what I consider freedom of speech, freedom of expression, and freedom of thought.

To prevent me from performing my show you are saying that you do not believe in these freedoms. If you do not believe in these freedoms, you are imprisoning everyone's mind. When a mind is imprisoned, then our spiritual life dies. When the spirit dies there is

(continued)

Prevendite fiacche per lo show di stasera

Torino a quota 20 mila

Come vanno le prevendite per il concerto di Madonna? «I biglietti ci sono, non è ancora esaurito», dicono alla Good Music di Torino, promoter del *Blond*... 40 mila lire più 4 mila di diritti di prevendita.

Al di là delle polemiche che hanno pre...

La Saci...

La...

di NIKI BARBA...

Raiuno trasmetterà in diretta il concerto di Ma-

la Repubblica Spettacoli
13 luglio 1990

Intervista alla star contestata

dal nostro inviato
LAURA PUTTI

Incontriamo la cantante nel ritiro di Portofino, del suo concerto di Torino. Ci parla cinema, del suo delle p...

> no reason to live.
> Every night before I go onstage I say a prayer—not only that the show will go well but that the audience will watch with an open heart and an open mind and see it as a celebration of love, life, and humanity.

"No, a nessuno chiederò scusa"

Madonna: lo show è fatto con ironia

Accanto, qui sotto e in alto, **tre momenti dello spettacolo "Blond Ambition" che Madonna sta portando in giro per il mondo e che oggi approda a Torino, dopo le polemiche sollevate nei giorni passati**

Pace fatta con la Rai
vedremo il concerto

DON'T CRY FOR HER!

There hasn't been a fun Hollywood feud since Crawford versus Davis, but there may be one brewing if Madonna and Meryl Streep cross paths. The Oscar-winning actress wanted to play Evita Peron so desperately, she auditioned by singing the entire score! And Streep was so outraged to learn she'd lost the role to Madonna that she spat, "I could rip her throat out. I can sing better than she can, if that counts for anything."

When asked if she admired Streep or thought she could do a better job, Madonna tactfully replied,: "I look at Meryl Streep and I say she's a fine actress. And I'm different. I think I'm a good actress, and I'm going to get better."

Photos courtesy of Ron Galella

BLOND-O-METER

"I think that the most important thing a woman can have—next to talent of course—is her hairdresser."—Joan Crawford

"Being blond is definitely a different state of mind. . .The artifice of being blond has some incredible sort of sexual connotation. Men really respond to it. I love blond hair, but it really does something different to you. I feel more grounded when I have dark hair, and I feel more ethereal when I have light hair. . . I also feel more Italian when my hair is dark."—Madonna

Doesn't it feel like Madonna changes hair color twice daily? Our estimated blondline gets to the root of the matter (ouch!):

1958-1982	Brunette
1983	Blond-streaked
1984	Blond-streaked
1985	Blond-streaked until July
July, 1985	Red
August, 1985	Blond-streaked
1986	White blond—no roots
1987	Yellow blond with roots
1988	Brunette
1989	Brunette, then brunette with a blond forelock in the Pepsi commercial
—	Blond by early spring
1990	Blond—and ambitious
1991	Brunette for Woody, blond for *Truth or Dare* publicity photos
May 1991	Brunette

Photo courtesy of Ron Galella

Photo courtesy of Ron Galella

Photo courtesy of Ron Galella

THE MADONNA MYSTIQUE

"All women should be as Madonna as possible."—Performance artist, Karen Finley.

"It seems that traditional feminists persistently misread Madonna, either because they feel threatened by her victories, or because they wish she'd keep her clothes on, or because they want a more serious examination and resolution of feminine objectification."—Lonette Stonitsch in *Exeter*

"The old-guard establishment feminists who still loathe Madonna have a sexual ideology problem. . . . I perceive Madonna's strutting sexual exhibitionism not as cheapness or triviality, but as the full, florid expression of the whore's ancient rule over men."—Camille Paglia

"Many feminist women perpetuate a sort of alternative puritanism which can be very boring indeed. . . . The absence of makeup and presence of body hair can't be criteria used to determine whether someone's a good feminist or not. . . . It was never just the self-presentation or representation of Madonna as a woman that worried feminists, it was also what she connoted in politics: the Thatcherite spirit of free enterprise."—Shelagh Young

Is she or isn't she a feminist?

Betty Friedan may be one of the rare old-guard feminists who likes Madonna. Madonna's penchant for stirring up controversy has polarized feminists, pitting young against old in a battle between the *sex*. In an MTV interview Friedan said, "Madonna—in contrast to the image of women that you saw on MTV—at least she had spirit, she had guts, she had vitality. She was in control of her own sexuality and her life. She was a relatively good role model, compared with what else you saw."

(continued)

Madonna is certainly pro-female, but she would probably call herself a humanist—one who champions *both* sexes' right to dignity, self-expression, and the pursuit of carnal happiness.

In her own words:

What does exploitation mean? In a revolution, some people have to get hurt. To get people to change, you have to turn the table over. Some dishes get broken.

Some people would say that I hate men and that I like to do things to take power away from them, but you don't have to get that analytical. . . . Look, you only take balls away from people when they give them to you.

The essence of femininity is to absolutely love being a woman.

It seems to me that one of the pitfalls of the women's movement was that women wanted to be like men. They felt they had to dress like men and behave like men to get anywhere, to be respected or to be in control. . . . I think that's bullshit. I think women have always had the power; they just never knew it.

I don't think of what I'm doing as gender specific. I am what I am, and I do what I do. I never set out to be a role model for girls or women. I'm a strong woman, a successful woman, and I don't conform to a stereotype. You know the idea—that you need to be like a chain saw or an army tank to play in a man's world. Well, I don't act like a man and I play in a man's world.

Photo courtesy of Ron Galella

IT'S IN HER STARS

Is there such a thing as astrological destiny? Madonna was born on August 16, 1958, under the fire sign Leo. If you read the work of eminent astrologers Linda Goodman and Joyce Jillson, you'll discover Madonna's a classic Leo woman. How much of the following sounds like our favorite ambitious blonde?

Leo's affiliation with that proud jungle king, the lion, is no accident. Think drama. Think ego. Leos love the spotlight and they're persistent enough to get to the top of any profession. Leos love managing other people's lives—they'd rather be relied upon than forced to ask for help. But all their roaring guards an ego that's surprisingly vulnerable to criticism and shamelessly responsive to flattery. They're relentlessly driven to prove themselves, gauging their own importance by others' reactions. Better to humor a Leo than critique one.

Leos are dedicated workers and terrific managers because they plan thoroughly. The work ethic was practically invented for Leos—they strive for supremacy in all they do. And they've got extremely high standards. What do they do with the payoff? Leos like living on a grand scale among beautiful, expensive objects.

Though their arrogance and bossiness frustrates, Leos are loyal friends, outspoken about their feelings. They're impatient, hardheaded, and amusing all at once. Leos feel protective toward their siblings and tend to gravitate toward the parent of the same sex. "Love me, love everything I do," says the Leo, demanding unstinting, uncritical support.

Leo is aligned with the Fifth House, the house of creativity. They make good actors (witness Dustin Hoffman, Robert Redford, Mae West, and Lucille Ball). Musically, they want to lead the band, not play second fiddle (Count Basie). Leos' self-confidence lets them be

(continued)

extremely generous with time and money when fellow artists need a boost. Leos need fan clubs and *must* be rewarded for their creative endeavors. Gifted with good timing, Leos set trends more often than they follow them.

The Leo woman is generally the most popular, energetic, radiant, clever, sexy, flirtatious female in any gang. She'll sometimes act submissive to get her way, but this is no domesticated house cat! She's jealous and possessive. She likes costly gifts and the glamorous life. Most Leo women have careers outside the home—they need the applause. Constant admiration helps a Leo woman mask the fear that she's not feminine or desirable enough.

Other famous Leos include Napoleon, Fidel Castro, Julia Child, Cecil B. DeMille, Dorothy Parker, Jacqueline Onassis, Aldous Huxley, and Alfred Hitchcock.

WHAT'S A WEBO

Madonna's music-publishing company is called Webo Girl. In Spanish street slang *webo* means ball-shaker, but it's also the name of a dance popularized in Manhattan discos during the early 1980s. The Blond One explained : "It's the way everybody was dancing a while ago, and I named my publishing company that because me and this girl Debi and this girl Claudia were the only white girls that could webo at the Roxy. And Kano, the graffiti artist, painted on the back of our jackets one of his paintings and it said 'Webo gals.'"

MADONNA'S FAVORITE MUSIC

As a kid Madonna grooved to the sounds of the Archies, Bobby Sherman, and David Cassidy. When she hit her teens it was Carole King and Joni Mitchell ("The *Court & Spark* album was my bible for a whole year")

What blasts fron her boom box these days?

Prince, Technotronic, NWA, Nenah Cherry, Tanita Takaiam, Don Henley, Chrissie Hynde, Rickie Lee Jones, Debbie Harry, Bronski Beat, Chaka Khan, Aretha Franklin, Boy George, C&C Music Factory, Black Box, George Micheal, Sinead O'Connor.

Madonna's favorite classical music includes anything baroque, Vivaldi, Bach, Pachelbel, Handel's *Water Music*, Mozart, and Chopin.

Her good taste also embraces Billie Holiday, Cole Porter, Irving Berlin, Ella Fitzgerald, Sarah Vaughn, old Sinatra, and Sam Cooke.

MTV

MTV was born on August 1, 1981, sired by Nickelodeon's "Popclips," itself the brainchild of ex-Monkee (and heir to the liquidpaper fortune) Michael Nesmith. (And hosted by then-unknown vee jay, Howie Mandel.) Warner Amex Satellite Entertainment Co. launched MTV on a $20-million budget, targeting their new network aimed at twelve-to-thirty-four year-old viewers. On average, they show about two hundred videos a day.

"MTV is a product of the eighties much as the masked ball was a creature of the Middle Ages, and cubism was a child of the early 1900s," wrote Lisa St. Clair Harvey in *The Journal of Popular Culture*. Like the eighties, MTV is all about consumption. E. Ann Kaplan, in *Rocking Around the Clock*, wrote: "MTV evokes a kind of hypnotic trance in which the spectator is suspended in a state of unsatisfied desire but forever under the illusion of *imminent* satisfaction through some kind of purchase." Another critic commented: "Music videos erase the boundary between commercial and program. . . . MTV is pure environment."

First and foremost, MTV sells music and sells it well. MTV revived the recording industry. which was floundering badly by the 1970s. In the beginning MTV favored English acts because with more rock shows on British television, they simply had more product. American rock and rollers were forced to redefine themselves visually to survive. Today some videos cost more than the album to produce, proving that it's better to look good than to play good. If album rock characterized the 1970s, MTV brought back the supremacy of the pop single. Beyond music, MTV markets trends by communicating fashions and fads with breathtaking speed.

No one's made better use of MTV as a promotional tool than Madonna. She has thirty-six videos in rotation, more than any other act, and some call MTV Madonnavision. When MTV marked its anniversary, nearly every birthday article featured a photograph of Madonna. She epitomizes the network"s vision of itself as the meeting ground of aesthetics and an irresistible move-to-the-groove backbeat that sets your feet tapping.

PHOTO

SPECIAL ROCK STARS

MADONNA:
LES PHOTOS DU
CLIP INTERDIT

LE RAP
MADE IN U.S.

L'ALBUM
INTIME DES
STONES

DAVID BOWIE
STING
NENEH CHERRY
PRINCE
MICK JAGGER
GRACE JONES
SINEAD O'CONNOR
IGGY POP
MICHAEL JACKSON
CYNDI LAUPER

SHE'S IN THE MONEY

In 1985, biographer Mark Bego asked Madonna, "Do you have good business sense?" She replied:

It's not very good. If someone says you're getting a half-million-dollar advance, I go, "Big deal!" I don't care. I'm not interested as long as I have enough money to pay the rent and buy all my rubber bracelets and stuff! I'm not really money oriented. That's probably bad because I should be thinking about making investments. . . . I forget I'm spending more than my credit card has left. I bounce checks all the time.

By 1990, Madonna ranked as our top-earning female performer (and eighth-highest-paid entertainer) of the year and made it to the cover of *Forbes*. Their paean to her business acumen, entitled "A Brain for Sin and a Bod for Business," estimated her pre-IRS earnings at $39 million for 1990. Since 1986, according to *Forbes*'s guesstimate, she's earned at least $125 million.

Madonna pays manager Freddy DeMann 10 percent of her earnings capped at $1 million. Bert Padell, her business manager, and Paul Schindler, her lawyer, both earn 5 percent of her income, capped at $1 million each. On a smaller scale, Madonna employs personal trainer Robb Parr, household help, and personal assistant Melissa Crowe. When she tours, there's the outlay of salaries and per diem expenses for her musicians and backup performers (her dancers are the highest paid in the business), plus a slice for the tour agent, who pockets 10 percent of her concert revenues.

Pepsi paid $5 million for Madonna's endorsement. They canceled American broadcasts of the ad—but not the check. And while much is made of her "scale" wages for playing Breathless Mahoney in *Dick Tracy*, only *Forbes* remarked that her contract's fine

(continued)

VANITY FAIR

APRIL 1991/$2.50

print gave Madonna a percentage of the gross box office revenue for film and video, plus a percentage of all merchandising profits.

What's she really worth? No one knows for certain. The secrecy starts at the top. Madonna prefers we think of her as an artist rather than a savvy executive. "Part of the reason I'm successful is because I'm a good businesswoman, but I don't think it is necessary for people to know that." To guard her secrets, "everyone that is employed by me signs a privacy contract, from my maid to a backup singer. It's a way of protecting myself before I get to know people and know that I can trust them."

Do Madonna's hired guns really mastermind all the wheeling and dealing? Doubtful. She's a self-confessed control freak who takes an active part in every aspect of Madonna Inc.—which includes her film company, Siren; Slutco, for videos; and Boy Toy, for music.

So was Madonna pulling Bego's leg or did she take a crash course at Harvard Business School?

Madonna
WHO CAN JUSTIFY HER LOVE? by Lynn Hirschberg
DEATH IN TUNIS
How Arafat's Man Was Betrayed, by T. D. Allman
OSCAR WYATT
Saddam Hussein's Texan Connection, by Marie Brenner
THE NEW POWER AT CNN by Peter J. Boyer
THE NINE LIVES OF 'FAT CAT' NICHOLS by Fredric Dannen

Madonna BIG-TIME GIRL TA[LK]
ROLLING STONE INTERVIEW by CARRIE FISH[ER]

ISSUE 606 • JUNE 13TH, 1991

RollingStone

PLAYING FAVORITES

Not since Cher displayed hers on prime-time television has a belly button been so discussed, so analyzed. In 1985, Madonna told reporters that forced to choose, she'd rank her belly button as her number one favorite body part: "The most erogenous part of my body is my belly button. I have the most perfect belly button—an inny, and there's no fluff in it. When I stick a finger in my belly button I feel a nerve in the center of my body shoot up my spine. If one hundred belly buttons were lined up against a wall I would definitely pick out which one was mine."

But the only thing constant is change. In 1989—uncannily repeating herself—Madonna told a reporter that her *hands* won the contest for number one favorite body part. And she likes them best because they're callused and because she would never recognize them if they were attached to someone else.

NAKED 'TRUTH': MADONNA ON HER NEW MOVIE

entertainment WEEKLY

NO. 66 FROM FRIDAY, MAY 17, 1991

An astounding media blitz accompanied the release of *Truth or Dare*, and the interviews proved more revealing than the flick.

$1.95 (CAN $2.50)

BLOND ON BLOND

"She has no charm, delicacy, or taste. She's just an arrogant little tail-twitcher who's learned to throw sex in your face."—Nunnally Johnson

While it sounds like a swipe at Madonna, Johnson's nasty crack was meant for Marilyn Monroe. From her first pelvic thrust, the press have compared Madonna with that other breathtaking blonde, and Madonna's taken full advantage of the parallels. She aped Monroe in "Material Girl," recreated her most famous poses in photography sessions, and for a time, dyed her hair whiter and whiter.

As early as 1985, Holly Brubach wrote: "Not since Marilyn Monroe has a performer seduced the camera so expertly.... Both Madonna and Marilyn put their sex appeal at the service of ambition.... Marilyn was clearly out for love; Madonna is out for power and money."

Madonna's favorite lie about herself is the one started by the *National Enquirer* when it announced she was Marilyn's reincarnation—impossible since Madonna was four when Marilyn died! Madonna *does* love Marilyn, but claims their differences far outnumber their similarities:

At first I enjoyed the comparisons . . . I saw it all as a compliment: she was very sexy—*extremely* sexy—and she had blond hair and so on. Then it started to annoy me because nobody wants to be continuously compared to someone else. You want people to see that you have a statement of your own to make.... I don't see myself as Marilyn Monroe. I'm almost playing with her image and turning it around....

I *do* feel something for Monroe. A sympathy . . . I think she really didn't know what she was getting herself into and simply made herself vulnerable, and I feel a bond with that . . . but I'm

(continued)

THE FACE

No 33/JUNE 1991 £1.50 • US $4.95

EMF
New brats on the block

JODIE FOSTER
on female heroes

Paul Weller

Ninjaman • Omar

De Niro & the Red Scare

MOO! How James, Carter, Ned's and Inspirals make money on your backs

determined never to let it get me down. Marilyn was a victim, and I'm not.

I don't claim to know her and can barely believe most of what's been written about her. I know how untruthfully people write about you and how it ends up being about one thing and not a million things, which is what a person's made up of. But the impression I get is, she didn't know her own strength and didn't know how to nurture it. . . . I don't have an addicted personality. I don't drink a lot and take pills a lot and try to make myself forget my life because I love my life.

Actress/director Lee Grant agrees. She's said, "Madonna hasn't a *clue* what Marilyn Monroe had. It was vulnerability. What she is, is Jean Harlow."

If Madonna truly wants the comparisons to end, she'll have to stop posing for photo spreads like the one called "The Misfit" for the April 1991 issue of *Vanity Fair*. Marilyn's iconographer, Bert Stern, was so incensed by Steven Meisel's duplication of his photos of Monroe that he contemplated legal action. "Madonna's body snatching Marilyn," he complained. "It goes beyond similarity. It's copying. . . . These people are making a lot of money from plagiarism, and it dilutes the impact of the originals."

MADONNA
THE INSIDE STORY

Photo courtesy of Ron Galella

THE AGONY AND THE ECSTASY

Like many lapsed Catholics, Madonna's life shows the effects of a strict Catholic upbringing and parochial education. Her work brims with religious imagery—some say blasphemy—and her beliefs are hotly debated.

Madonna believes in God:

> God seems to be there when things are really horrible. If something's really horrible and I say enough prayers, it will get better. . . . I do try to remind myself—I know this sounds corny—to be thankful for things when they're good, to be conscious of God.

And in sin:

> When I do something wrong . . . if I don't let someone know, I'm always afraid I'm going to be punished. I don't rest easy with myself. . . . That's something you're raised to believe as a Catholic. Everyone's a sinner . . . and must constantly be asking God to cleanse your soul.

But not in the confessional:

> I never told the priest what I thought I'd really done wrong. I'd make up smaller crimes. I thought . . . if I've done something wrong, I have a private line to God, and I'll just tell him in my bedroom.

Or attending church:

> I don't practice Catholicism now. Catholicism is a really mean religion and it's incredibly hypocritical. How could I be supportive of it? But it plays a role in my life because you can't get a lot of things out of your head, such as what Jesus Christ looks like and that divorce is a horrible thing.

Because she likes sex:

> The Catholic Church completely frowns on sex. . . . Your sexual life is supposed to be dead if you're a good Catholic. That's wrong. It's human nature to be sexual, so why would God want you to deny your human nature?

MADONNA COLLECTIBLES

The following collectibles can be purchased through Madonna's American fan club. For membership information, current prices, and ordering information, contact The Official Madonna Fan Club at 8491 Sunset Boulevard, #485, West Hollywood, California, 90069. Their order fax line is 213-850-6572.

Posters

Truth or Dare	$ 6.99
Immaculate Collection	6.99
Blond hair over one eye	6.99
Bare back in bed	6.99
"Vogue"	6.99
"Express Yourself"	6.99
"Like a Prayer"	6.99
Leather hat, exposed bra	6.99
Breathless collage	6.99
Breathless in fedora	6.99
"You Can Dance" door poster	11.99
"Like A Prayer" video door poster	11.99
Poster book (nine-color tear-outs)	11.99
Desperately Seeking Susan wall hanging, full-color	17.99
Desperately Seeking Susan wall hanging, black-and-white	17.99
"*Vogue*" wall hanging	14.99

Tour Memorabilia

Blond Ambition tour jacket	$129.99
Blond Ambition backstage pass	9.99
Blond Ambition die-cut stand-ups	
eighteen inches	9.99
life size	24.99
Blond Ambition lithograph with tour schedule	14.99

T-shirts and Clothing

Blond Ambition, profile in hat	$14.99
sleep shirt	17.99
Blond hair over one eye	14.99
sleep shirt	17.99
Who's That Girl?	14.99

(continued)

Memorabilia courtesy the Bill Ryan Archives
Photo by David Palmore

Truth or Dare	14.99
Truth or Dare close-up	14.99
Who's That Girl? baseball cap	12.99
Dick Tracy baseball cap	9.99
"Justify My Love" bikini pants (women's)	11.99
For Bed and Bath	
True Blue beach towel	$27.99
Like a Prayer beach towel	27.99
"Express Yourself" pillowcase	12.99
Breathless pillow	17.99
Desperately Seeking Susan pillow	17.99
Immaculate Collection pillow	17.99
Miscellaneous	
1991 calendar	$10.99
Twelve-pack of assorted postcards	8.99
Eight-by-ten-inch postcards	
Breathless #1, three-pack	8.99
Breathless #2, three-pack	8.99
Two-inch button assortments	
"classic" six-pack	7.99
new six-pack	7.99
Dick Tracy four-pack	4.99
Two-inch die-cut pins, two-pack	
"Vogue" and "Express Yourself"	4.99
Six-inch buttons	
Bare back in bed	3.99
"Express Yourself"	3.99
Three-pack of refrigerator magnets	5.99
"Express Yourself" sports bottle	4.99
"You Can Dance" 250-piece jigsaw	12.99
Breathless Gold Digger Club card	4.99
Breathless wallet	5.99
Breathless fanny pack	7.99
Madonna postage stamp from Grenada	19.99
Watches, Jewelry, Key Chains	
Quartz watches in neon/deco colors	
"Like a Prayer"	29.99
"Vogue"	29.99
"Express Yourself"	29.99
	(continued)

Immaculate Collection	$14.99
"Vogue"	49.99
"Express Yourself"	49.99
"Express Yourself" electronic L.E.D. watch	9.99
Breathless enamel jewelry	
necklace	14.99
earrings	12.99
pin	12.99
"Express Yourself" earrings	5.99
Leather medallion necklaces and keychains:	
Blond Ambition (n)	9.99
Blond Ambition (kc)	9.99
"Justify My Love" (n)	9.99
"Justify My Love" (kc)	9.99
Backstage pass key chain (brass)	9.99
Acrylic key chains (three-pack)	8.99

For additional merchandise information, try sending a self-addressed, stamped envelope to: Madonna c/o Rock Express, P.O. Box 59, San Francisco, California, 94101.

Another Madonna Fan Club may be found at: 99 Powerhouse Road, Room 108, Roslyn Heights, New York, 11577.

June 1991 marked the debut of *Madonna Monthly*. For information contact: Fiona Bramzelle (editor) 6 Chapel Street, Cambridge, CB4 1DY, England.

Memorabilia courtesy the Bill Ryan Archives.
Photo by David Palmore.

MADONNA'S ART COLLECTION

Wealthy people traditionally become patrons of the arts, and Madonna's an old-fashioned gal. Her impressive, still-growing art collection wins her a place among America's top collectors. So what does she own? *Vanity Fair* reports that Madonna's homes contain: a Nadelman sculpture; a personalized David Salle drawing; a veritable Tamara de Lempicka museum; a gold-framed Langlois of Endymion and Diana; Salvador Dali's *The Veiled Heart*, Fernand Léger's *Composition*; several Frida Kahlos, including *My Birth*; a Diego Rivera nude; an Irving Penn photo of Joe Louis; Man Ray's portrait of Kiki de Montparnasse; and countless more photos by masters such as Ilse Bing, Weston, Weegee, Tina Modotti, Matt Mahurin, Lartigue, Drtikol, Blumenfeld, Herb Ritts.

When *Vanity Fair* asked what three paintings she'd bring to a desert island, Madonna named pieces in her personal collection: *My Birth* and *Self-Portrait With Monkey* by Frida Kahlo, plus *L'Heure Bleu* by Tamara de Lempicka.

From the personal collection of Curtis Zales

MADONNA'S BOOKSHELF

"Man, I lo-o-ove to read."
—Madonna

Madonna's favorites include: all biographies, James Agee, Charles Bukowski, James Joyce, Henry James, F. Scott Fitzgerald, Hemingway, J. D. Salinger ("If I were a writer, I think that's how I would write"), D. H. Lawrence, Thomas Mann, Balzac, Guy de Maupassant, Françoise Sagan, Marguerite Duas, V. S. Naipaul, Milan Kundera, Lawrence Durrell, Jack Kerouac, Kurt Vonnegut, Alice Walker, Raymond Carver, Anne Tyler, Louise Erdrich, Rainer Maria Rilke, Anne Sexton, and Sylvia Plath.

Memorabilia courtesy the Bill Ryan Archives.
Photo by David Palmore.

Memorabilia courtesy the Bill Ryan Archives.
Photo by David Palmore.

Memorabilia courtesy the Bill Ryan Archives.
Photo by David Palmore.

The Official
MADONNA
FAN CLUB
MADONNA
FAN CLUB
MEMBER
icon
Madonna
3 INCH CD SINGLE
MADONNA
3 INCH CD SINGLE
WHAT'S NEW
(9月号)
8月25日発売
リミックス・プレイヤーズ
REMIXED PRAYERS
日本特別企画
マドンナ
ミニ・アルバム
8-25 ON SALE
ライク・ア・プレイヤー
MADONNA
3/16 ON SALE
マドンナ/ライク・ア・プレイヤー
ライク・ア・プレイヤー
MADONNA HOT LINE
Express Yourself
madonna
Express Yourself
madonna
エクスプレス・ユアセルフ
EXPRESS YOURSELF
MADONNA マドンナ
ルック・オブ・ラヴ
THE LOOK OF LOVE
Madonna
マドンナ
レスキュー・ミー
RESCUE ME (ALTERNATE SINGLE MIX)
DRESS YOU UP
マドンナ
MADONNA
MADONNA ANGEL
DANCE
HOLIDAY
No.1
2661

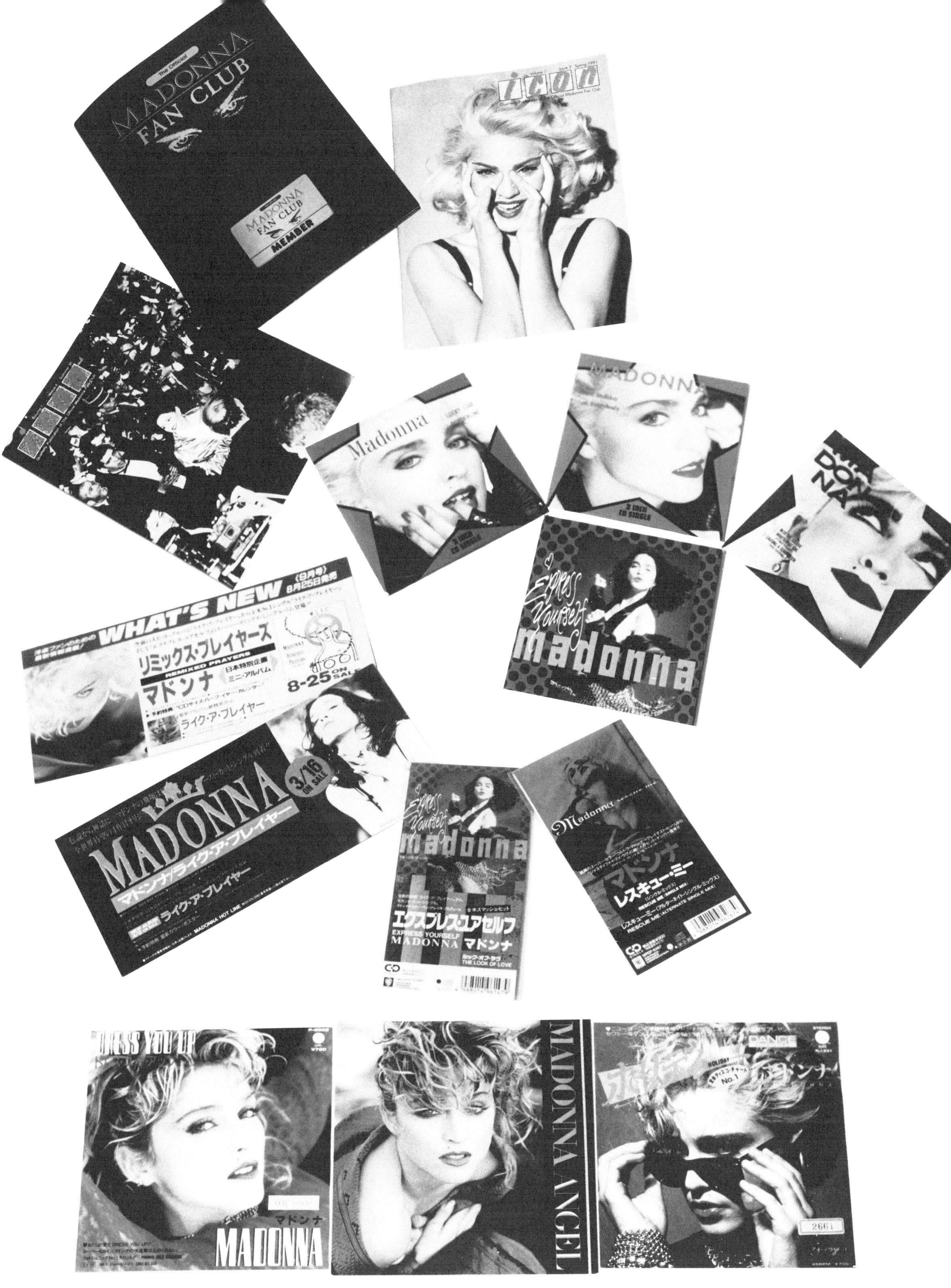

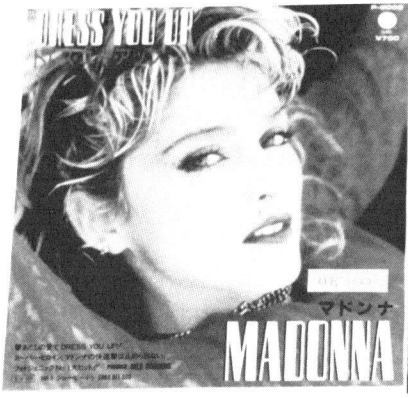

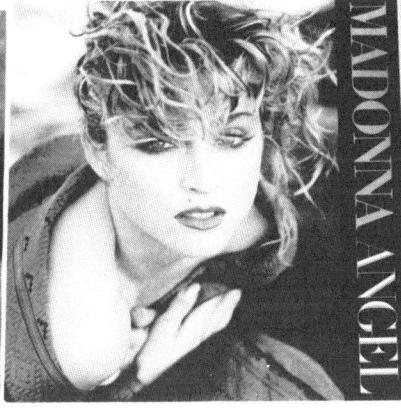

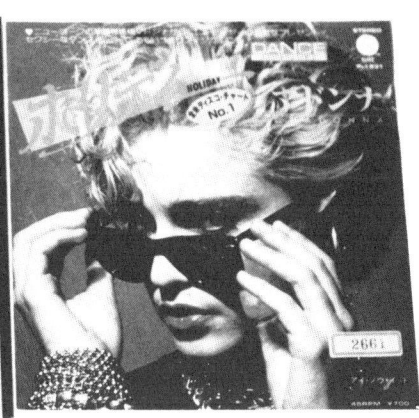

Photo courtesy of Ron Galella

Memorabilia courtesy the Bill Ryan Archives.
Photos by David Palmore.

Photo courtesy of Ron Galella

Photos courtesy of Ron Galella